THE GENERAL AND THE BOMB

WILLIAM LAWREN

THE GENERAL AND THE BOMB

A Biography of General Leslie R. Groves, Director of the Manhattan Project

DODD, MEAD & COMPANY • NEW YORK

Published by Dodd, Mead & Company, Inc.
71 Fifth Avenue, New York, N.Y. 10003
Manufactured in the United States of America
Production supervision by Mike Cantalupo

Designed by Laura Stover

First Edition

1   2   3   4   5   6   7   8   9   10

Library of Congress Cataloging-in-Publication Data

Lawren, William.
    The general and the bomb: General Leslie R. Groves, director of
the Manhattan Project / by William Lawren.
       p.   cm.
    Includes index.
    1. Groves, Leslie R., 1896–1970.   2. Generals—United States—
Biography.   3. Military engineers—United States—Biography.
4. United States. Army. Corps of Engineers. Manhattan District.
5. Nuclear weapons—United States—History.   I. Title.
UG128.G76L39 1987
aa2 B 19—dc355.8/25119/   87-26334
    ISBN 0-396-08761-2

To the memory of my parents,
Robert and Edith P. Lawren

Contents

Acknowledgments

All books are artifacts of shared labor, and this book is no exception. I would like to thank the many people who contributed so unselfishly to make this book a reality. Edward Reese at the Modern Military History branch of the National Archives first unlocked the door to Groves's invaluable personal papers, then guided me to important corollary documents when those papers were exhausted. Allison Kerr and Roger Meade at the Los Alamos National Laboratory archives went far beyond their job descriptions to locate interesting material and steer it through the nearly intractable labyrinth of government classification procedures. General Richard H. Groves gave generously of his own time, of information available nowhere outside his family album, and of a son's priceless perspective.

My own friends and family did much to relieve the writer's natural loneliness. Stephen Dane provided a steady source of interest and encouragement throughout this book's abnormally long gestation period, and Jack Rosenblum did the same in the latter stages of research and writing. My friend and agent Wendy Lipkind absolutely refused to give up on a project that seemed to have questionable potential as a piece of commerce and in general proved herself a throwback to a time when publishing was the business of gentlemen and gentlewomen. Carole Dunn coped admirably and graciously with my long and undoubtedly disruptive stays in her Washington home. Most of all, my wife Ana Maria and my son Daniel were consistently understanding and supportive, often putting their own needs aside to help me with mine.

Preface

Writing a book about the atomic bomb or about any of the figures involved in its making is by nature an emotionally loaded proposition. Most books on the subject—especially the more recent ones—make the mistake of ascribing today's moral reservations about the bomb to a time when those reservations were all but subsumed by a fierce national desire to put a fast end to a devastating war. In this book I have done my best to avoid moral hindsight, to be faithful to the wartime *Zeitgeist*, and to present General Groves and his handiwork as part of an American mentality that was necessarily and almost unrelievedly martial. This, I think, is the first task of the journalist and the historian: to present the subject in context, as part of the spirit of the time.

As to Groves himself: I was asked many times during the course of research why I was writing a book about him. His contributions, I was told, had been carefully enumerated in a number of other books, most notably Hewlett and Anderson's excellent *The New World*, and Groves himself had written a version of his story in his own book, *Now It Can Be Told*. I say "a version" of his story because my own research had convinced me that Groves's book was more remarkable for its restraint than for its revelations and that there remained an untold story about his role in the making of the bomb and about his relationships with Manhattan Project scientists—especially with the complex and controversial J. Robert Oppenheimer. Groves's personal papers, which for fifteen years lay neglected in the National Archives, confirmed this impression and told a fascinating new story of their own.

In telling that story I have deliberately, if unfortunately, given short shrift to some of its subplots. Groves's activities ranged far beyond the supervision of the building of the bomb itself: during the course of the war his office engaged in everything from international diplomacy to global uranium prospecting, and these two enterprises in particular came to consume increasingly greater amounts of the general's time. But to tell all these stories in appropriate detail would have required a book of at least twice this length, so I have tried to focus more narrowly on those aspects more directly related to the making and dropping of the bomb itself.

Groves's reputation did not survive the threshing of history, for reasons that this book will make apparent. In the end I came to see it as my job not so much to praise Groves as simply to resurrect him, to try to restore to him the position he so obviously earned at the very front and center of the history of the atomic bomb.

Part One

IN THE BEGINNING

Chapter One

The sound started as a faint drone, the sort of steady, faraway buzz that a mosquito makes when it has found your room but has not yet homed in on your neck. Hearing the sound, Edith Plant came instantly awake in her Cape Hatteras home. Her nine months in the Ground Observer Corps (GOC)—she had joined the day after Pearl Harbor—had so sharpened her ears that now, although she had just passed her seventieth birthday, she could be awakened from a sound sleep by the sound of the farthest, faintest buoy off the shores of her Cape Hatteras, North Carolina, home— or, in this case, by the unmistakable hum of an approaching airplane.

Fifteen seconds later, as the sound grew louder, Edith picked up the phone and hurriedly dialed the Army Filter Center in Norfolk, Virginia. Over the sound of her own racing heartbeat—so loud she was sure the sergeant could hear it—she gave her name, location, GOC number, and the approximate position of the incoming plane. The sergeant took the data, then briskly told her to stay on the line. Within thirty seconds he was back on the phone.

"It's okay, Mrs. Plant," he said. "That one's ours." Then his voice relaxed and became more personal. "But thanks," he said. "You never know."

"You never know," Edith repeated as she hung up the phone, her heart still drumming wildly. Indeed you didn't. For on that day, September 17, 1942, the war news was very bad indeed. That morning *The Washington Star* blared the dismal headline that Hitler's Sixth Army, 250,000 strong, was nearing the gates of Stalingrad, the heart of Russia itself, while in the Pacific the resolute and seemingly unstoppable Japanese were pushing grimly south toward Port Moresby, New Guinea.

To Edith the war seemed increasingly and frighteningly close. More and more often she heard talk of an Axis invasion, once unthinkable. Already she had seen the night sky over Cape Hatteras rent by the flares

3

and explosions of offshore sea battles, and in the harbor lay the wasted hulks of two American freighters that had been sunk by Nazi U-boats only a few miles off the North Carolina shore.

The country, she knew, was preparing to defend itself against a possible sea invasion. The people of Georgia had organized a volunteer army that bustled about in tireless patrol of the state's virtually un-protected coastline. Even in Wisconsin, fifteen hundred miles from any ocean, the American Legion proposed to repel any Nazi invasion by way of the St. Lawrence River with an unlikely army of twenty-five thousand deer hunters.

The real fear, though, was of an attack by air. Along both coasts and up to three hundred miles inland, six hundred thousand of Edith's colleagues in the Ground Observer Corps kept their eyes and ears trained on the skies, reporting all incoming aircraft to Army Filter Centers in major cities. Throughout the country Civil Air Patrol planes conducted mock air raids, pelting the citizenry below with flour-filled paper "bombs," while Boy Scouts scurried about administering ersatz first aid. In Maryland, blackout regulations imposed a five-thousand-dollar fine on any driver who kept his or her headlights on within a mile of the beach, while New York City "dim-outs" had left determined theatergoers feeling their way from Sardi's to the Shubert. There was a great national hue and cry for air-raid shelters; proponents advocated everything from the conver-sion of immense Wyoming mine shafts to *House and Garden*'s luxurious "garden or pool shelter," complete with gas locks, air filters, and up-to-the-minute libraries. All in all, as many as seven million Americans were actively engaged in the massive civil defense effort — a fivefold increase in less than six months and a reflection of growing national nervousness about a possible Axis invasion.

In some quarters this feeling of national vulnerability — new to a country that had not felt the sting of attack since the British burned the Capitol during the War of 1812 — was heightened by persistent rumors of a new Nazi superweapon. Anyone who had read reporter Ansel Talbert's October 1939 article in the New York *Herald Tribune* or William Laurence's 1940 pieces in *The Saturday Evening Post* and *The New York Times* knew that a potential new source of energy had been found in the heart of the uranium atom and that this energy could conceivably be fashioned into a bomb of unprecedented, almost nightmarish destructive power. They would also know from the newspaper and magazine reports that the breakthrough discovery had been made in Germany; with only the simplest of deductions they would realize that if this terrible bomb were ever to become a reality, the Nazis had a substantial and frightening head start.

Had Talbert and Laurence's readers known the whole truth, they would have been even more alarmed. For the American effort to keep pace with the Nazis in the grim race to develop an atomic bomb—an effort that by September 17, 1942, was already more than three years old—was mired in uncertainty, indecision, and misunderstanding. Scientific and military leaders eyed one another suspiciously over stacks of unsolved equations and heaps of unfinished blueprints.

Indeed, it seemed to many of the key scientists, politicians, and military officers who were in on the secret that if America were to lose the race for the superweapon, it would be for lack of a leader.

Chapter Two

As usual, the colonel was in a hurry. His walk, as he strode through the halls of Congress, was a study in incongruity: his 220 pounds of haphazardly arranged bulk were contradicted by the light, quick stride of an accomplished tennis player. Today, the colonel's step was even lighter than usual, and veiled behind his characteristically stern demeanor, his cool gray eyes were full of anticipation. For Colonel Leslie Richard Groves the dream of a lifetime and the ambition of every professional soldier was about to become a reality: after three years of West Point preparation and twenty-four years of peacetime service in the Army Corps of Engineers, he was about to be offered a combat post.

Colonel Groves felt sure it would be an overseas commission. His boss, General W.D. "Fat" Styer, had already placed him at the top of a list of officers who "might be considered for key assignments." And Groves was already planning to move his wife and daughter (Dick, his eighteen-year-old son, was following the family tradition at West Point) from their Washington home to a Delaware farm for the duration.

It seemed to Colonel Groves that nothing, not even the tedious congressional hearing at which he had just testified, could dampen his high spirits. Then, as he continued walking down the Capitol hallway, he ran into General Brehon Somervell, the elegant southerner who as commander of the Army's Services of Supply was not only Groves's boss but Styer's as well.

"General," said Groves, "I've got some good news. I'm going overseas."

To Groves's immense surprise, Somervell shook his head. "Sorry, colonel," he said. "You can't leave Washington. The secretary of war has picked you for a very important assignment."

In an instant Groves's good humor evaporated as he suspected what Somervell was talking about. Ever since early that summer Groves's office

7

in the Construction Branch had been advising the Syracuse District of the Army Corps of Engineers about a new project that had fallen into the Army's lap. Although he knew that the project involved the design of a bomb that, if successful, would make the detonation of the world's hitherto most powerful weapon look like the explosion of a small firecracker, he also knew that the scientists involved had been essentially unable to agree on how the major problem—the production of the esoteric material needed to fuel the bomb—should be tackled. He had sensed that some of the scientists' frustrations were being projected onto the Army, and he suspected an imminent change in the project's military leadership. Styer was the logical choice, for he had been working closely with the scientific leaders since June. But now Groves's worst fear was about to materialize: Styer was passing the buck to him.

General Somervell soon confirmed Groves's uncomfortable suspicion. Instead of going overseas, Groves was ordered to supervise the mysterious new entity that he himself had helped form and that he had named: the Manhattan Engineer District, or MED.

The colonel's heart sank. A career-making opportunity was disappearing before his eyes, replaced by a project that had the unmistakable look not only of a gigantic boondoggle but of a monumental personal comedown. After all, the construction phase of the Manhattan District was expected to cost only about $85 million in total, while as deputy chief of construction in charge of all military building in the United States, Groves had been spending eight times that amount every *month*.

Seeing the colonel's consternation and guessing its cause, Somervell tried to cheer him up. "If you do it right," he said, "it could win the war."

Groves sighed with the resignation of a soldier under orders. "Oh," he said by way of showing his disappointment, "that bomb thing."

Chapter Three

Four years before, in the winter of 1938, "that bomb thing" had consisted of little more than a set of scrawled equations in a battered notebook of an aging Austrian physicist who had suddenly been turned by German National Socialism into a political refugee. Warned by her colleagues that Hitler was about to deny exit visas to all Jews, the physicist Lise Meitner was now fleeing across Germany, trying to escape the country where she had worked peacefully and productively for many years but that was now intolerable. In fleeing, she was leaving behind a career—she was the head of the physics department at Berlin's prestigious Kaiser Wilhelm Institute—that had been more than twenty years in making and a collaboration with chemist Otto Hahn that had approached an intellectual marriage.

The equations in her notebook represented the culmination of that long and fruitful collaboration. Meitner hardly suspected that she and her colleague had been on the verge of unlocking a secret that would change the world.

Her train reached the Dutch border. Just before it crossed, five Nazi soldiers filed through the coach, intently reviewing the passport of each traveler. Meitner was terrified: her Austrian passport had expired, and Hitler had declared open season on escaping Jews. Her worst fears seemed realized when one of the soldiers took her passport and disappeared. For ten minutes she sat and waited—ten minutes during which her life seemed to have frozen in place. Finally the soldier came back and without a word handed her back her passport. Two minutes later she was in Dutch territory and free.

Keeping her purse and notebook tight to her side, she immediately made for Stockholm and then for the seaside resort of Kungelv. There, in the midst of a gray Swedish winter and alone in a cheerless boardinghouse, she waited restlessly for a letter from Hahn.

In Kungelv she was joined by her nephew, Otto Frisch, a top-ranking German physicist then working in Copenhagen with the legendary Niels Bohr. Like his aunt, Frisch had been involved in pioneering experiments with the atomic nucleus, the results of which were then being fervently debated in the international physics community.

But Frisch had come to Kungelv on vacation. When a letter from Hahn finally arrived—a letter full of talk about barium and lanthanum and nuclear disintegration—he wanted no part of it. To avoid his aunt's impassioned discourse, he strapped on a pair of cross-country skis and fled across the winter landscape. But the ground around Kungelv was maddeningly flat, so his determined aunt, slogging along on foot, was able to keep up with him. Finally, overcome by frustration and annoyance, Frisch stopped to listen. As he did, it soon became clear to him that his aunt's colleague had precipitated a scientific revolution. In a series of elegant experiments, Hahn and Fritz Strassman had found that the nucleus of the uranium atom, when bombarded by neutrons, actually disintegrated into recognizable fragments. What brought that discovery from the realm of science into the realm of world politics was that in the process of fragmentation, a tiny portion of the uranium atom's mass could be converted—in accordance with Einstein's thirty-year-old formulas— into an estimated 200 million electron volts of pure and potentially usable energy.

The news put a prompt and premature end to Frisch's winter idyll. After an evening of frenzied discussion with his aunt, he hurried back to Copenhagen and immediately relayed the information to Bohr, who a few weeks later carried it to an astonished group of physicists in the United States at Princeton University. From there the news flashed to the great centers of American physics: to Columbia University, where the Pupin Laboratory now buzzed with the experiments of Nobel Prize winners Enrico Fermi, Harold Urey, and I.I. Rabi, and to the University of California at Berkeley, where young Phillip Abelson was independently recapitulating Meitner and Hahn's discovery and where Nobel Laureate Ernest Lawrence and a group of his disciples were gaily smashing atoms using the enormous energies generated by their massive cyclotrons.

But as the news of fission circulated among the physicists with the speed and impact of a guided missile, the larger world was experiencing the first paroxysms of what was already being called World War II. The question that was raised almost simultaneously by both sides in that war was both fascinating and frightening: Could the colossal energies liberated in the fission process be controlled, and if so, could they be forged into a weapon that would change the face of war—and perhaps the face of peace—forever?

In the United States this question had been troubling not only the physicists but also a thoughtful and sharp-eyed economist named Alexander Sachs. Considered something of a Renaissance man, Sachs had made a small fortune in investment banking while at the same time making a series of accurate forecasts that ultimately attracted the attention of President Franklin D. Roosevelt. As time went on and Sachs continued to impress him with his acute mind and timely prognostication, the President drew him closer and closer into his circle of unofficial but influential advisers.

Sachs was a great believer in the impact of technology on the world at large. As such he followed developments in science—particularly in physics—quite closely. In 1936 he had traveled to Cambridge to listen to one of the great Ernest Rutherford's growling lectures, which had left him powerfully impressed by the potential of nuclear reactions. It had also left a nagging suspicion in his mind that somewhere in the physicists' equations lay the embryo of the most powerful weapon the world had ever seen.

Sachs read the reports by Hahn and Strassman and by Meitner and Frisch with avid interest. Then Roosevelt told him of a curious meeting between Enrico Fermi (the Italian whose pioneering discoveries in nuclear physics had earned him the nickname "the Pope") and Admiral Stanford C. Hooper of the United States Navy. As head of the Navy's Technical Division, Hooper had in 1937 made a cursory investigation of atomic energy and had been told by physicist Henry Andrews of Johns Hopkins University that "a small pitcher of uranium could be substituted for all the fuel required by a battleship to cross the Atlantic." Although Andrews made no mention of a bomb, Hooper had remained greatly interested in the possibility of a virtually inexhaustible atomic fuel.

In January 1939, at the urging of Columbia physicist George Pegram, Fermi paid Hooper a perfunctory visit. Hooper listened attentively while Fermi explained in broken English and a strange, foggy voice that although it might be possible to generate an energy-producing reaction in uranium, the problems involved were grave and unprecedented and at present the idea seemed to him a "chimera." Impressed by Fermi's reputation and obvious intelligence, Hooper asked him to keep the Navy posted despite the physicist's cautious negativity. At the same time, though, the Naval Reseach Laboratory had declined to recommend a major research effort, saying that fission was unlikely to be of use during the current war. There, in Roosevelt's estimation, the matter lay.

But Sachs was not inclined to be a mute witness to a scientific stillbirth. Knowing that a sizable number of the world's best scientists— including not only Hahn but also Nobel Prize–winning physicist Werner Heisenberg and his distinguished colleague Carl von Weiszäcker—had remained in Germany, and concerned that the Nazis might soon be able to "terrorize the world with an atomic detonator," he began to wonder if there were physicists in the United States who shared his worries and his sense of terrible urgency.

He soon found a pair of like minds in Hungarian physicists Leo Szilard and Eugene Wigner. The two were very different in personality: Szilard was loud and impulsive, with a mind that swept broadly but did not alight long on any one subject, while Wigner was quiet, almost painfully polite, and intellectually meticulous. But they had in common that both were Jewish refugees, that both shared Sachs's estimate of the German danger, and that both were convinced that the U.S. government should be alerted to the alarming possibility of a Nazi atomic bomb. Sachs knew that Roosevelt felt his hands were tied by the Navy's negative recommendations, and the economist felt that if he were to have any hope of reversing what he saw as dangerous inertia, he would have to enlist a scientist of even greater international renown than either Szilard or Wigner.

The two Hungarians had already approached Albert Einstein, who worked virtually side by side with Wigner in Princeton and who had often discussed politics with him during their rambling afternoon walks. Sachs agreed that Einstein would be the perfect physicist to address the President. Szilard and another Hungarian physicist, Edward Teller, drafted letters to Roosevelt advising him of the discovery of nuclear fission—a phenomenon, they said, that could conceivably lead to the construction of "extremely powerful bombs." They urged him to "speed up the experimental work" on the chain reaction. Einstein, who later said, "I really acted only as a mailbox," signed the letter.

It now fell to Sachs to deliver the message to the White House. On October 11, 1939, he placed a large dossier that included Einstein's letter on the President's desk. Although distracted by the increasingly serious situation in Europe, Roosevelt did seem interested.

But the problem, he told Sachs, was that the Navy had already said that the research was not worth pursuing. That being the case, the President did not see how he could justify reconsidering it.

Sachs was crestfallen. He simply *had* to find a way to persuade the President to do something. During a sleepless night at the Carlton Hotel, he wondered how to impress the President with the severity of the situation and how to resolve the impasse created by the Navy's recalcitrance. Finally, near dawn, the solution occurred to him. Wangling a breakfast appointment with Roosevelt, the exhausted Sachs launched into a long soliloquy about Robert Fulton, the inventor of the steamboat. Fulton had offered to build a fleet of steamboats for Napoleon, but he was turned down on the grounds that there could be no such thing as a ship without sails. If Napoleon had shown more imagination, Sachs concluded, the United States might be a French-speaking country.

Roosevelt remained silent for several moments. "Alex," he said finally, "what you're after is to see that the Nazis don't blow us up."

"Precisely," Sachs replied.

The President was silent for a moment. Then he brought up his old objection: How could he promote research on a military development when his own military had already told him that the development was worthless?

This time Sachs was ready with an answer. He explained that for the moment—at least until the possibility of a nuclear chain reaction could be established—universities would conduct the research and it could be coordinated and supervised by the Bureau of Standards. If the research scientists showed that the reaction was possible and that the production of a bomb was feasible from an engineering point of view, the military could be brought in then.

Roosevelt listened carefully. When Sachs was finished, he pointedly offered him a glass of Napoleon cognac. Then he summoned his personal adviser, General Edwin M. "Pa" Watson.

"Pa," said the President, handing him Sachs's dossier, "this requires action."

Chapter Four

Roosevelt's proclamation was both dramatic and forceful, but the reaction of the American research community was somewhat hesitant. Part of their hesitation was due to the nature of the effort itself: it would be a constant push against the frontiers of physics, a perpetual battle with the unknown. In the fall of 1939 no one knew whether a self-sustaining chain reaction in uranium—the first of what seemed an infinity of steps toward the tapping of fission energy—was possible. No one knew if fission occurred in the 238 isotope of uranium or in the far less plentiful 235 isotope. And scientists were beginning to suspect that the "slow" neutrons being sought for precipitating a controlled chain reaction might be incapable of provoking the explosive reaction necessary for a bomb. If this were so, then the possibility of an atomic bomb was so slim that many scientists were ready to write it off entirely.

In the absence of concentrated and central control for a scientific attack on these problems, American nuclear research was scattered among over a dozen universities. Despite the flurry of excitement that followed the discovery of fission, many physicists still communicated with each other haphazardly, in the pipe-and-slippers style to which they had become accustomed by years of peacetime intellectual luxury. Theoretically this problem should have been solved by the appointment of the Bureau of Standards as a coordinating agency. But Lyman Briggs, the Bureau's chairman, was constitutionally disinclined to move quickly. A dignified, tight-necked physicist of the old school, Briggs was the sort of scientist who, according to one of his colleagues, "would spend twenty years of his life doing one experiment."

Despite constant prodding from Sachs and despite repeated displays of interest from Roosevelt, through the spring of 1940 Briggs and his Uranium Committee continued to move only in inches. His first request for funds was limited to three thousand dollars—for an effort on which, Sachs thought, the Germans might already be spending millions. As far as Sachs was concerned, Briggs's snail's pace was not only frustrating but increasingly dangerous.

The economist had good reason to worry. The Nazis had already overrun Belgium, so that huge deposits of uranium ore in the Belgian Congo were now endangered. In an ominous move Hilter had halted all sales of uranium from the ancient Joachimstal mines in Czechoslovakia. Worse, there were persistent rumors from Germany that the Kaiser Wilhelm Institute—where Hahn, Heisenberg, and von Weiszäcker were all thought to be working—had mounted a determined and systematic push to solve fission's many problems. If there were a race for the bomb, it looked to Sachs as if the Nazis had come out of the blocks with terrifying speed. The United States, on the other hand, seemed content merely to stand and survey the course.

If America were to make up its lost ground, Sachs thought, Briggs would have to be bypassed if not actually replaced. In May, at Sachs's urging, Roosevelt brought in a new protagonist: the energetic New England mathematician Vannevar Bush. Spry and deceptively boyish, with a lock of hair perennially falling over his forehead, Bush had parlayed the chairmanship of the National Defense Research Committee (NDRC)—a federal agency whose job was to bring the fruits of science to bear on the war effort—into a virtual scientific czardom. From his Washington office the acerbic Yankee all but controlled the dealing of federal dollars to the country's hungry and increasingly defense-minded universities.

But Bush proved no easy convert. From his vantage point at the top of the NDRC he could survey the whole of wartime scientific enterprise. In comparison with such already fruitful projects as radar and submarine research, the fission idea seemed little more than a pipe dream to him. Hadn't Szilard, the most enthusiastic of the few optimistic physicists, been stymied when asked in a meeting to outline a course of research that might end in an atomic bomb? Besides, as a newly shaped scientific politician, Bush had little desire to step on the toes either of Lyman Briggs or of the many university laboratories who were competing with increasing ferocity for government money. "Uranium research," he wrote in the spring of 1941, leaves "no clearcut path to defense results of great importance."

With Bush unconvinced and Briggs apparently unready, the fission project seemed suspended in a leaderless vacuum. Except for Sachs— who as a political figure could not hope to lead a group of academic scientists—and Szilard, whose pugnacious personality and intellectual flightiness rendered him suspect among many of his colleagues, no one seemed able to firmly take charge. On the research front most of the effort was still focused not on a bomb but on the use of fission as a source of energy; few of the vital questions on chain reactions, isotopes, and explosive fission had been answered to anyone's satisfaction. To the small group of scientists who saw the German effort as a growing threat to world civilization, the situation had begun to look very dark indeed.

Fortunately for the Americans, the British approach to a possible atomic bomb was decidedly more energetic. Organized in 1940 under the chairmanship of George Thomson, Britain's MAUD Committee had relentlessly pushed its researchers toward the development of a war-ending atomic weapon. As a result of this almost monomaniacal pursuit, the British were coming up with information that looked increasingly promising.

A formal report on their progress reached Vannevar Bush by October 1941. Emboldened by the British optimism, the Americans finally began to stir. On October 9 Bush carried the news of the British achievements to the White House, where he told Roosevelt and Vice President Henry Wallace that although not yet proven, the atomic proposition was looking increasingly feasible. Cheered by the report, Roosevelt told Bush to expedite the research "in every possible way."

Bush took the President at his word. Out of a series of noisy conferences in the winter of 1941 a plan of attack began to emerge. Research on chain reactions and the preparation of fissionable material— some of it already under way—was further organized and parceled out among the various universities. Funding, which after two years of Briggs had still been discussed only in terms of hundreds of thousands of dollars, now suddenly became a matter of hundreds of millions, with a top estimate of $130 million as the total cost of the bomb. Perhaps most important, Bush and the scientists now began to talk about constructing pilot plants to take fundamental research out of the laboratory and toward the production of a real bomb.

But Bush sensed—even if many of the scientists did not—that the making of a bomb would ultimately require the construction of immense industrial installations, sprawling "fission factories." Their design and building would present problems that no one could foresee and that no group of research scientists could expect to solve without outside help. When the planning of that construction began—hopefully, Bush thought, in the summer of 1942—scientific brainpower would have to make room for engineering expertise. Bush could think of no more expert group than the engineers of the United States Army.

By May 1942, Bush thought the research results were promising enough to actually bring the Army into the picture. He consulted with Army Chief of Staff General George C. Marshall, who immediately appointed General "Fat" Styer—a competent engineer thoroughly experienced in massive construction projects—to act as liaison. But Styer was already overburdened with his duties in General Somervell's Services of Supply, and Somervell was loath to donate any of his aide's valuable time. Styer could continue to supervise from a distance, but to coordinate and push through the vital day-to-day operations, the Army would have to bring in a fresh, new face.

Chapter Five

Colonel James Marshall was puzzled. Summoned from his office in Syracuse the day before, he was now ensconced in Washington's Willard Hotel, his desk strewn with the contents of a mysterious folder cryptically labeled "S-1." In fact, his instructions from Styer on that June 1942 day had been scarcely less cryptic: the general had told him that he had a new job supervising the construction of something called an atomic bomb.

Marshall could not even guess what Styer was talking about. In place of an explanation the general had given him this folder.

Now, in his dimly lit hotel room, Marshall struggled over the envelope's contents. In obscure and baffling terms it told him of the possibility of fashioning an incredibly destructive bomb from uranium or from a recently discovered manmade element called plutonium. There were five ways, the report said, to produce the required ingredients; each way would eventually require the construction of a separate industrial plant. All in all, the building of the plants was expected to cost in the neighborhood of $85 million.

Marshall, a handsome and courtly man who was known to his fellow officers as "Gentleman Jim," was as experienced an engineering officer as the Army had. His background included four years as an engineering professor at West Point and the successful supervision under the Syracuse District of a gigantic $250 million civil-military construction program. But the S-1 folder, choked with scientific vocabulary and obfuscated by oblique references to unknown objects, seemed like a missive from Oz. What, Marshall wondered, was a cyclotron? a centrifuge? heavy water? Through a sleepless night, Marshall tried to make sense of it. "I had never heard of atomic fission," he said later, "but I did know that you couldn't build much of a plant, much less four of them, for $85 million."

A meeting with General Styer and Vannevar Bush the next day cleared up some of Marshall's confusion. Four of the possible paths to the bomb, Bush explained, involved separating the U-235 isotope, which constituted only .7 percent of natural uranium ore, from the far more abundant U-238 isotope. Since the chemical properties of the two isotopes were exactly the same, this was an extremely tricky proposition.

Nonetheless, scientists thought they had a bead on a series of possible solutions. At the Naval Research Laboratory, Ross Gunn and Phillip Abelson were trying to capitalize on the tendency of the slightly "lighter" U-235 isotope in liquefied uranium to move toward the hotter of two concentric pipes, an approach known as liquid thermal diffusion. At Columbia, Nobel Prize winner Harold Urey was looking at gaseous diffusion, a process in which a uranium gas would be passed through a series of porous "barriers" that would separate U-235 atoms from the slightly heavier U-238 atom. At the University of Virginia, Jesse Beams was spinning powdered uranium in a massive cylinder, using centrifugal force to separate one isotope from the other. And on the West Coast, Ernest Lawrence was applying his stable of cyclotrons—the invention of which had helped him win a Nobel Prize—to the separation of the two isotopes by means of a powerful electromagnetic current.

The fifth method depended on the production of an entirely new element. In December 1940 Glen Seaborg and Joseph Kennedy, a pair of talented young chemists at the University of California, had bombarded uranium with deuterons, the nuclei of atoms of heavy hydrogen. The collisions had produced two new elements, the like of which had never before been seen on earth. The elated chemists and their colleagues— Abelson, Edwin McMillan, Emilio Segrè and Arthur Wohl—named the new elements neptunium and plutonium after the last two planets in the solar system. Of the two, plutonium soon proved tantalizingly fissionable. Best of all, it became evident that the new element was almost certain to be a by-product of any chain reaction of uranium. If this were so, then a uranium-based nuclear reactor could itself be used as a "factory" to produce material for the bomb.

When Bush finished his exposition, Marshall sat back in relief. Fine, he thought; at least the whole thing sounds doable. But two weeks later, when he sat down with the scientific leaders themselves—including Lawrence, Urey, and Arthur Holly Compton, who was heading reactor and plutonium work at the University of Chicago—he was shocked back into reality. Of the four prospects for uranium isotope separation, he was told, only Lawrence's was anywhere near the stage where practical industrial planning could begin. At Chicago, progress toward a uranium chain reaction was going slowly, and almost no weighable amounts of plutonium had been produced. Worse, Lawrence and Compton were already arguing about where to locate an industrial plant, which, given the current state of the research projects, could not even be designed, let alone built.

Colonel Marshall was jolted. It seemed as if he were back in the Willard Hotel reading that incomprehensible report. As the summer wore on and the situation remained essentially unchanged, he began to feel more and more as if he were wading through an impenetrable swamp. Finally, in desperation, with the thoroughly inadequate figure of $85 million fixed firmly in his mind, he made a decision that fatally compromised his position as a leader. Since, he assumed, only one plant could be built with the allotted money, and since only Lawrence's electromagnetic method showed any realistic promise of success, he would build that plant and that plant only, abandoning not only the other three isotope-separation processes but the plutonium process as well.

This was precisely what Bush did not want to hear. He had no desire to put all of fission's eggs in one basket and was firmly convinced that until one or the other of the processes proved infeasible, all five should be pursued with equal vigor. In fact, he had already said as much in his recommendation to Roosevelt. In general, it had been noticed over the course of the summer that the deferential Marshall seemed to lack the drive necessary both to command the respect of his superiors and to successfully coordinate the scientific and engineering aspects of the bomb effort. As disturbing rumors of German progress continued to reach Washington, the American project, which had seemed to finally acquire some momentum in June, was now not only stagnant but actually moving in reverse. Clearly, Bush thought, it was time for a change.

As August rolled into September, Bush outlined his plan. A Military Policy Committee consisting of two high-ranking Army officers and one Navy officer—and bolstered by the presence of Bush and his assistant, Harvard University President James Conant—would run the project as a sort of board of directors. This board would then choose a single Army engineer officer to run the day-to-day operations and build the necessary plants. That officer, Bush assumed, would be someone with whom he already had a good working relationship. Specifically, he wanted Styer.

But Somervell outmaneuvered him. Rather than lose Styer for the duration of the war, he casually proposed that the full-time running of the fission effort be turned over to a certain Colonel Leslie Groves. Bush tried to hold him off, saying that it would be up to the new Military Policy Committee to select the leader and that Styer had already proved himself capable of working comfortably with the scientists. But Somervell had already decided that Styer would stay exactly where he was and that Leslie Groves would become the atomic project's next "victim."

Thus Bush was shocked and chagrined when Groves presented himself on September 17, 1942, as the new officer in charge. The scientist listened with growing discomfort as the brash colonel, supremely confident of himself, briskly described his notion of how things should be organized.

Groves said he would never get anything done if all his decisions had to go through a committee. There would be endless arguments, and everything would slow down. The colonel was used to working independently, on his own authority. If Bush didn't like the way he handled his job, he was welcome to fire him.

After Groves left, Bush sat back in his chair, deeply troubled. First of all, Somervell had beaten him with a smoothly calculated end run. Second, he was apparently going to be deprived of the services of Styer. But the personality of this new officer was the worst blow of all. Although he certainly seemed to have the requisite drive, Bush doubted that he had the tact and diplomacy to deal with the scientists, many of whom had substantial egos of their own and a deep suspicion of all things military.

Quickly Bush pulled out pen and pencil and dashed off a memo to Harvey Bundy, his liaison in the office of the Secretary of War.

"I fear," he wrote, referring directly to the obstreperous colonel, "we are in the soup."

Part Two

FIRST STEPS

Chapter Six

For Leslie Groves, September 17, 1942, was no happier a day than it had been for Vannevar Bush. After his encounter with General Somervell in the Capitol, he had gone straight to General Styer's office. He and Styer had long been friends, and although they needled each other mercilessly about their respective weights, they had a deep and enduring respect for each other's ability. Despite Styer's higher rank, they had worked as virtual coequals in Somervell's Services of Supply division. Because their relationship was so close, Groves felt no qualms about unburdening himself to his erstwhile boss.

The appointment to head the atomic bomb project, he complained, would cost him his only chance to get out from behind a desk and into combat. Furthermore, although he knew very little about the bomb project, what he did know had not impressed him. As far as he could tell, all the scientists had done was come up with a series of vague and as yet unproven theories. There was, as far as he could see, absolutely nothing to indicate that the effort would be more than a weak shot into an almost impenetrable dark.

Styer tried to calm him. The scientific work, he assured Groves, was just about finished. All the colonel would have to do was go out and build a few plants, make a few bombs, and the war would be over.

Groves was not so sure. He had worked with scientists before, and although he did not deny their intelligence and capability, he felt that they tended to be impractical. Instead of sticking with a perfectly good design and seeing it through to the production stage, they were forever tinkering with it, forever improving it, forever drifting off on interesting but not-quite-relevant tangents.

Furthermore, despite the fact that a great many of them seemed to hate the sight of a uniform, he had found that many of them were themselves secretly and quite rigidly rank-conscious.

25

If he was going to work with scientists, he told Styer, he would have to be able to command their respect. With only a colonel's rank and without complete authority to run the project, he might have trouble getting them to listen to him.

Styer agreed. On the spot he decided to promote Groves to brigadier general and to put him entirely in charge of the whole project.

To Groves the promotion must have meant that he would at least get something out of the unwelcome assignment. As soon as his new rank was a fact, he would start meeting with the scientists. In the meantime there were other things he could do.

Groves actually knew a great deal more about the fission project than he had let on to Somervell or even to Styer. During Marshall's tenure he had handled the project's funds through his office, securing, after some difficulty, the allotted $85 million from a special presidential fund. (Roosevelt and Bush had agreed early on that the money should not come through Congress, whose investigating committees—one of them led by a feisty little bulldog senator from Missouri named Harry Truman—were always ready to make a public show of big-money projects.) Groves had advised Marshall to secure the services of Boston engineering firm Stone and Webster to begin the design of the pilot plants and had continually urged him to press both the scientists and the engineers into formulating an organized, coherent program. Groves had even scrapped the project's name—Designated Substitute Materials—as so mysterious as to arouse unwanted questions and had substituted the name Manhattan Engineer District as more suitably innocuous.

More important, Groves's three-month involvement with the MED had enabled him to pinpoint its problems. As he saw it, there were three major obstacles. All of them were surmountable in his estimation, but they had stymied Marshall to the point of procrastination. Now, with authority in his hands and a treasured promotion in his pocket, with twenty-four years of experience and a singularity of purpose that at times seemed to border on monomania, General Leslie R. Groves set out to break through the logjam.

Chapter Seven

Five months earlier, on a fine spring day in April 1942, three members of the NDRC's Planning Board set out on a leisurely drive through the Tennessee River Valley. Although their pace that day was slow, their mission was urgent. They were looking for land on which to build the world's first atomic factory. If a bomb were ever to become a reality, they knew, the fission project would eventually—and the sooner the better—have to move out of the scientific laboratories and into at least one full-size, functioning industrial installation.

The Planning Board's drive through the Tennessee hills was the penultimate phase in the exhaustive and systematic search for a site for the "fission factory." After some consideration of the Great Lakes area (preferred by Arthur Compton because of its proximity to his Chicago base) and over the loud protests of Ernest Lawrence (who wanted the plant built near *his* home base in Berkeley), the Planning Board had focused on the area around Knoxville, where a number of broad and healthy rivers rolled out of the Appalachians and where the mighty Tennessee Valley Authority could guarantee hundreds of millions of watts of crucial electricity.

As they rounded a series of curves near the tiny town of Elza, they knew immediately that their search was over. Here was a series of invitingly buildable valleys surrounded by low hills, with Louisville and Nashville Railroad installations available to provide transportation. Very little of the nearby land was being cultivated, which meant that few families would have to be moved. A dam a few miles upstream rendered the Clinch River free of the sediment that would have made excavation and construction difficult if not impossible.

When the Planning Board submitted its report on the Elza site, everyone connected with the project (except Ernest Lawrence) agreed that it seemed a happy choice. Bush liked the security provided by its location in the heart of the country, where it would not be vulnerable to coastal attacks by Axis bombers. After a quick inspection, Arthur Compton was won over—the site, after all, was only a few hundred miles from Chicago. And even Ernest Lawrence ultimately dropped his objections and joined the bandwagon. Noting this rare unanimity among the scientists, Styer recommended in June that the site be purchased immediately.

But Colonel Marshall had hesitated. Reluctant to proceed with the acquisition until what he called "the Compton process" (i.e., plutonium production) was proven, he called for a detailed survey by Stone and Webster and proceeded nearly to sink the endeavor under a weight of unnecessary paperwork. Finally, at the end of July, he ignored Styer's recommendation and decided that there was really no reason to go ahead with the purchase until sometime in late autumn.

Groves had watched all this foot-dragging with growing impatience. He had earlier concurred on the site, not only because it met all the criteria but also because the area offered a large supply of what he called "friendly" (that is, nonunion) labor. He could not understand Marshall's reluctance to proceed with the acquisition, and he repeatedly urged him to move forward "with all due speed." The project as a whole, he knew, was badly in need of new momentum, and the purchase of land for a plant— with the implication of a construction start soon thereafter—might be just what was needed to get things going.

After his promotion, when he had the authority to get the Manhattan District off the ground, Groves moved with lightning speed. On September 23, the day after his promotion to brigadier general was finalized, he attended a top-level meeting in the office of Secretary of War Henry Stimson. Besides the aging secretary, present were General George Marshall, Bush, Conant, Somervell, Styer, and Stimson's assistant Harvey Bundy. But Groves was not one to be intimidated by titles. In the middle of the meeting, surrounded by people who outranked him on all scores, he suddenly stood up.

"Gentlemen," he said, "you'll have to excuse me. I'm going out to Knoxville to have a look at that land, and I've got a train to catch."

With that he turned and left the room, leaving behind a group of astonished VIPs. "It was a shock to most of them," he said later, "because they weren't used to hearing anyone talk to the secretary that way. Most of them would have just sat there and missed the train."

For his part, Somervell could only grin. "I told you he'd move fast," he said.

By 6:30 the next morning, Groves was in Knoxville. After a hurried breakfast at a local cafeteria, he drove out to the Elza site, where Colonel

James Marshall was waiting to meet him. In the blue mist of the Cumberland Mountain morning they walked the trails of Black Oak Ridge, the northernmost of the five pine-covered outcroppings that had originally caught the eye of the Planning Board. Groves saw that the reality of the site was even better than the maps and site surveys had suggested. Not only did the lay of the land provide both access and isolation; it also allowed for extensive expansion along the chain of sleepy valleys below, in case everyone had underestimated the size of the "fission factories."

By the end of the day Groves was absolutely certain that the MED had found its spot. Not content to wait until they returned to Washington, he immediately telephoned his office, instructing that condemnation proceedings—the first step in any large government land purchase—begin at once on fifty-six thousand acres of the Tennessee site. Within a few weeks the acquisition of that site—which would soon and forever after be known as Oak Ridge—was a fait accompli. Always a good soldier under orders, Groves had put aside his personal reservations about the project's viability, and was already attacking his new job with his customary energy and forcefulness. A controversy that had mired the project in uncertainty for three months had been resolved, and Groves had shifted the Manhattan District from reverse into first gear.

Chapter Eight

But if the bomb effort were ever to move from first gear into second, it would have to be supplied with a virtual mountain of raw materials. This included thousands of tons of steel, hundred of miles of copper wire, and acres of glass, as well as a long and continually growing list of such rare items as uranium ore and high-grade nickel. Up until Groves's appointment, the battle to get access to these materials had been tremendous and ongoing, a battle that the underpowered Manhattan District had seemed likely to lose.

The coming of war—which a reluctant public and an isolationist Congress had stubbornly tried to wish away—had caught the nation short-stocked; its industries were vastly underprepared to meet the wartime crunch. In the aftermath of the bombing of Pearl Harbor and with the entry of the United States into the great struggle, demands on American production capacity had doubled, and then doubled again.*

The nation's producers scrambled to convert their assembly lines from manufacturing peacetime products to manufacturing those needed for war. Simultaneously, the collective appetite of the country's consumers—especially the now-insatiable military—grew at a rate that must have seemed astronomical. To assuage that appetite, the government pumped some $2.3 billion a month into the economy—enough, as one analyst later put it, to build two Panama Canals every day.

Amid the banging of hammers and the whining of drills had arisen a new and far more disconcerting noise: the sound of thousands of harried factory managers and an equal number of insistent captains clamoring for the same raw materials at the same time. But despite the heroic efforts of

---

*In 1941, for example, the United States produced 309,000 tons of aluminum. By late 1943 that figure—bloated by the wartime needs of the aircraft industry—had risen to almost 1,200,000 tons, a fourfold increase.

the miners and manufacturers, there was simply not enough of anything to go around. Laissez-faire economics had to be suspended for the duration; in its place the government installed an orderly system of priorities to determine who should get what when.

The national agency responsible for establishing these priorities and dealing out the raw materials was the War Production Board, created by a Roosevelt executive fiat in January 1942. At its head the President installed Donald Nelson, a huge, bald bear of a man who had made his reputation as an executive for Sears, Roebuck. Within two months, in concert with the Army-Navy Munitions Board, Nelson had developed a system that rated each individual military project (proximity fuses, for example, or Sherman tanks) according to its perceived importance to the war effort. The higher the rating, the faster that project got the raw materials it needed.

Naturally, this system did absolutely nothing to alleviate the murderous competition for raw materials. For the military, it meant establishing a delicate balance among a number of crucial war efforts, including radar, sonar, jet aircraft, and possibly most important, synthetic rubber. (Not only the military but industrial civilization itself ran on rubber, and the Japanese, with their victories in Southeast Asia, had cut off a large portion of the world supply.)

Exacerbating this already monumental problem was an ongoing battle royal between General Somervell and Donald Nelson. Essentially, the civilians, whose needs were championed by Nelson, were lined up against the military, which was seen as an avaricious gobbler of raw materials that cared not a whit if civilians went unclothed, unhoused, and untransported. Over and over again, whether the issue was spare parts for the coal mining industry, new factories to meet civilian needs, or even the allocation of newsprint (the Army argued that the printing of Sunday comic strips was a frivolous waste of critical materials), Nelson and Somervell locked horns. The former retailer accused the patrician southerner of "trying to turn the War Production Board into the Army's errand boy."

Against this backdrop of confusion and acrimony, the fledgling fission project struggled to fill its needs for raw materials. The effort was further hamstrung by Bush's early skepticism about the possibility of making an atomic bomb—skepticism that had led him to relegate the project's priorities below such ongoing and apparently more promising developments as radar and even DDT. His failure to support the program more aggressively in its earlier stages had allowed the Army to treat it with summary disregard, which in turn was reflected in the estimates of the military majority of its chances for success.

Even after Bush began to raise his voice on the Manhattan District's behalf, the attitude of the Army remained a considerable obstacle. General Lucius D. Clay, a hardworking Georgian whose popularity with Congress had led Somervell to put him in charge of championing the Army's priority needs, was among the most stubborn. In June 1942 he had grudgingly offered Marshall a blanket AA priority for the MED—a high priority but not the highest available. Marshall started to exercise that priority, but he found that Clay had actually given him not the respectable and potentially useful AA-1 but a routine AA-3. This meant that the Manhattan District, a project that was working on the cutting edge of the world's most sophisticated science, was forced to compete with the construction of barracks and mess halls in Stateside Army camps. The rating served, as one MED staffer noted, to make the project seem "miscellaneous and unimportant"; and as far as the MED leadership was concerned, it would cause delays that would all but hopelessly cripple the project.

Throughout the long summer of 1942, Marshall and Bush fought for a higher rating. Still, Clay stood firm. Even when Bush threatened to take the problem to General George Marshall himself, Clay vowed to fight him all the way.

But Clay had not reckoned with Groves. The day after his appointment and briefing by Styer, the new MED leader paid Clay a call. Clay was an old friend of Groves, a former classmate at the Army Engineer School and a colleague in Somervell's office. Now Clay eyed Groves warily across his desk. Just a few days before, he had given the then-colonel the responsibility of filling the lumber needs not only of the Army but of the Navy as well. Now here Groves was telling him about this new job.

"Groves," said Clay, "I don't like this. I'm an expert on military history, and I can tell you that no war has ever been won by a new weapon. And this atomic thing is a dream of the highest order. It was sold to the president by a bunch of hare-brained scientists, and for some reason he bought it." The general paused dramatically. "There's another reason I don't like it," he said.

Although he was secretly amused to hear Clay voice sentiments that were very close to his own, Groves did not show it. "What's the other reason?" he said.

"I can handle Colonel Marshall," Clay responded. "I don't expect to be able to handle you."

Clay had good reason to be concerned. Groves knew full well how obstinate Clay could be and had already developed a plan of his own. First of all, Groves felt that not even an AA-1 priority rating was high enough. If the atomic bomb were going to be ready in time to counter the German effort—a proposition that at that point looked highly dubious—it would have to be pursued with terrible speed. Even an AA-1 rating would mean endless competition for materials, especially with radar and synthetic rubber, and this in turn would mean a series of unpredictable and intolerable delays. If the project were to move at what Groves saw as the necessary velocity, only a blanket rating of AAA—the highest possible—would suffice. To get that rating, he knew, he would have to bypass Clay altogether. He would have to deal directly with the top.

Clay may have sensed this when he predicted that his friend would be hard to handle. He would have been right. Even as he met with Clay on September 18, the new head of the Manhattan District had an ace up his sleeve. The day before, Groves had drafted a letter for Donald Nelson to sign:

> Dear Groves:
>
> 　　I am in full accord with the prompt delegation of power . . . through you to assign a AAA rating to those items of delivery which cannot otherwise be secured in time for the prosecution of the work under [your] charge.
>
> Very truly yours,
> Donald Nelson

On September 19, the day after his meeting with Clay and only two days after his appointment to head the Manhattan District, Groves appeared in Nelson's office, thrust the letter under the bureaucrat's nose, and asked him to sign it. It was, the new general assured him, extremely urgent.

Nelson blanched. From his point of view it must have looked like another Army attempt to steam-roller him. But calmly, in his low-key, soft-spoken voice, Groves explained the nature of the Manhattan District's mission, emphasizing that the President himself had ordered it pursued as quickly as possible. "If you don't sign the letter," he concluded, "I'm going to write the president and recommend that the project be cancelled."

Actually, the move was a bold and skillful bluff. As direct and uncompromising as he was, it is doubtful that Groves would have made good his threat. But he knew that Nelson owed his position to Roosevelt's patronage and had surmised that the War Production Board chairman's reputation for affability reflected a character that was weak and malleable. Putting his knowledge of his opponent together with the nature of the situation, Groves must have guessed that Nelson could be bulldozed.

It turned out that Groves guessed right. After a few moments Nelson reached for his pen and signed the letter. Groves thanked him gravely and put the letter into his briefcase. Only after he reached the hallway might he have allowed himself a slight smile of victory.

The confrontation with Nelson was a major triumph. No longer would the Manhattan District have to stand in line for its vital supplies or compete with the construction of outhouses and the manufacture of pesticides. From that point forward, Groves knew, all other wartime research and development would take a back seat to what would be recognized as the most important project of all: the effort to beat the Nazis in the grim and terrible race for the atomic bomb.

Chapter Nine

Groves's coup had essentially secured for the Manhattan District first rights to all its necessary *materiae primae*. But there was one raw material, the most crucial of all, that could not be had simply with the stroke of a pen.

Until 1939, that material had been considered so humble by the industrial community that the contemporary edition of Funk and Wagnall's Dictionary solemnly declared that it had "no commercial purpose." (In fact, it did have an obscure use as a dye in the manufacture of certain kinds of glass and ceramics. It made, the ceramics people said, a lovely yellow.)

The material, of course, was uranium. Discovered in 1789 by the German chemist Heinrich Klaproth, who distilled it from the black, radium-producing ore known as pitchblende, uranium was of little interest except for its curiosity value as the element with the highest atomic weight. In the last years of the nineteenth century it was found by Henri Becquerel to emit radioactivity (which, incidentally, the excited chemist erroneously took to be X-rays). Even then, outside the small circle of European scientists who were experimenting with radiation, uranium attracted almost no attention at all.

But in 1939 came the discovery of fission. In the wake of Hahn and Meitner's reports came the realization that the obscure yellow metal might well become the handmaiden of an atomic future.

One of the first to grasp the significance of uranium's new status was Edgar Sengier, a worldly Belgian who had the rollicking spirit of an adventurer—he had spent five years of his youth building tramways in the mountains of China—and the elegant manners of a continental diplomat. Now in his midsixties, pale and slight, Sengier's self-effacing presence and unshakable discretion masked the fact that he was, in the estimation of at least one observer, "one of the most powerful men in the world." One of the thirteen directors of the Bank of Belgium—which, because of Belgium's rigorous neutrality, occupied a position at the very center of

European financial affairs—Sengier was also the chairman of the executive committee of the Union Minière du Haut Katanga, a multinational mining concern whose holdings in the mineral-rich Belgian Congo produced a full 7 percent of the world's copper, 5 percent of its zinc, and an incredible 80 percent of its cobalt.

From its mines in Shinkolobwe, in the southeastern Congo, the Union Minière also produced a substantial percentage of the world's high-grade uranium ore. But a depression in the world market had caused the price of radium, which was laboriously processed from uranium, to drop from $6 million an ounce in 1912 to $600,000 an ounce; uranium salts themselves were selling for as little as $1.50 a pound. So the Shinkolobwe mines had been all but abandoned. Outside the main shafts, which were flooded with water, a 2,200-ton pile of uranium tailings sat neglected in the African sun alongside a collection of rusting machinery.

Then in May 1939, Sengier paid a visit to the London office of Lord Stonehaven, his fellow director on the board of the Union Minière. Sengier was surprised and puzzled when his cohort asked him to speak briefly with Sir Henry Tizard, a well-known scientist who at the time was director of London's Imperial College of Science and Technology. What, Sengier wondered, could a British scientist possibly want of him?

He quickly found out. Without so much as an explanatory preamble, Tizard asked Sengier to grant the British government an option on any and all uranium that could be extracted from the Shinkolobwe mines. For Sengier this meant that he would have the wealthiest of buyers for what up to then had been a virtually unmarketable product. But the financier's business instincts prompted him to immediately refuse the strange offer. As he left Stonehaven's office, Tizard took him by the arm.

"Be careful," said the Englishman. "Never forget that you have in your hands something which may mean a catastrophe to your country and mine if it were to fall into the hands of a possible enemy."

The remark, coming as it did from a famous scientist, impressed and intrigued Sengier. A few days later he met in Paris with a group of French physicists, headed by Frederic Joliot-Curie, the son-in-law of the discoverer of radium. Sengier listened transfixed as Joliot-Curie explained the process of fission in uranium. As if this startling news weren't enough, the Frenchman further astonished Sengier by proposing a grand scheme: he, Joliot, would retire with his group to the deepest Sahara, where, with Sengier's help, they would build and test the world's first atomic bomb— thus beating not only the Germans but also the British and the Americans to the punch. It was the kind of notion that appealed immediately to the adventurous Sengier, who agreed on the spot to furnish the uranium and even to provide some of the financing.

But in September the war broke out, isolating Joliot-Curie and effectively putting an end to his atomic aspirations on behalf of France. But his meeting with Sengier was ultimately of enormous benefit to the Allied cause, for the Belgian was alerted both to the tremendous significance of uranium and to the extreme danger posed by the advanced state of German nuclear physics. Anticipating a Nazi invasion of his own country, he took immediate steps to ship to the United States and Great Britain the 120 grams of radium that represented Belgium's entire stock. He also ordered all the uranium ore that stood warehoused in Oolen, Belgium, to be sent to the United States. But because of an administrative delay the order was not carried out immediately. A few months later the Nazi blitzkrieg overran the Low Countries, and it was too late.

There still remained, however, the neglected pile of tailings at Shinkolobwe. Toward the end of 1940, as a German invasion of the Congo began to seem more and more likely, Sengier—who by then had fled his native country to take up residence in the United States—ordered over half the pile shipped to New York. In the fall the freighters *West Humhaw* and *West Lashaway* set out from the Congolese port of Lobito, their holds concealing what would become the war's most important cargo: 1,200 tons of high-grade uranium ore. For two months Sengier sweated in his New York office while the freighters slowly crossed the Atlantic Ocean, which was bristling with U-boats. But the crossing was made without incident. By December all the ore was sitting safely (if idly) in a Staten Island warehouse.

With the entry of the United States into the war a year later, Sengier thought he saw an opportunity both to secure a buyer for his neglected ores and to provide the Americans with a running start on an atomic weapon. Within days of the bombing of Pearl Harbor he was in touch with Thomas Finletter, a high-level State Department official who was then assistant secretary for strategic materials. But Finletter proved to be an unfortunate contact. Possibly because of the extreme intracabinet rivalries within the Roosevelt Administration, the State Department was essentially in the dark about the existence of the fission project. Thus, when Finletter and Sengier met face-to-face in April 1942, the Belgian's urgent appeals made little impression. The assistant secretary, it seems, was far more interested in cobalt.

Meanwhile the Americans had found a source of uranium in Canada. Years before, in the spring of 1929, a young prospector named

Gilbert "Lucky" LaBine had set out for the Yukon Territory in search of silver and gold. Instead, he found pitchblende. Over the next decade, LaBine turned his Eldorado Mining Company into one of the world's principal suppliers of uranium. Although meager in comparison to the glory days of production at the Shinkolobwe operation, by 1942 Eldorado was able to modestly boast of a surplus of some three hundred tons of ore and a production capacity of about three hundred tons a year. Tipped by the Canadian government, which in turn had been alerted by the British, one of Vannevar Bush's fission committees had in April 1942 agreed to buy some two hundred tons of LaBine's suddenly precious ore.

Perhaps the ongoing availability of this other supply accounts for the coolness of both Bush and Finletter to Sengier's repeated offers. But if Bush and Finletter were cool, Groves definitely was not. Even before his appointment as head of the Manhattan District, he knew that the three hundred tons a year from Eldorado could only scratch the surface of the project's eventual requirements. Besides, he thought, if the Germans were truly engaged in the atomic race, it would be wise as a purely preventive measure to buy up all the uranium in sight.

Thus in July 1942, when Finletter finally forwarded Sengier's correspondence to Manhattan District offices, Groves immediately sat up and took notice. Here, he thought, was a potential source of supply that could not only satisfy the project's current needs but might well put it over the top for the long haul. Wasting no time, he urged Marshall's assistant Colonel Kenneth Nichols to check the offer thoroughly from all angles— including an exhaustive security check on Sengier that involved not only FBI and military intelligence reports but elaborate wiretaps of the mine owner's New York hotel room. (He warned Nichols to keep the whole thing secret—Belgium was involved, after all, and the Nazis owned Belgium.)

But even though Sengier passed all these tests with flying colors, then-Colonel Groves could only sit and fume as the project leadership continued to ignore the Union Minière uranium. Only after LaBine himself tried to buy five hundred tons of Sengier's ore to satisfy the Manhattan District's growing needs did Bush begin to stir, but even then he did little more than suggest that the ore be tested for purity.

With Groves's assumption of authority in mid-September, this leisurely attitude came to an abrupt halt. On the afternoon of his appointment, even before his first meeting with Bush, he ordered Nichols to go to New York the next day to buy all the uranium that Sengier would sell.

The next afternoon Colonel Nichols, dressed in civilian clothes, presented himself at Sengier's Manhattan office. The Belgian cast a suspicious glance at the bespectacled young officer in the ill-fitting suit and tie. Nichols looked so incongruous that Sengier asked him to produce identification. Not even the colonel's military ID quite satisfied him.

"You want to buy uranium," Sengier said. "But do you have the authority to buy it?"

"I probably have more authority," Nichols shot back, "than you have uranium."

The answer seemed to please Sengier. But in his mind one vital question remained. Why did the Army want this uranium in the first place?

When Nichols seemed reluctant to tell him, Sengier explained himself. He had no desire to sell the uranium if it was going to be used to make yellow stoplights. If he were to sell it, he wanted assurance that it would be used for military purposes. "You don't have to tell me specifically what those purposes are," he said. "I think I know. But I will need your assurance."

Nichols had grown increasingly uncomfortable under Sengier's questioning. He had a mandate not only from Groves but from the President himself to keep the Manhattan District's ultimate objective entirely secret. But now he felt somewhat relieved. Sengier obviously already knew that the uranium would be used to make a weapon but had deliberately and delicately left that unsaid. Here, Nichols must have thought, was someone with whom the MED could do business.

"You have that assurance," he said solemnly.

"Good!" said Sengier, smiling at last. "Then I suggest we come to terms on price."

A half-hour later Nichols emerged from Sengier's office, a piece of yellow notepaper tucked firmly into his briefcase. On that paper, in eight sentences of scrawled handwriting, Sengier had agreed to sell not only the Staten Island ore but also the entire remainder of the tailings pile at Shinkolobwe to the Manhattan Engineering District. In one swift coup Groves had pierced the uranium curtain and ended a year of stalemate. At the bargain price of $1.60 a pound, he bought the raw material from which would be forged, if all went well (an *if*, the general would soon discover, of monumental proportions), the most awesomely destructive weapon the world had ever seen.

For Groves it had been an eventful week. The course of his life, apparently headed for overseas duty and the possibility of a combat command, had been drastically changed. His new assignment was supremely difficult, frustrating, and in the end quite possibly intractable. (In the privacy of his thoughts he estimated the chances of the project's success at no better than 60 percent.) But it was now beginning to look like an appetizing challenge, and he had already responded with speed, boldness, and his characteristically unquenchable vitality. In the course of one week his adroit maneuvers—the securing of the Tennessee land, the successful priorities gambit, and the quick purchase of the Belgian uranium ore—had broken through a three-year accumulation of stubborn obstacles. A project that only a week earlier had seemed dangerously stagnated was now once again in motion. If it was at all possible to build an atomic bomb in time to beat the Germans and to influence the outcome of the war, Groves was determined to do it.

The project leadership—Bush in particular—was alternately alarmed, bemused, and encouraged by Groves's swift and forceful grasping of the reins. To everyone but Styer and Somervell the new general was unknown. But had they been aware of Groves's personal and professional history, they would have been less surprised. For in reality Groves's confident assumption of responsibility, his bold and authoritative push at the project's many obstacles, and even his abrasive personal style were consistent with attitudes and qualities that had characterized him all his life.

Chapter Ten

A knock at the door one day in 1916 took young Dick Groves (only those who didn't know him ever called him Leslie) by surprise. Despite the fact that he was a handsome and vigorous twenty-year-old, a fine athlete, and an accomplished student in his junior year at MIT, few people ever found their way to his Boston boardinghouse room. For Dick Groves was a loner, an intensely businesslike and almost precociously serious young man whose exaggerated self-confidence and bristling sarcasm tended to keep potential friends at a distance. Had they bothered to try to penetrate his rather considerable armor, they might have found in Dick Groves a nascent gentleman, a man whose values—pride and loyalty, duty and responsibility—belonged more to the century in which he had been born than to the one in which he now, somewhat uncomfortably, found himself. They might have found in the end that his almost swaggering ego, his air of superiority, and his intellectual posturing masked a confused social awkwardness and a sincere and genuine puzzlement as to how people really went about understanding one another. But few bothered.

This particular knock at the door, it turned out, was no curious classmate with a penchant for social ground-breaking. Instead, it was a Western Union delivery boy. That was unusual, for Dick's father, an Army chaplain for whom thrift was one of the godliest of virtues, was not inclined to spend good money on idle long-distance communication.

The telegram, like both its sender and its recipient, was essentially and ultimately serious. Dick's older brother Allen, who was working at a Department of Agriculture experimental farm near Arlington, Virginia, had suddenly come down with pneumonia. There was no cure, and now, a week after the illness had struck him, Allen had taken a turn for the worse.

As usual, Dick wasted no time. Packing a bag on the run, he left immediately for Washington. But by the time he got there it was too late.

43

The disease had ravaged Allen's lungs. Only two weeks after the first telling cough, he had died, gasping for breath.

His death hit the family hard. Allen had always been his parents' pride. No matter how impressive the achievements of his two younger brothers (Owen, younger than Dick and a scholar by nature, could literally read in the dark), somehow Allen had always been looked on as the household genius. Although he barely studied—as a boy he had done all his lessons standing up in a streetcar on the way to school—he rarely got anything less than an A. His memory was prodigious: he could look at a geometry theorem for thirty seconds and remember it for the rest of his days. His high school essay on moderate drinking won a national prize. "He may have had some influence on me," Groves would later admit, albeit grudgingly. "There may have been some desire on my part to keep up with him."

Allen's death galvanized Dick's planning for his own future. Ever since his junior year in high school he had wanted to attend West Point. But his father had opposed it. The chaplain had come to regret his military career, and his virtuous sensibilities were now offended by the Army, which he saw as a refuge for cursing, drinking lowlifes—"Anything," as one family member later put it, "but an intellectual oasis." A cultured and educated man whose most cherished recreation was reading the classics, Chaplain Groves's ambitions for his sons were primarily academic.

But Dick had his own ideas. All his life, especially since his third year in high school, he had wanted a military career. Earlier, while studying at the University of Washington, he had tried for a congressional appointment to West Point but had been passed over. Now Allen's death seemed to fire his own ambitions, to make him more determined than ever. Within weeks after the funeral he left MIT and enrolled in Shadman's, a well-known Washington D.C. prep school for the service academies. There he plowed through a seven-week cram course for the annual presidential competition for an at-large appointment. When the results came in, Dick had won a spot and the attendant prestige of a presidential mandate. "Entering West Point," he later said, "fulfilled my greatest ambition. I was deeply impressed with the character and devotion to duty of the Army officers I knew, and I was imbued with the idea that West Point graduates were normally the best officers." But there may have been another factor that kept young Dick in the military fold. "The Army in those days was like a family," his son later explained. "Leaving it would have been a major step."

In retrospect, Groves's devotion to the Army seems curious, for military life had placed him under extreme and unusual pressures almost since birth. Born in the manse of the First Presbyterian Church of Albany, New York, on August 17, 1896, the seventh-generation descendant of a Channel Islands farmer who had come to the Massachusetts Bay Colony in the 1660s as an indentured servant, Dick Groves had spent the first four years of his life waiting for the appearance of his father. The elder Groves had left the lay ministry to become an Army chaplain just before Dick was born; between 1896 and 1901 Chaplain Groves was perpetually shuttled from one tropical assignment to another—to Cuba and then the Philippines during the Spanish-American War and later to China, where the American Fourteenth Infantry was helping the British quell the Boxer Rebellion.

In his father's absence, young Dick's early development was so torpid that he spent his first four years without speaking. His worried mother, ill herself and struggling to run a fatherless four-person household, nonetheless found time to take her son on a diligent round of doctors, none of whom could find anything organically wrong with the speechless boy. Finally, just before his fifth birthday, young Dick uttered his first word: *cheese*. "I am always grateful," he wrote later, "that I was brought up in the days before the psychiatrist and the pediatrician gained such power. What a terrible time I would have had under modern conditions."

The return of Chaplain Groves in 1901 brought little relief to his son's austere boyhood. The chaplain himself was a severe man, a teetotaler (one of Groves's first memories was of asking his father about the smell of stale beer in an Army barracks and being regaled with a long lecture on the evils of drink) and a stern disciplinarian who considered any leisure-time activity other than reading, hunting, and fishing to be a frivolous waste of time if not downright diabolical. Well educated and academically minded, he had graduated from New York's Hamilton College. As a lawyer he had successfully argued cases before the New York State Supreme Court, and when he changed course toward the ministry, he ultimately graduated high in his class from Auburn Theological Seminary. The chaplain loved to spend his evenings reading *The World Almanac*, an activity to which his sons also dedicated themselves with such ferocity that by the time they were ten, they could easily recite not only the names of all the Presidents and Vice Presidents but the names and exact populations of each of the country's one hundred largest cities.

This atmosphere of quiet but inflexible discipline was made even grayer by a long and ultimately tragic series of family illnesses. While on duty in Cuba, Chaplain Groves contracted both malaria and yellow fever, which left him so weakened and emaciated that during the return journey from Siboney he could barely drag himself to the ship's deck to perform last rites for those whom the diseases had already vanquished. In 1899, when he was transferred to the Philippines, his post commander entered a strong plea to keep the chaplain out of unhealthy tropical climates, but the duty-bound Groves insisted on going. His reward, other than an appreciative citation from his commanding general ("No other officer worked as hard," wrote the Fourteenth Infantry's A.S. Daggett; "His horse was more often ridden by soldiers than by himself"), was a long and desperate bout with tuberculosis, which meant, on his return from China, separation from the family and a series of seemingly interminable confinements in a New Mexico Army hospital. In fact, the chaplain's general state of health remained so fragile that until 1908 he could spend only one month a year at home with his family.

But the chaplain was not the only member of the family to suffer from serious diseases. In 1906 young Dick himself was diagnosed as having a pronounced heart murmur. To strengthen what he saw as a weak organ, he enticed his brother Allen into an endless series of breakneck footraces around the Victorian porches of their various homes. Their younger sister Gwen was so severely crippled by an extreme curvature of the spine that to relieve the pressure on her back she had to spend four hours a day stretched out on the living-room floor, her body painfully confined in a rigid wooden frame. This "therapeutic" torture, fashionable at the time, went on for almost four years. "It was not a pleasant experience," Dick would recall, "and it was particularly hard on my mother." Although courageous and resourceful enough to run what amounted to a family hospital, Mrs. Groves herself was substantially slowed by a heart condition.

Had the chaplain not been so resolutely dedicated to a military career, young Dick might have had a chance to develop outside friendships that would have both checked his growing ego and relieved the tensions of a sick and physically disunited family. As it was, he resigned himself to the peripatetic childhood of a service brat. Indeed, Groves's youth was a dizzying series of family moves, a blurry parade from one place to another—Albany, New York; Vancouver, Washington; Fort Hancock, New Jersey; Fort Wayne, Michigan; Helena, Montana; Pasadena, California; Fort Apache, Arizona. This meant constant uprootings, a sort of ongoing geographical insecurity that must have made investment in youthful friendships seem emotionally risky. Difficulty in forming close and deep friendships would mark most of Groves's adult life.

If rootlessness and loneliness were serious and constant problems, the family's financial situation sometimes bordered on the desperate. Army salaries were abysmally low; as a chaplain, Groves's father sent home only $125 a month. With his health a perpetual worry, the boys were early and often expected to chip in in the form of housework or outright wage-earning. At the age of seven Dick was collecting groaning armloads of driftwood for the family fireplace and single-handedly carrying the luggage of all the family's female guests the half-mile from their house to the Fort Hancock dock—an effort for which, he would recall, "I got hardly a thank-you." In Pasadena at the age of ten, he picked grapes, peaches, and walnuts, working for up to eleven hours a day to bring home a single dollar. A fifth-grade classmate noted that his hands were perpetually stained black from their daily soaking in walnut juice. Even this work, which young Dick likened to "forced slavery," was not enough for his taskmaster father, who, he recalled, remained "quite disappointed in my ability to stay at work, and termed me a very lazy little boy."

All this left its mark. A photograph of Dick Groves at the age of thirteen reveals a man in boy's clothing. The face is darkly mature, precociously handsome, and full of quiet confidence; the eyes are intense but a little angry and perhaps fundamentally sad. It is a face that brings to mind the last words of novelist Evan Connell's protagonist Mr. Bridge: "No," he had finally decided, "joy was for simpler minds."

But if outright joy was not a common feature of Groves's work-laden childhood, there was nevertheless a series of fond memories and simple pleasures. Many of these were of the family's constant travels. The transcontinental train rides fascinated Dick. He pressed his nose to the window and marveled at the seemingly endless expanse of prairie dog cities and at the wild horses that galloped past the lumbering train as if it were standing still. There was the mule-drawn school wagon in Vancouver Barracks, with the children racing to claim its cherished brass seats, and the clopping to school amid rows of blossoming cherry trees. There was Fort Hancock, with its sweeping view of the channel entrance to New York Harbor, where young Dick could watch the stately, never-ending parade of the world's grandest merchant ships. There was the trip from Vancouver to Pasadena, passing through San Francisco in the immediate wake of the disastrous 1906 earthquake. Dick was amazed to see thousands of people camped out in the rubble-strewn streets, cooking aromatic stews on huge outdoor stoves. In Pasadena there were the cakes and pies of the sidewalk vendors, which Dick and Owen earned by surreptitiously recycling tin cans; and there was Dick's pony Napoleon, so congenitally thin and ragged that one of the neighbors accused the boy of mistreating him.

Perhaps the happiest days of Groves's childhood were the summers he spent with his family in Fort Apache, Arizona. Years later he would remember with amusement the long stagecoach ride from Pasadena, bouncing across the high Arizona desert with the family dog running along beside. In Fort Apache itself they lived in the house of the famous Indian fighter General Miles, a rustic, seven-bedroom mansion "big enough," according to Mrs. Groves, "so you could drive an escort wagon right through it." Here there was the usual housework (after finding a fly "nicely grilled" into his mess hall steak, Dick took over all the cooking chores, in addition to dishwashing and gardening) and the long evenings reading in the post library; but there was also trout fishing in the White River, chasing bears on horseback through the woods, and best of all, long, solitary rides through the still pine forests and dazzling Alpine greenery of the White Mountains.

The three summer sojourns in Fort Apache marked the end of Groves's childhood. The rigor of his father's discipline, the long hours of work and constant traveling, and especially the responsibilities he had assumed for the welfare of the family in his father's absence had combined to mold a confident and independent adolescent. "He had always been with people who needed a lot of support," his own daughter would say later. "I think this need to support people had a lot to do with his own strength."

But the discipline and hard work had not kept him from developing a healthy curiosity about the world around him—especially the female half of that world. On a train ride from Pasadena to Helena, Montana, where his father was transferred after being given a clean bill of health in 1911, he and the chaplain found themselves involuntarily cloistered in a car in the company of a traveling burlesque show. Outraged at this indignity, the chaplain insisted on moving to a car in which the company was more suitably civilized. "I was a bit disappointed," Dick recalled dryly, reflecting the new, earthy concerns of a young man. "The ladies of the group were rather attractive. But like a good little boy, I said nothing at all to my father."

For fifteen-year-old Dick, life in Helena was anything but idyllic. The landscape was bleak—vast, open vistas barely broken by treeless brown hills—and the winters were brutally cold. But the summers came, and with them a ninety-mile ride through the northern Montana wilderness ordered by President Theodore Roosevelt, who had been disgusted by the condition of the Army officers he had seen in Washington. Permitted to go along with his father, Dick soon found himself trotting alongside the post commander, "a small colonel," he recalled, "on a very large horse." The colonel quickly impressed Dick with his courtesy and his surprising physical endurance. By the time the ride was over, he and Colonel Richard H. Wilson were fast friends.

As the friendship grew, Dick came to appreciate the colonel even more. He found he was a man of broad and genuine knowledge who spoke five languages fluently and read Greek and Latin for recreation. Yet unlike the chaplain, the colonel fully enjoyed the pleasures of the world. He loved a good baseball game (even, to the chaplain's undisguised horror, on Sundays), and his Montana house was full of lush classical music, beautiful paintings, and sumptuous food.

Dick's appreciation of the colonel was fully reciprocated. Wilson was quick to notice the boy's intelligence, his unflagging dedication, and his remarkable appetite for hard work. Reassuring the chaplain, who, in Wilson's private opinion, was much too hard on his youngest son, he said, "Groves, that boy of yours will go far."

But even more attractive than the colonel's praise was the fact that he had a daughter. On New Year's Eve 1912, the Wilsons invited the Groveses to their annual party. There, next to an enormous silver candelabrum that had been taken during the Fourteenth Infantry's raid on Peking, stood Grace Wilson, only fourteen and small for her age but already showing signs of an accomplished linguist, a talented artist, and a gracious and charming young woman. Chaplain Groves brought his not-too-reluctant son — who at fifteen already towered over most of the men in the room — to Grace's side. In his curious upstate New York diction, the chaplain presented his son: "I want," he said, "you should know my little boy Dick."

For her part, Grace Wilson later recalled that "there was absolutely nothing little about him." For his part, Dick Groves decided on the spot that he had met the girl he would marry.

Chapter Eleven

For the time being, however, marriage would have to wait. In early 1913 the Fourteenth Infantry was transferred to Fort Lawton in Seattle, where Dick was immediately enrolled in Queen Anne High School. Quickly bored with the standard series of English, German, Latin, and mathematics courses, he took an accelerated course that would allow him to enter the University of Washington at age sixteen. Although his father opposed it—the other two boys were already in college in the East, and the salary of a major could not be stretched to support a third college student—Dick prevailed, cramming his way through the advanced summer course and earning outstanding grades.

At the University of Washington, Groves quickly and easily adopted the life of a college student. Electing a mathematics major, he breezed through courses in algebra, analytical geometry, and differential and integral calculus. He kept a promise to his father to spend as little money as possible and lunched on ten-cent hot dogs; quelling his considerable appetite with a "main meal" that consisted of a fifteen-cent bag of roasted peanuts. On Saturdays he played tennis, and on Sundays he rode horseback through the misty hills near Fort Lawton.

Intent on pursuing his mathematical bent in the best of all possible worlds, Groves left home the next year and struck out for Boston and the famous Massachusetts Institute of Technology. His first experience there was anything but auspicious. He had been sent by a helpful student to a $2.50-a-week boardinghouse in Boston's West Rutland Square and was immediately accosted by his next-door neighbor, an attractive young woman who, Groves recalled, was "most friendly indeed." He realized that he had been sent to a pension-cum-whorehouse and immediately moved to another residence, where, he said, "some of the female residents were of easy virtue, but they were more discreet about it."

Groves shrugged off the low comedy of his surroundings and plunged into the academic life of the country's best technical school. For the next two and a half years he dedicated himself to studying descriptive geometry, drawing, physics, chemistry (his most difficult subject), and, at the insistence of a senior professor, a repeat of his University of Washington calculus course. (Groves's protest that he had already worked every problem in the book was to no avail: "You'll take the course anyway!" his professor shouted. Later, at West Point, he would repeat it for a third time.) In his second year he tutored in both mathematics and physics. What little spare time he had he spent playing tennis at the YMCA and catching an occasional Boston Braves baseball game.

In his third year came the turning point: Allen's death, the cram course at Shadman's, the personal triumph of the presidential exam. In June 1916, Groves reported to West Point, twenty years old and already with three years of college under his belt. The other plebes, many of whom were eighteen and straight out of high school, were impressed by his age, his supposed worldliness, and his undeniably advanced intellect— impressions that Groves himself did nothing to dispel. "Some of the plebes were overawed," recalled one of his classmates. "Others thought he was an intellectual snob."

As time went on, Groves's general unpopularity increased. As a "flanker"—a cadet who because of his superior height stood at either side of company formations—he tended to lord it over the shorter "runts," who were envious enough as it was. The few cadets who tried to get close to him almost inevitably gave up, unable to see through his aloof manner and his often biting sense of humor. His habit of doing his own wash to avoid Academy laundry charges won him both a reputation for tightfisted- ness (in fact, he kept a daily account of his expenditures, which he dutifully reported to his father) and a nickname, "Greasy," that would haunt him not only through his West Point years but also through years of post–World War II controversy. Because Grace Wilson came to see him only once during his three years at the Academy—it was a rainy prom day, she later recalled, during which Dick adamantly refused to be seen walking under an umbrella—he was undeservedly disparaged as a "woman-hater" in his West Point yearbook. "I think he was unhappy the whole time he was at the Academy," said classmate Willard Holbrook. "He was unpopular, and he was lonely."

Perhaps to compensate for his lack of friendships and youthful sociability, Groves racked up an impressive series of accomplishments. From an academic ranking of twenty-third in his plebe class, he moved steadily up so that by his final year he stood at the head of his class, with a three-year overall ranking of fourth. As his reputation grew, frantic athletic coaches increasingly asked him to tutor their physically gifted but academically underpowered charges.

Thanks to his adolescent expeditions in Arizona and Montana, he was one of the Academy's best riders; as a marksman he quickly won an expert's rating. Although he never played organized football in high school or college, he tried out for the Army team and soon earned a position as a second-string center—beginning a love affair with Army football that would last the rest of his life. As a plebe he came in second in the light-heavyweight wrestling division but lost to fellow flanker Holbrook in the finals. "We became friends after that," Holbrook recalled. "He always respected anyone who could lick him."

Perhaps even more important than his academic and athletic achievements were Groves's accomplishments as a leader. In his second year he became his company's first sergeant, in which position he effectively ran the outfit for the cadet officers. "Here," said one of his classmates, "Groves was clearly outstanding. He knew his people, knew their capabilities better than anyone." As a cadet sergeant he began to develop the soft-spoken but strong-willed style that stayed with him throughout his career. "He never harangued anyone," Holbrook would recall. "He worked quietly, simply gave instructions that things be done. But there was always a sense of authority in the way he said things."

In the middle of his third year, with graduation drawing ever closer, it became time for Groves to choose his branch of the Army—a decision that amounted to a choice of career. Tradition made the decision for him. The Academy had originally been founded in 1802 by Thomas Jefferson primarily, if not exclusively, as a school for engineers, and for fifty years it had remained the only bona fide engineering college in the United States. Its graduates, including Zebulon Pike and Henry Abbott, had explored the unknown West and had built the Capitol, the Library of Congress, and nearly every fort, dock, and canal in the country. The work of Army engineers—far more interesting than shuffling along with the infantry or shooting at invisible targets with the artillery—inevitably attracted the best officers in West Point; in Groves's class, for example, every one of the top twenty-seven students went with the Corps of Engineers. In fact, this tendency was so imbued in Academy tradition that the top students, called "intellectuals" or "grinds" in other colleges, went naturally and unremarkably by the name "engineers."

His choice made, Groves left the Academy in 1918, a year early. The powers that be in Washington had thought the war in Europe was going badly and so had ordered the abbreviation of the West Point course to make new officers available. But Groves was still a few months too late to fulfill every cadet's dream: a combat command in the European war. Swallowing his disappointment, he began the itinerant career that is the lot of every Army officer: nearly two years at Engineer School in Fort Humphreys (now Fort Belvoir), Virginia, and a year as a company commander in Fort Benning, Georgia.

In the summer of 1921 he got what may have been his most fortunate transfer: an assignment to Fort Worden, a coastal defense fortification on Washington's Puget Sound. Within days of his arrival he appeared on the doorstep of one Grace Wilson, whose father had recently retired in the Seattle area. Although the young lady was pledged to a naval officer by the name of Rocky, Groves persisted; and finally, one dark and rainy afternoon in February 1921, the two were married. (Rocky, it was reported, had to be restrained by his shipmates from jumping overboard.)

A few months later Groves was transferred to the Presidio in San Francisco. Amid the pines and cypresses of this lovely coastal outpost, the young couple set up housekeeping. In their rambling, furnitureless frame house they narrowly averted disaster: a secondhand gas stove on which Grace was cooking suddenly exploded, leaving her face badly burned and forcing her to spend months with her head swathed in bandages. Her young husband dutifully brought her orchids and also displayed a strange sense of humor that would later make him unfathomable to his colleagues and acquaintances: "I'll always love you, darling," he told her, "even without a face."

Grace had barely recovered when they were transferred to a Pacific idyll—to the palms and poinsettias of Schofield Barracks in Honolulu. Lieutenant Groves undertook to train the enlisted men of F Company on the rifle range; the company soon had the post's top marksmanship rating. They also won the post tennis championship in both singles and doubles. Grace dedicated herself to cooking on a coal-burning stove and to taking their baby, Richard, on exploratory drives around Oahu, the new baby securely bundled into a laundry basket on the back seat of their new Ford.

Although life in Hawaii was pleasant and Groves's labors as a training officer quietly rewarding, the lieutenant itched to do the engineering work for which he had been thoroughly educated. He got his chance in 1925, when he was transferred to Galveston, Texas, and assigned as an assistant to the Army Corps district engineer. This job kept him away from his family for one month out of every two for the next two years; his assignment was to open the harbor around Port Isabel, an historic port that had lain clogged and useless since the beginning of the century. By 1927 Groves and his men had effectively cleared the harbor, deepened its interior channel, and built a series of jetties for merchant ships that steamed in from the Gulf of Mexico. In the years to come new groups of engineers would build on Groves's work to develop the important modern ports of Brownsville and Harlingen.

With this work finished and with a glowing recommendation from his superior ("Groves," said the major, "is the best officer I've ever had"), the lieutenant was transferred to the 1st Engineer Regiment in Fort DuPont, Delaware. There he was given an assignment that almost cost him his career and even his life. In the winter of 1927 his company was sent to Vermont, where an exceptionally bitter cold spell had frozen the Winooski River so severely that the ice-locked bridges had to be blasted free with dynamite. In the course of the operation a grenade unexpectedly went off in the hand of a sergeant standing at Groves's side. The sergeant was killed, and the explosion drilled pieces of his bones like shrapnel into Groves's hand and face. Groves was so severely wounded that he spent weeks in a Burlington hospital; because of the injury to his hand he was never able to fire a pistol competitively again. He also suffered a loss of hearing in one ear that lasted the rest of his life. The incident was so dramatic and the results so serious that the local commander called for a hurried investigation. Groves was found negligent, and an official censure was inserted into his record—the only negative note in a service career that lasted over thirty years.

If the Winooski incident nearly precipitated Groves's downfall, his next assignment gained him a large measure of redemption. Congress had for years been fascinated by the idea of an alternative to the Panama Canal. In 1929 it ordered the Corps of Engineers to survey a potential route along Nicaragua's San Juan River. To perform the survey, the company sent a company of engineers, of which Groves's battalion formed a part.

The lieutenant slogged through the jungles with his men, battling heat, mosquitoes, snakes, and his soldiers' congenital drunkenness. In spite of all this, and due in part to Groves's unswerving discipline (on arrival in the seaport town of Corinto he billeted his men in a second-story barracks so that no overly merry trooper could sneak in without passing the stairway guard), the fieldwork for the survey was finally finished in 1931 and duly reported to a curious Congress. In the meantime, Grace Groves had arrived in 1930 to ensconce herself and the two children (a daughter, Gwen, had been born in Delaware) in a colonial house in one of the best sections of Granada. Grace learned how to cook arroz con pollo and empañadas while six-year-old Richard recited all the Spanish profanity his Nicaraguan schoolmates could teach him.

But just before Groves and his company were to pull out, Managua was suddenly struck by a tremendous earthquake. The city was reduced to a burning rubble and a large percentage of its population was summarily wiped out. In the devastating aftermath the survivors, many of them injured and homeless, were left entirely without water. Groves and his men were quickly assigned to repair the city's only water main, which lay inside and at the base of a steep volcanic crater. Once inside the crater, which constantly rumbled and shook with the quake's many aftershocks, Groves found that the force of the earthquake had literally torn one of the two main pipes in two and had left the second line looking "like a piece of taffy in the process of being pulled."

"I had four enlisted men with me," Groves recalled. "We were using impressed labor, and the only way you could keep them on the job was to have an armed guard at the top of the crater. In addition, we had earthquakes throughout the day, so that boulders kept rolling down the field of the slope onto our workers down below."

Despite being the targets in a natural shooting gallery, Groves and his men got the job done and restored water to a city that without it would have suffered even more desperately. In recognition Groves received a Nicaraguan Medal of Merit and a grateful citation from President J.M. Moncada, a citation that, in words later echoed by many of his American commanders, praised the lieutenant's "technical knowledge, spirited direction, and inexhaustible energy."

His energy served Groves well in his next assignment—a job that perhaps more than any of the others prepared him to take on the Manhattan Project. Sent from Managua back to Washington, D.C., he was placed in the Military Supply Division, where his task was to supervise the development of new equipment. It was not an easy job; the older officers, still captivated by the Army's swordsman-on-horseback image, had to be repeatedly urged to modernize. Groves was at them constantly with his recommendations to replace picks and shovels with jackhammers and bulldozers; to develop infrared detectors to pick up high-flying aircraft (once developed, under Groves's supervision, these detectors were the state of the art until the development of radar during World War II); and perhaps most exemplary, to develop a new mass production technique for the manufacture of huge metallic searchlight mirrors, a job that Groves's assistant Charles Holle would later liken to "a Manhattan Project in miniature."

During his four years in the Military Supply Division—the last year as its chief—Groves maintained, for the first but certainly not the last time in his life, steady, day-to-day contact with scientists and with imaginative inventors. In Holle's words, they "were never quite through with their inventing. They were always saying 'give me another two months and I'll come up with something even better.'" Under the pressure of the Army's immediate demands, Groves's response to this was practical to the point of hardheadedness. "He rode herd on them," Holle recalled. "He was always saying, 'Let's get something we can work with now, and save the improvements for later.'"

It was a phrase that later rang in the ears of many a Manhattan Project scientist.

Chapter Twelve

By July 1940 the war in Europe was nine months old. In Washington, the generals were realizing, painfully and belatedly, that the war had caught the country's armed forces almost entirely unprepared. Obviously the size of the Army would have to expand; and the expansion would require more Stateside military facilities—a building boom for which the Quartermaster Corps, then in charge of all military construction, was unprepared and ill-equipped to handle. As the Army stirred from its peacetime slumber, orders poured in for new camps and schools, hospitals and industrial plants. The Corps of Engineers' workload jumped from a manageable $20 million to more than $10 *billion*. This exponential growth not only threatened to bring the machinery of the Quartermaster Corps to a groaning halt, but it actually brought its assistant chief, General Hartman, to the point of a nervous breakdown.

Faced with a potential disaster, Quartermaster General E. B. Gregory turned for help to an old friend. Gregory had known Dick Groves since boyhood; now, with the approval of Chief of Staff General George C. Marshall, he moved the young major from the general staff to be his special assistant. Within months as Director of Operations, Groves was overseeing the labors of a million men, the spending of $8 billion (at one point his office was buying over half the country's lumber), and the building of every new barracks, depot, port, and airfield in the country.

It was a high-stress job. As the Army geared up to add 25,000 new troops, then 40,000, and then 125,000 by the fall of 1941, the pace of construction grew furious. In Groves's Washington office it took two shifts of secretaries working around the clock to keep up with him; according to one assistant, Groves "worked early and late." He traveled ceaselessly, troubleshooting the building of a chemical warfare plant in Arkansas, a financial dispute with a railroad in Florida, and a bottom-to-top re-modeling of an Army camp in Indiana.

Through all the harried traveling, the half-eaten breakfasts, and the complaints of overwrought contractors, Groves's technical expertise, his low-key manner, and his relentless efficiency calmed pressure-frayed nerves and kept the jobs on schedule. At one ordnance plant in Buffalo a conflict between the Army engineers and a contractor had the contractor in a sullen mood and the job more than a month behind schedule; Groves spent an entire day with the man listening to his complaints and pains-takingly analyzing every aspect of the floundering project. By the end of the day the formerly hostile contractor was beaming and nodding his head. Three weeks later, the once-moribund construction effort was humming along ahead of schedule.

As Groves raced about the country, he was followed by a fierce and unshakable beast: a congressional investigating committee chaired by spirited Missouri senator Harry Truman. Truman's job was to hawkeye every dollar that the Army in general—and Groves in particular—spent to gear up for war. Truman had locked horns with Groves before, in a 1936 conflict over the letting of Army contracts to small arms manufacturers in St. Louis; now, with a much fatter fish to fry, Truman kept the flame under Groves turned up high. But Groves remained unshaken even when Truman publicly grilled him about why the hospital at Camp Mead, Maryland, had been moved from one end of the base to another, at a cost of a million dollars.

"Rumor has it," said Truman at an April 1941 congressional hearing, "that the commanding officer moved the hospital to make way for a golf course."

"I don't know," Groves replied. "I'm not a golfer myself, so I wouldn't hesitate to put the hospital right in the middle of the eighteenth green."

This answer may have satisfied Truman and the Senate end of Capitol Hill, but Groves still had to deal with the ramifications of a high-profile project that he had inherited from General Somervell and that was beginning to raise important hackles in the House. This was the building of the Pentagon, the massive military office building that on completion became the largest such structure in the world. Its radical design ($17\frac{1}{2}$ miles of concentric corridors) and eye-opening cost (ultimately some $83 million) had earned it the name "Somervell's Folly" even in the planning stages. (Ironically, the building was constructed on the site of the Department of Agriculture farm where Allen Groves had contracted his fatal pneumonia.) From the moment the plans hit the House for approval, the Pentagon was subject to unrelenting and at times almost hysterical attacks from a group of tightfisted congressmen who saw the building as an enormous military boondoggle.

Undeterred by the highly public criticism, Groves drove the building toward completion. Under his supervision 13,000 men worked twenty-four-hour shifts. First they moved some six million cubic yards of earth; then they dredged the Potomac for the 680,000 tons of sand and gravel necessary to make 410,000 cubic yards of concrete. (Everything about the Pentagon was massive: even the *plans* weighed several tons.) Yet despite the protests of Congress, *The Washington Post*, and even the Washington Commission of Fine Arts, despite endless bickering among the military brass, each of whom wanted to put his personal imprint on the building's design, and despite overruns that more than doubled the projected cost, Groves had the building up and ready for occupation by January 1943 (even after his appointment to head the Manhattan District he remained in charge of Pentagon construction)—only a little more than a year after the groundbreaking. It is still considered one of the great feats of modern engineering.

By now Groves had moved up the promotional ladder. Although the movement was slow at first—he had remained a lieutenant for seventeen years as a result of an Armywide freeze on promotions after World War I—the achievements of his last three years accelerated his advance at a pace that, for the slow-moving Army, seemed almost breakneck. Only five years had passed between his captaincy, which came in 1935, and his 1940 promotion to colonel—a promotion that sent him skipping two ranks and leapfrogging over the heads of West Point graduates ten years his senior. (Although the unprecedented promotion had Washington officers buzzing, Grace Groves celebrated the news in a characteristically low-fuss fashion: she went out and bought herself a new dishpan.)

By now Groves had developed the hard-charging, straight-ahead style that characterized his entire career. "He was all business," Holle remembered. "There was no foolishness in his office—no one sat around telling jokes." He attacked sloth and incompetence with dedication that at times bordered on ruthlessness. At Camp Forrest, Indiana, where a wasteful design and an overinflated labor force were crippling a construction project, Groves summarily eliminated 27 percent of the buildings and fired six thousand workers. When a project in Pine Bluff, Arkansas, moved too slowly for his liking, and when the commanding officer continued to drag his heels after several warnings, Groves swiftly arranged to transfer the offending colonel to the South Pacific.

More than anyone, Groves's own subordinates most often came to feel the pressure of his exacting standards. "His philosophy," said General William Wannamaker, "was to delegate wherever he could, and then put the screws to the delegees." His men, who had considerable and surprising freedom to do their jobs without interference, were sometimes taken aback to find that the boss was checking on them. "He sent me once to take care of a problem," recalled Robert Furman, a young Princetonian who weathered the fire and became one of Groves's most trusted assistants, "and when I came back with my report, he pulled out of his desk another report by another officer on the same problem." He drove his people mad with constant demands for rewrites ("The reports had to be not just good," said Holle, "but good enough for Groves")—a tendency that had the door of his secretaries' office constantly turning. While in the Construction Branch, he once went through six secretaries in six weeks.

At times his demands seemed to his subordinates little more than power plays. To William Potter, whom Groves once sent tramping twenty miles at night through the Nicaragua jungle just to pick up a payroll, Groves was "cold as hell." To Kenneth Nichols, whom Groves sometimes kept waiting on a bench in his office for as long as five hours, he was "the biggest son of a bitch I ever met." His son-in-law Alan Robinson put it just as succinctly: "He was a taskmaster. He was proud of the fact that people were scared of him."

But for all his gruffness and insensitivity, Groves almost never lost his temper. "He never swore," recalled one of his officers, "and he never raised his voice." "If he was mad at you," said engineer and patent attorney Ralph Carlisle Smith, "you got the silent treatment." For those who put up with this and saw in his sarcastic teasing a clumsy but genuine attempt at camaraderie, Groves was someone to be respected and even appreciated. "I liked him," said Joseph Volpe, expressing a sentiment that was echoed by the majority of those who worked with him closely. "Once he knew that I would stand up to him, he treated me very well."

This—along with the competence and dedication that were his prerequisites for a staffer—was the key to winning Groves's respect. Self-contained and himself unimpressed by rank, he tended to like those qualities in the people who worked for him. "He didn't like being kowtowed to," said physicist Robert Bacher, who came to know Groves well. "In fact, the more people kowtowed to him, the worse they got along with him. I think he liked a demonstration of spirit and independence in the people he worked with."

Spirit and independence, so important in his subordinates, were also the key features of Groves's own working style. Impatient with the tangles and delays of bureaucracy, he developed methods for quick bypass, including channels and techniques that were almost uniquely Grovesian. He kept his own staff small and his bureaucratic baggage as light as possible, supervising the initial phases of the Manhattan District from a tiny, two-room office. He got all his information about any given job by talking to the man on the spot, avoiding the delays and "telephone games" involved in talking to their desk-bound superiors. If he needed supplies, he found ways to end-run the bureaucracy and simply take them. (As deputy chief of construction he sent his men to every surplus auction in the country, neatly cornering the national markets in used lumber and iron. These he later graciously turned over to exasperated naval supply officers who had scoured the country to no avail.) If he needed something done he used any means at his disposal. When, for example, he wanted to convince his bosses that every barracks in the country should be painted, he arranged to have Eleanor Roosevelt driven past the shabbiest Army buildings he could find. "The order to paint," he noted with satisfaction, "came two days later."

His combination of inventiveness, practicality, and sheer drive won Groves admiring evaluations from his superior officers. "Outstanding in all respects," wrote Colonel C.R. Sturdevant of the Missouri River District. "Excels in capacity for work, resourcefulness, and accurate judgment." "Original, independent thinker," said General A.L. DeWitt of the Army War College; "Open-minded, views problems from all angles." General E. Reybold, chief of the Corps of Engineers, praised his "superior knowledge of his profession"; while Reybold's assistant, General T.M. Robins, noted his "energy" and "reliability." In the opinion of General Somervell, Groves was "forceful, intelligent, and loyal" and had "handled a difficult position extremely well."

But General Styer, the sometimes-colleague, sometimes-superior who may have known Groves better than anyone else in the Army, perhaps best summarized the qualities that above all others earned him the Manhattan District job: "He knows what he wants," Styer wrote, "and he knows how to get things done."

At the time of his appointment to head the Manhattan District, Groves was forty-six years old. Jowled and stern, his weight at the point of getting the best of him, he was nonetheless a rather handsome man. His smile, on the relatively rare occasions when he showed it, was, according to one of the secretaries in his office, "more charismatic than Roosevelt's." His personality and character were fully formed and reflected in large part his father's example—the seriousness, the impatience with frivolity and anything that smacked of impracticality, the devotion to duty and gentlemanly values—as well as the puzzling isolation of his youth. His intelligence, though perhaps not profound and certainly not philosophical, was shrewd and capacious; his memory was truly remarkable. ("He never took a note," Nobel Laureate I.I. Rabi recalled. "He kept the entirety of that enormous bomb project in his head.") He was in general a man of action, not of introspection; and his few heroes, like General William Tecumseh Sherman, were also men of action. When it came to making a decision, he tended to trust his own instincts over detailed and detached analysis and was perhaps most impatient with what he perceived as indecisiveness in others.

Groves had missed World War I by a few months and with it the opportunity to distinguish himself as a combat commander. Still, his career was full of impressive accomplishments—Port Isabel and Managua, the Army construction program and the Pentagon—that undeniably made their own solid and substantial form of history. But his new job presented him with his biggest challenge. A successful response to that enormous challenge depended on Groves's ability to order the efforts of some of the greatest scientists in the world. One of those scientists later confessed, "The physicists tried to run things for three years, and couldn't get to first base." It remained to be seen if the new general could do better. The outcome of the greatest war in history and the fate of human civilization itself might well be at stake.

Part Three

THE ATOMIC WHEEL

Chapter Thirteen

It is hard to imagine a more tranquil setting than that of the Naval Research Laboratory (NRL) in Anacostia, Virginia. Once ringed on its perimeters by oaks and ancient elms, the Laboratory looks out over the Potomac River and across to the gentle woods and accommodating hills of southern Maryland. But like the Potomac, whose smooth, unhurried appearance conceals vicious undercurrents that drown dozens of people every year, the drowsy, semirural setting of the Laboratory was deceptive.

It was especially so on September 21, 1942, when General Leslie R. Groves came to pay a call, the brass on his new star gleaming with fresh polish. For the previous five years, starting even before the breakthrough discoveries of Lise Meitner and Otto Hahn, the Navy had been working steadily to turn the theory of fission into the reality of a nuclear power plant. Groves was eager to see just how far they had progressed.

If an atomic bomb were ever to be teased out of the physicists' notebooks, Groves knew, there would have to be a sound, practical way to convert delicate laboratory work—where, in the scientists' words, "invisible quantities were being weighed with invisible measures"—into a full-scale, broad-shouldered industrial effort. Specifically, this would mean producing explosive fissionable material in absolutely unprecedented quantities. The scientists, as we have seen, were working on five different methods for achieving that production; though each method had its own set of peculiar and perplexing problems, Bush and Styer assured Groves that at least four of them looked capable of delivering the finished product. Groves's job, they had hinted, was simply to take laboratories and turn them into factories.

With this in mind, the general had set off on a grand tour, in the course of which, if Vannevar Bush and General Styer were right, he would see heartening progress on the scientific front. Although his own preappointment contacts with the MED had left him with nagging doubts—doubts that had been reinforced by the frustrated skepticism of Colonel Marshall and Colonel Nichols—he was willing to put his reservations aside for the time being and let the scientists amaze him with their accomplishments.

Groves already knew that 99.3 percent of the uranium found in nature was the U-238 isotope, which was useless in making a bomb. The American effort needed workable quantities of the radioactive uranium isotope U-235. But that isotope was supremely and maddeningly elusive. First of all, it constituted only .7 percent of natural uranium. Because its chemical characteristics were essentially the same as those of U-238, it could not be separated from U-238 by the existing, relatively inexpensive chemical techniques. Instead it had to be strained out of U-238 virtually atom by atom, using a science—isotope separation—that for all practical purposes was yet to be born. The Naval Research Laboratory's attempts to separate the uranium isotopes by the process known as liquid thermal diffusion represented some of that science's first and most pronounced labor pains.

But the head of the NRL program, physicist Ross Gunn, was a somewhat reluctant midwife. Gunn had been a member of one of the early government bomb committees; but partially because Roosevelt did not want interservice rivalries to interfere with work on the bomb, he had been dropped when the Army took over. Groves got the distinct impression that Gunn's feelings had been hurt. In general he doubted the strength of the physicist's commitment to the research and found his attitude annoyingly condescending.

Perplexed and put off by Gunn's recalcitrance, Groves sought out Phillip Abelson, a scientist who despite his youth—he was not yet thirty—was already considered one of America's top nuclear physicists. In fact, three years before, Abelson had been pursuing a series of experiments at the University of California that would have led him independently to discover the process of nuclear fission. Hahn and Strassman had beaten him by no more than a few weeks.

Now, at the Naval Research Laboratory, Abelson was spearheading the research on the liquid thermal diffusion process. Basically, this process depends on taking uranium, converting it to a hexafluoride gas, then cooling the gas until it turns to liquid. The liquid was then circulated in the small space between two concentric pipes, with the inner pipe cooled by water and the outer heated by steam. The lighter isotope, the fissionable U-235, collects along the wall of the hot pipe and the heavier U-238 on the wall of the cold pipe. Convection then carries the U-235 to the top of the column of pipe, from where it can be "harvested." Given enough steam, enough time, and long enough columns of pipe, Abelson thought that the uranium product could at least theoretically be enriched sufficiently for use as fuel for an atomic bomb.

But Groves's earlier experience with scientists had taught him to beware of the word *theoretically*. As he learned more about it, he found that the process's appetite for steam was expected to be truly monstrous—in fact, some estimates placed the steam costs at as high as $2 to $3 *billion*. But at this point, Groves was still working with a budget of $85 million for the entire construction program. Clearly, the liquid thermal diffusion approach was unthinkably expensive.

Abelson himself was impressive, obviously yet unpretentiously competent. But Gunn's lingering bitterness would make establishing a mutually confident working relationship difficult if not impossible. "No," Groves must have thought as he stepped outside into the brilliant Virginia autumn, "this is not what I'm looking for."

His visit to the Naval Research Laboratory was a major letdown. Of the five production processes under consideration, liquid thermal diffusion had the longest history and the biggest headstart. But Groves's practical eye found it thoroughly unfeasible.

Swallowing his disappointment, Groves moved on to Pittsburgh, the next stop on his inspection tour. There he hoped he would find a workable process for producing the material for the bomb.

The huge steel drum stood on its mounting and spun in a leisurely horizontal motion as Groves contemplated it from below. The enormous rotating drum was part of a method of separating uranium isotopes that, if the scientists here at Westinghouse Laboratories were right, was as uncomplicated as separating cream from milk. As the drum, or centrifuge, spun, the lighter, radioactive U-235 isotope of a uranium gas would collect at the center and the top of the cylinder. If one drew this off and ran it through a second centrifuge, the concentration of the lighter isotope would be increased. Run it through a third centrifuge, and the concentration would be increased still further. With enough centrifuges you could theoretically—there was that word again—attain a uranium gas that was highly enriched in U-235.

The principle seemed so appealingly simple that Lyman Briggs had earlier recommended it as the quickest and surest way to manufacture fissionable material. And Groves had to admit that—on paper, at least— the centrifuge method was powerfully attractive. But there were problems. First of all, the basic laboratory research under Jesse Beams at the University of Virginia was proceeding in what Groves called "the usual academic fashion"—that is, slowly. In fact, Groves discovered, Beams was running his program on what amounted to a charity donation from the Navy and had a staff consisting entirely of two overworked graduate students. Even more disconcerting as far as Groves was concerned was Beams's nonchalant practice of closing on Sundays and holidays, as if the lab were somehow exempt from the pressures of war.

Still, Beams had managed to develop a prototype centrifuge that actually achieved a minute amount of isotope separation. Soon afterward, the focus of the work had shifted to Westinghouse, whose facilities were more capable of producing and testing centrifuges in industrial quantities. Unfortunately, the enrichment was only about 60 percent of the amount predicted by theory, so that the number of one-meter centrifuges necessary to produce a hundred grams of U-235 a day was no longer 8,800 but over 25,000. Since the cylinders were extremely difficult to manufacture—they had to be strong enough to spin at almost unheard-of velocities yet precise enough to keep vibrations from shaking them to pieces—this was enough to dampen all but the most extreme optimist's enthusiasm for the method's future.

There was still a chance, though, that these problems could be alleviated by using a cylinder of a new design. It was this new state-of-the-art cylinder that Groves was now reviewing in Westinghouse's Pittsburgh Laboratory.

But something, he felt, was not right.

"How fast do these drums have to spin before you start getting separation?" he asked one of the Westinghouse scientists.

"About twice this speed," came the reply.

"And how long do they have to run?"

"Just about continuously."

"Do you ever run them continuously?" Groves asked, fearing that he already knew the answer.

"Oh no," said the scientist, apparently astonished at the question. "We only run them about five minutes at a time." Groves's face must have shown his displeasure, for the scientist hastened to explain, "This is the only model we've got. If we ran it continuously, something might happen to it."

The answer confirmed Groves's darkest suspicions. Even with the improved design, over twenty-five thousand of these devices would have to be built, tested, and run continuously for at least a year if any significant production of U-235 were to be achieved. Against this need, the Westinghouse scientists had no more than one working prototype, a prototype that they had not tested under anything remotely approaching operating conditions. Even more disturbing, they seemed in absolutely no hurry to do so. To Groves, their attitude toward an urgent and revolutionary wartime project seemed lackadaisical to the point of being cavalier.

Another method of isotope-separation was now well on its way to being ruled out. The flustered scientist and the uselessly spinning centrifuge were soon left behind as symbols of a doomed approach.

At Columbia University's Pupin Hall, still another production method was embodied in a piece of dully gleaming metal foil no bigger than a silver dollar. The foil, made of a nickel alloy, was the latest in a long line of possibilities for a radical new isotope-separation process known as gaseous diffusion. In late October, Professor John Dunning was explaining the process to Leslie Groves. Cheerfully, in his rapid-fire, breathless style— "He had one of those mouths," Groves said later, "that words just poured out of"—balding Professor Dunning gesticulated and stabbed with a pointer at a handmade chart.

The process started with uranium hexafluoride gas, the professor explained. The gas would be pumped through a long series of minutely porous metal barriers. If the pressure on one side of the barriers was lower than on the other side, molecules of the lighter U-235 isotope would be drawn to the low-pressure side. From there they could be collected and pumped through a second barrier, where the same process would enrich the gas a bit more. If the gas were pumped through a thousand or so stages, the end product would be a uranium gas highly enriched in U-235.

Groves was impressed by Dunning's dynamic energy and by his obvious enthusiasm for the gaseous diffusion approach. But not even the physicist's optimism could hide the fact that finding a suitable material for the barrier was a tremendous problem. First, the material had to be a metal that would stand up to uranium hexafluoride, a gas so diabolically corrosive that it could eat through a thick sheet of steel as if it were Kleenex. Even more troublesome, for the gas to pass through, the barrier had to be almost impossibly porous, with billions of identical, microscopic holes no bigger than one ten-thousandth of a millimeter.

Under Nobel Prize winner Harold Urey, teams of physicists from three universities and two private companies had been sweating for over a year, performing hundreds of tests on dozens of metals to find something that would fill this maddening prescription. Now the round-faced Urey held up a possible answer for Groves's examination. Urey was convinced that this nickel alloy was the barrier material for which he and his researchers had been searching for more than a year.

The sample was brittle, fragile, and not quite uniform, Urey admitted. But with a few improvements, he thought it would do the trick.

But for Groves perhaps the most important question of all was, How much of the material was available? Dunning had told him that a full-blown gaseous diffusion plant would require acres of barrier material, but all the researchers could show him was this one, dollar-size piece. Had the scientists developed a method for scaling up production so that the barrier material could be produced in the massive quantities necessary?

Urey was sanguine. Although a method for scale-up had not yet been found, the researchers were hard at work. The problem would be solved, he assured Groves, in another two weeks.

In the face of the obviously heartbreaking difficulty, Groves found Urey's optimism almost flippant. But something he sensed about the physicist's character disturbed him even more. Despite his evident intelligence—his scientific colleagues often described him as "brilliantly precise"—to Groves Urey seemed somehow flighty, insubstantial. His restless mind, which the general would later liken to a "a squirrel in a cage," refused to alight for long on any particular subject or to develop solid and predictable attitudes. As an administrator Groves saw him as weak and threatened, willing enough to let Dunning run the show but somehow resentful of his colleague's straight-ahead style and uncomplicated energy. The tension between the two seemed almost palpable, which made the program, already beset with tremendous technical problems, look even more iffy from an administrative point of view.

On his way back to Washington, Groves apparently pondered the problem. Urey, he knew, was a key figure in the gaseous diffusion program, but he loomed as a potential negative. Groves had little doubt as to what he would do in an ideal situation: "If this were a military organization," he said, "I would see how fast I could get rid of Urey."

"But since it was an academic organization," he lamented, "what on earth could I do?"

Chapter Fourteen

If Groves found Harold Urey ill-suited to lead a scientific project that might have a critical impact on the outcome of the war, the reverse seemed true of Arthur Holly Compton. Indeed, Compton seemed almost typecast for the role of scientific administrator. Tall and powerfully built (like Groves, he had been a college football player), his massive eyebrows, bristling moustache, and prominent chin gave him the authoritative look of a movieland preacher—Elmer Gantry, perhaps, as portrayed by Errol Flynn. In fact, so pronounced was this impression that Groves later took to calling him "Arthur Hollywood."

At the same time, Compton's tact, his ready smile, and his cordial competitiveness had won him the respect and affection of a great number of America's best physicists, who saw him as one of their natural leaders. "Smooth," Groves came to describe him, "but a battler from start to finish."

Compton was placing his bets for bomb material on plutonium, the new element discovered by Glen Seaborg and his young colleagues at the University of California. Theoretically, plutonium could be obtained as a by-product of a controlled chain reaction in a uranium "pile." Fully committed to the effort, Compton had skillfully propelled himself to the leadership of the plutonium program. As early as the spring of 1940 he had recognized the need for haste in the face of German accomplishments and had joined Ernest Lawrence as one of the fledgling project's scientific spearheads.

Impatient with the glacial pace of the Briggs Uranium Committee, however, he soon took it upon himself to organize a research program at the University of Chicago that would try to resolve some of the many uncertainties about nuclear reactions and the development of the nuclear reactors, which, it was hoped, would ultimately produce plutonium for the bomb.

With the coming of the war, Compton had moved swiftly to bring the best physics brains in the United States under the roof of the University of Chicago's new Metallurgical Laboratory, or Met Lab. Using his status as a Nobel Prize winner and project leader as an entrée, he mercilessly raided the laboratories of the country's top physics departments. From Columbia he shanghaied the great Fermi himself, and Fermi brought with him the pioneering Hungarian Leo Szilard as well as the talented young Americans Walter Zinn and Herbert Anderson. From Princeton he rounded up Eugene Wigner, the meticulous Hungarian who had consorted with Szilard to help get the American bomb effort under way, and the amiable and precociously able "Smiling John" Wheeler, who at twenty-five had already copublished with the legendary Niels Bohr. From Berkeley came Glen Seaborg, the lanky, long-fingered chemist who had made his reputation with the discovery of plutonium, and young experimental physicist John Manley. From Iowa State came Frank Spedding, already considered one of the top men in the world in the experimental manufacture of uranium metal. From New York University came the able department chairman Martin Whittaker. It was, quite simply, one of the greatest collections of scientific talent that had ever been gathered in one American university.

Unfortunately for Groves, many of the assembled brains were of a decidedly antimilitary cast. Supremely confident of their abilities both as individuals and as a collective, many of the Met Lab scientists saw the Army's participation in the project as superfluous and undesirable. Others, especially the large contingent of younger scientists, looked at the military with a wary and antiauthoritarian eye, while those who had fled fascist regimes in Europe tended to view the Army's presence as downright dangerous. In fact, Compton himself had written to James Conant in May 1942 that he "questioned the desirability" of placing the project under military control. Szilard, who was endowed neither with Compton's tact nor with his circumspection, was a self-confessed, out-and-out brass-baiter.

It was into this lion's den that Groves confidently strode on October 5, 1942. The morning began quietly as Compton took the general on a proud and paternalistic tour of his domain. First came a round of the laboratories themselves, where the scientists were bustling about with enthusiasm that Groves found highly exhilarating. In the uranium section Edward Creutz (late of Princeton) was working on purifying orange-size lumps of the radioactive compound uranium tetrachloride, mixing them with metallic calcium, and then heating and cooling the mixture in an airtight steel drum. In the graphite section Fermi's team was checking the neutron-absorbing properties of graphite, which would surround uranium in the chain-reacting "pile." In the plutonium section Seaborg's chemists had been breathlessly weighing the world's first samples of plutonium— 2.77 millionths of a gram, about one-millionth the weight of a dime—on a quartz fiber balance so excruciatingly thin that the whole process had to be called a new name: *ultramicrochemistry.*

If all this activity struck Groves as absolutely appropriate to the extraordinary task at hand, the final stop on Compton's tour must have taken him aback. Physicists Martin Whittaker and Walter Zinn had assembled a messy-looking stack of black graphite bricks that constituted Compton's pièce de résistance. Spaced between the graphite blocks were lumps of yellow-orange uranium metal. The objects of almost two years of frantic research, they were now as pure as Spedding, Creutz, and their avant-garde techniques could make them. These six-pound lumps were the heart of the structure, and the structure—known as an "exponential pile"—in turn was the heart of the fission project itself. Its purpose was nothing less than to determine the ultimate viability of the entire effort to make an atomic bomb.

For if a bomb were ever to be the outcome of all this furious effort, it would first have to be shown that a chain reaction could be sustained in uranium. Thanks to Meitner and Hahn, the physicists knew that the uranium nucleus could be split by a flying neutron. Later experiments had shown that on splitting, the nucleus would emit more neutrons. The scientists thought, although it had not been quite proven, that these stray neutrons would then go on to perpetrate more fissions in nearby nuclei. The vital factor, indeed the sine qua non of the atomic bomb itself, was the average number of neutrons emitted by each fissioning nucleus, a number that the scientists were cryptically calling the value k. If k were less than one, then a chain reaction would shut itself down before reaching the critical point of self-sustenance. In that case, to keep the reaction going new neutrons would have to be fired in from outside—a ponderous process that would make a bomb impossible. But if k were one or greater—that is, if the uranium nucleus could be counted on to throw out enough of its neutrons to then perpetrate fissions in other nuclei—then the reaction could run on its own. Without that vital self-sustenance the chain reaction—and thus the atomic bomb itself—would never be more than a set of numbers on the physicists' blackboards.

Experiments in August and September had produced hopeful results: the estimated value of k had risen to 1.014. With purer uranium, Compton thought, the value would go even higher, which meant that the self-sustaining chain reaction would ultimately become a reality. But

Groves's engineer's eye was not satisfied with estimated values or sanguine predictions. He wanted proof, and proof would become available only when Compton's men built a pile large enough to "go critical"—to create and sustain a chain reaction. Apparently, Groves had come to Chicago ready to witness such a pile in action or at least under construction. But Whittaker and Zinn's pile was not critical, only "exponential," meaning that it was still too small to generate a self-sustaining chain reaction. Construction on a critical pile had not yet begun.

As far as Groves was concerned, he was looking at yet another major disappointment. There was still no proven chain reaction, which meant that not only plutonium production but the very notion of the bomb itself was still nothing but an enormous question mark. Still, Compton and his men seemed to combine optimism with the confidence and commitment to see the job through. There was to be a large meeting that afternoon in which the scientists were supposed to put all their specialized efforts into the larger and more coherent perspective vital to the pursuit of the bomb. In that meeting, Groves hoped, he would finally get the solid answers he was looking for.

Just after lunch Compton ushered the general into Room 201 of Eckart Hall, a plush, librarylike setting with thick carpeting and roomy leather easy chairs—"Just about the richest-looking place," Groves recalled, "that I'd ever seen." Into that room filed a group of some twenty physicists, a group that represented the collective scientific brain power of two continents. There was Enrico Fermi, bald, pleasant, with his perpetual secret grin; Eugene Wigner, short and scholarly, wearing his exquisite courtesy like a pin-stripe suite; James Franck, the modest German whose pioneering work in quantum physics had inspired many of the men in the room; Leo Szilard, whose paunch preceded him like the cowcatcher of an outdated locomotive; Walter Zinn, tall and rugged, with the incongruous face of an Irish boxer; and Herbert Anderson, boyish and handsome.

As they took their seats, Groves tried to size them up. What kind of people were they? Some of them, especially Fermi and Franck, came from Axis countries. Would their loyalties be divided? Would they ultimately balk at making a bomb that might be dropped on their own homelands? So far, there seemed little question that they were doing their best for the Allied cause, but still, Groves thought, "it was the kind of thing you had to be thinking about."

One of the young physicists got up and launched into an energetic lecture on the amount of uranium or plutonium needed for the actual making of a bomb. This was precisely what Groves had come to hear. As an engineer, it was crucial that he have a precise estimate of the project's material needs, and no single need was as important as this one. Up to now, he'd gotten no clear answer to this simple but absolutely essential question. Maybe, he thought, the answer had finally come.

The young physicist went excitedly on. His words rushed together, and his hand filled the blackboard with a torrent of equations. Although many of the expressions and most of the formulas were entirely new to him, Groves found that his calculus stood him in good stead: he could follow the discussion, in its outline if not in its entirety.

But then the general noticed something wrong. A figure in the fourth row of an especially long and tortuous equation had somehow changed when carried to the fifth row. What was going on? Groves wondered. These people were supposed to be geniuses—how could they make such a schoolboy mistake? Or was it a mistake after all? Might it be a deliberate attempt to trick him, to show him up as a mathematical inferior?

With some trepidation, the general took the bait. "Excuse me," he said, "but that 10^{-5} in the fifth row; shouldn't it be 10^{-6}?"

Distracted, the physicist looked back at the figures, contemplating them for a long moment. Then he summarily erased the second figure with the tip of his finger and wrote in the correct number. "You're right, General," he said.

But Groves could not shake the feeling that he was being tested. He listened with even more careful attention as the physicist finished his discourse.

"We think," the physicist said, "that to get an explosive reaction, we're going to need a critical mass of about five kilograms of uranium, maybe a little less of plutonium. That's correct to a factor of ten."

Immediately Groves broke in. "Excuse me," he said. "Would you mind explaining that factor of ten? Engineers usually express accuracy as a plus-or-minus percentage."

The physicist looked puzzled. "Well," he said, "it means just what it says. It's a factor of ten."

"In other words," Groves said, "you're telling me that instead of needing five kilograms you're actually going to need somewhere between half a kilogram and fifty kilograms?"

"That's right," said the physicist.

Groves sat back in his chair, thoroughly dissatisfied. He felt like a chef preparing a wedding banquet for a host who couldn't tell him how many guests were coming. In impatient silence he listened to the rest of the presentations, which now seemed to confirm his lingering suspicion that

the physicists had very little to say that was concrete and that they were
trying to steam-roller him with vague and obfuscatory mathematics. If that
was true, he thought, it was time to set things straight.

"Gentlemen," he said when the presentations were finished, "as
most of you probably know, I don't have a Ph.D. But I think you should
know that after I left West Point I spent ten years doing nothing but
studying. No outside jobs, no teaching—just ten years of pure study.
Now, that should be about equal to two Ph.D.'s, shouldn't it?"

The remark was followed by stony silence, which Groves interpreted
as agreement on the part of the physicists, a sign of newfound if grudging
respect. But actually the general had made a serious gaffe. In the
academic world it was considered extremely bad form to make an overt
display of one's background; education at the highest level was a simple
given and was not to be discussed. To many of the men in the room the
general's speech had displayed not his education but a lack of grace and
tact that bordered on boorishness. It was an impression that for many
would last a lifetime.

"You see?" exploded Szilard after Groves had left the room. "How
can we work with people like that?"

Minutes later, in a small office in Eckart Hall, Groves and Szilard
confronted each other face-to-face. Ostensibly they were meeting to
discuss alternate methods for cooling the critical pile; actually they were
wrestling for nothing less than control of the project itself. For almost ten
years, ever since he had had a vision of a nuclear weapon on a London
street corner, the bumptious Hungarian had felt himself the intellectual
and political Ground Zero of bomb research, the prime mover among the
politicians, and a sort of paterfamilias to the fission researchers. As far as
Szilard was concerned, he and his fellow scientists needed no help from
the Army or even from the "Washington scientists," Bush and Conant,
whom Szilard saw as outsiders, as meddling scientific bureaucrats with no
training in nuclear physics. In Szilard's estimation, he and the Chicago
scientists could build the bomb themselves.

In reality, though, Szilard's role in the American project and his
standing in the community of physicists was complex and contradictory.
For every physicist who stood in awe of his undeniably brilliant mind—
which seemed to issue bold new ideas with the speed of a machine gun—
there was another who found him intellectually flighty, lacking in depth,
and unable to stay with one idea long enough to pursue it to a satisfying
conclusion. "Leo," one of them said only half jokingly, "should be put in
suspended animation, awakened for a day every hundred years so his ideas

can be harvested, and then put back to sleep." Perpetually jobless, he lived from loan to loan and grant to grant, moving restlessly from hotel to hotel, university to university. His tumultuous personality alienated many of the project's best physicists, especially Fermi and Arthur Compton. "We called him 'the general'," Wigner later recalled. "He wanted to run everything."

No one denied that "the general" had made important contributions to the bomb effort, especially early on. His efforts to alert the U.S. government to the dangers of Nazi physics would probably have come to nothing without the vital intervention of Alexander Sachs, but at least they stirred action among some of the Columbia physicists. And his pioneering experiments—performed in a borrowed Columbia laboratory with a gram of borrowed radium—had helped provide the first experimental evidence of the possible feasibility of an atomic bomb.

But the truth was that ever since these early efforts, Szilard had found himself moving toward the fringes of the project, so that by the fall of 1942 he was very nearly an outcast. At Columbia, where he never had a faculty position, Dean George Pegram had been at best lukewarm to his presence in the laboratory. At Chicago, he had alienated Arthur Compton by writing a long memo in which he insinuated that the Met Lab director was weak and unable to make crucial decisions.

But it was in Washington that Szilard had made his most serious enemies. Very early in the game, Bush and Conant had decided that all patents for inventions arising from government-sponsored war research should be retained by the government, and President Roosevelt had so decreed. Szilard had already applied for $750,000 worth of exclusive patents for the design of a chain-reacting uranium pile; he fought the declaration bitterly, pestering Bush and Conant with unsolicited letters. Soon afterward, Conant warned Groves that many of the project's leaders were finding Szilard's gadfly complaints increasingly irritating and that Groves himself could now expect to become the focus of those complaints. "Szilard will be very opposed to your being there," Conant had warned. "He wanted to have a committee in which he would be the dominant character, running the entire project while the government just poured in money."

Fully forewarned, the general now faced "the general" on his own ground. Szilard had been one of a Met Lab group assigned by Compton to investigate methods for cooling a uranium pile. There were four possible coolant materials: helium, water, heavy water, and metallic bismuth. Szilard's own favorite was bismuth, a preference that was logical in that he himself had been doing the research on bismuth cooling and had in fact applied for an exclusive patent on the process. But now, Groves summarily found his approach too expensive and chose to concentrate on the water and helium methods. This meant that Szilard's personal bailiwick was cut off from Manhattan District funding and would die of financial starvation.

But Groves was not satisfied with excising Szilard's ideas from the project; he soon tried to excise Szilard himself. Within two weeks of that first meeting he asked Compton to get the Hungarian out of Chicago. On October 26, Compton wired that he had "given Szilard til Wednesday to remove his base of operations to New York. . . . Anticipate possible resignation." To Groves not even this was enough: two days later he had no one less than the secretary of war write a letter to the attorney general firing Szilard and ordering him interned for the duration of the war as an enemy alien! The order was never executed; fearing an explosion among his already contentious scientists, Compton may have interceded. But Groves did what seemed to him the next best thing: he had his own agents tail Szilard everywhere he went.

Groves undoubtedly overreacted to Szilard and the potential threat he represented. "Groves sometimes got fixations on people," his security chief John Lansdale said later, "and Szilard was one of them." On the other hand, Lansdale saw Szilard as "almost a psychiatric case—very brilliant, but absolutely erratic and unpredictable. He would talk to anybody about anything, and he refused to be confined by the same regulations that applied to everyone else."

Whether Szilard was simply an open-minded, free-thinking scientist who chafed at security restrictions or, as Landsdale maintained, "disruptive and dangerous," the battle lines between Groves and the physicist, drawn before the two men even met, were tightened by their Chicago confrontation. Groves and Szilard would remain antagonists not only for the rest of the war but for the rest of their lives. For his part, the general made his feelings abundantly clear: "From the time I came in, the entire project would have been better off if Leo Szilard had simply disappeared."

There remained one thing that Groves wanted to know of Compton and his group: If an atomic bomb was possible, just how powerful would it be?

"We think," said Compton, "that it will be equal to five to ten thousand tons of dynamite."

This answer rocked Groves. He probably knew that the most powerful bomb then in existence, the ten-ton Grand Slam, had an explosive force of only about five hundred tons. The atomic bomb, then, would be not just an improvement on existing weapons but an exponential and absolutely unprecedented leap in humankind's ability to destroy.

"Can't you make it smaller?" Groves asked. "If you can make it the equivalent of five hundred tons, it will be available for military use without restriction. If you make it much larger, the conditions under which it can be used will become a matter of political decision."

Compton explained that unless the uranium or plutonium that went into the bomb were of a certain critical size, the bomb would not explode at all. As far as the physicists could tell, he repeated, that size would yield an explosion of five to ten thousand tons and could simply not be smaller.

This answer disturbed Groves. His reply, in essence, anticipated forty years of unrelenting controversy. "If this bomb is bigger than the biggest conventional bomb," he said, "we'll be in political trouble."

Chapter Fifteen

Groves must have left Chicago on October 6 with a sour taste in his mouth. Increasingly it looked as if the Manhattan District job would leave him in a "damned if he did, damned if he didn't" situation. On the one hand, if the bomb was successfully developed, endless political wrangling would forestall its use in the war. If it was unsuccessful, he would likely face what he imagined would be "the greatest Congressional investigation of all time."

Based on what he saw in Chicago, success seemed almost impossibly distant. There was no full-scale uranium pile and thus no incontrovertible proof that a self-sustaining chain reaction was possible. And even if that problem was solved, there would still be no proof that a chain reaction could be made explosive, as in "bomb." No one seemed to know just how much uranium or plutonium would be needed to make this as yet implausible weapon. As if all this wasn't enough, the Chicago group in general—and Leo Szilard in particular—seemed to have an attitude problem.

In the end, Groves could only shake his head and go grimly on to Berkeley, where the University of California's Radiation Laboratory, or Rad Lab, was the next stop on his tour. Waiting to meet him, his blue eyes shining behind rimless spectacles, was an eager and intense Ernest Orlando Lawrence. Tall, blond, and sporting a deep tan earned on the courts of the Berkeley Tennis Club, Lawrence was in many ways the prototype of the emerging twentieth-century scientist. As the inventor of the cyclotron—a massive and hugely expensive particle accelerator that could literally smash atoms to fragments—he had realized early on that the Bunsen burner-and-bailing-wire variety of science was on its way out, that the new basic knowledge about the workings of the universe would essentially have to be bought, and that the price would soar with the increasing sophistication of what he liked to call "our infernal machines."

With that realization Lawrence became a tireless organizer, a relentless scientific promoter, and an inspired grant-grabber. Using his ebullient personality like a rake, he had gathered in more money than any one university department had ever seen. This in turn had paid off in the form of the laboratory that had produced not only a stable of increasingly powerful cyclotrons but the discovery of the first transuranic elements: neptunium and the vitally important plutonium. The combination of Lawrence's dynamic energy and the best machines money could buy had attracted a core of brilliant young scientists and graduate students, at least four of whom—Glen Seaborg, Luis Alvarez, Emilio Segrè, and Edwin McMillan—would win the Nobel Prize.

From the train station in San Francisco, Lawrence now ushered Groves on a hair-raising, pedal-to-metal car ride through the Berkeley hills to the Radiation Laboratory, which perched on the summit with a sweeping view of San Francisco's beautiful bay and bridges.

As they left the car, Lawrence turned to the tight-lipped general, who was still shaken by the physicist's eccentric driving. "Everything you've seen at the other labs is a bunch of theory," Lawrence said. "Here you're going to see isotope separation at work."

Lawrence was referring to the electromagnetic method of separating fissionable U-235 from U-238. A year before, he had converted his thirty-seven-inch cyclotron from a particle accelerator into a sort of mass spectrograph, in which ionized uranium chloride gas was shot through a powerful magnetic field. The force of the field set the uranium ions chasing one another in a circular path around the inside of the chamber until they reached a collector on the other side, where the lighter U-235 ions clustered in a spot separated by a tiny fraction of an inch from the U-238 ions. In February 1942 the excited Lawrence reported that the converted cyclotron actually collected and separated about 225 micro-grams of 30 percent pure U-235—a fly-speck, admittedly, but it put the electromagnetic method at least 225 micrograms ahead of all the others. To Lawrence, the process looked like the salvation of the entire project. To the consistently skeptical Groves, it was "like looking for a needle in a haystack while wearing boxing gloves."

Even Lawrence knew that if he was ever to produce U-235 in the quantities necessary for a bomb, he would have to boost the power of his machine many times over. With that in mind he had built the Calutron, a whopping 184-inch dynamo that was far and away the largest cyclotron in the world. Now, glowing with enthusiasm and confidence, Lawrence guided Groves through a jungle of cables and a bevy of hardworking graduate students into the presence of the beast itself. No doubt the

Calutron, its immense magnet suspended twenty feet above the floor by a bright red gantry crane, was impressive to an engineer like Groves, especially after what he saw as the barren theorizing of the Chicago group. And Lawrence, with his boyish optimism, his air of certainty, and his openhanded friendliness, represented a refreshing improvement over Chicago's truculent condescension.

Barely concealing his pride, Lawrence cranked up his enormous machine to a satisfying hum. "More power, Jimmy!" he yelled to the graduate student at the controls. "Come on, give it more!"

Groves ignored the strange order that suffused the laboratory; Lawrence's biologist brother John was using an adjacent lab to do radiation experiments on animals; on an earlier visit Colonel Kenneth Nichols had noted "an atmosphere of cooking rats." Groves watched through an observation port as the Calutron began the mighty effort of creating an internal vacuum. At the same time, he saw the beginning of a massive electromagnetic field, signaled by the appearance of a shimmering blue arc. Two small bins on the far side of the field stood ready to collect the two isotopes as they were separated from the uranium gas. Had the Calutron operated at the same level as its smaller and more successful prototype, the fruits of separation would have shown up as a greenish smudge in the collection bins. That smudge—which Lawrence's technicians had been able to scrape off the collector of the smaller cyclotron—had been the first visible product of the atomic age.

But on this October 8 there was no smudge. Lawrence ran the machine for less than half an hour, then ordered it turned off. Groves, who had been expecting to see separation occur before his eyes, instantly came at Lawrence with a cluster of sharp questions.

"How long does this thing have to run to get real separation?" the general wanted to know.

"Well," hemmed Lawrence, "it takes fourteen to twenty-four hours to get up a sufficient vacuum in the machine."

"And how long do you run it?" Groves persisted.

"Never more than ten or fifteen minutes."

"Then what about separation?"

"Well, actually," Lawrence admitted, "the Calutron is still in the experimental stage. We don't get any sizable separation at all."

To Groves it was immediately evident that despite its pyrotechnics, the Calutron was no more advanced as a production method than any of the others. But what made the Calutron approach different from, say, the centrifuge was the presence and personality of Ernest Lawrence. Any momentary disappointment that Groves might have felt about the electromagnetic method was mitigated by his strongly favorable impression of the method's developer and the laboratory he directed. In Lawrence, Groves had found a man with whom he could identify: a minister's son, a conservative, flag-waving American, and a scientist who miraculously seemed primarily concerned with practical results. "He impressed me with his confidence and his ability," the general recalled, explaining his instant affinity for the Rad Lab's director. "And he didn't seem ill at ease with someone who wasn't academic."

Lawrence's confidence and his open acceptance of military leadership, so dramatically in contrast to the attitudes Groves had found in Chicago, were reflected in the atmosphere at the Rad Lab. Lawrence's hearty enthusiasm was obviously contagious, for the Lab throbbed with the kind of purposeful, unified activity that the general had found nowhere else in the project. "Lawrence's people acted like an industrial organization," he said, bestowing on them his greatest compliment. "As far as getting something done was concerned, they were right on the ball."

Back in his Washington office, Groves summed up his impressions of his tour. "I was shocked," he said, "by how little the scientists had in the way of real knowledge. It was as if the Wright brothers had come to see me after getting their first plane up in the air for twenty seconds and said, 'Okay, the work's all done. All you have to do is build some plants and start turning out airplanes.'"

With his vast experience in industrial construction, Groves knew better. All in all, it looked to him as if the making of an atomic bomb—if such a bomb was indeed possible, which even in December 1942 was far from certain—would require a concentrated industrial effort unprecedented in human history. Everything would have to be done backward. Instead of following the normal, orderly path in which research and development establish basic principles before production facilities are built, Groves and the Manhattan District would have to swallow their doubts and plunge feet-first into the building of huge multimillion-dollar factories, praying that scientific research would soon catch up with and justify them.

Success, if it were to be had, would depend on answering a hair-raising sequence of scientific unknowns; on the development of entirely new methods for dealing with unfamiliar and devilishly difficult materials; and on the construction of mammoth factories unlike any ever seen on earth. It would also depend on the design of elegant new equipment— everything from improved mass spectrometers to absolutely leakproof seals—built to specifications so impossibly perfect that armies of engineers and designers would gnash their teeth for the duration.

Against this mountain of problems, the project in its pre-Groves phase had made disappointingly little headway. Of the five possible methods of producing fissionable material, only the cyclotron had actually produced any, and that amount was negligible; Conant estimated that it would take some five hundred of the huge Calutrons—still entirely unproven—to produce as little as one hundred grams of U-235 a day. As for the gaseous diffusion method, the barrier problem seemed to defy solution; an enormous plant, featuring hundreds of acres of the still nonexistent barrier, would have to be built before it could be known if the method worked at all. And although Fermi's critical pile—to be built on a squash court under the University of Chicago football stadium—would soon show that the plutonium approach was theoretically feasible, the plant necessary to produce plutonium would ultimately require at least seven such piles, each hundreds of times bigger than Fermi's pioneering model.

Against all these difficulties, which had already sunk Colonel Marshall and which had threatened to sink the entire project, Groves moved with astonishing boldness. Two months after his visit to Berkeley, he made his recommendations through Bush and Conant to Roosevelt. Instead of concentrating on just one production method, as Colonel Marshall had so unfortunately suggested, Groves recommended pursuing three methods simultaneously. That way, he reasoned, at least one of them might bear fruit.

Groves concluded that the liquid thermal diffusion method could be dropped as too costly and the centrifuge as too poorly staffed. But gaseous diffusion should be pursued; despite its brain-racking technical problems and the apparent shakiness of Urey's leadership, construction of a full-scale gaseous diffusion plant should begin at once at the Oak Ridge site. The cost: some $150 million. This immense plant should be complemented by a pilot electromagnetic plant for $10 million and an enormous plutonium plant for about $100 million. All in all, Groves asked for some $400 million—almost five times the amount of Roosevelt's last authorization and some seventy *thousand* times the original 1940 allotment.

Even before he garnered Roosevelt's approval, Groves was already on the move. His report had estimated that there was a good chance that the first bombs could be ready by June 1945. This meant that Groves was now racing not only against the Germans but against his own optimistic estimate. Therefore, he was already furiously negotiating almost half a billion dollars' worth of contracts with industrial concerns big and small, trying to coax them into roles in a wartime extravaganza that, although he had had no hand in the script, was his to direct. "Nothing would be more fatal to success," he wrote, "than to try to arrive at a perfect plan before taking any important step."

At Columbia, at Berkeley, in the offices of dozens of contractors and subcontractors, and most especially at Chicago, Groves's drive, his unswerving practicality, and his relentless prodding were already beginning to be felt. Compton summed it up in a letter written to Conant in the immediate aftermath of the general's whirlwind tour of the Met Lab:

"I had not," Compton wrote, in perhaps the war's driest understatement, "anticipated such rapid action."

Chapter Sixteen

Colonel Franklin Matthias was puzzled. The day before, on December 14, 1942, General Groves had called him to his War Department office and issued a strange order.

"Matthias," he had said, "I want you to go to a meeting tomorrow in Wilmington. It's in the boardroom of the DuPont Company. Don't take any notes, because it's all top secret. I just want you to sit there and listen."

Although Matthias was used to unorthodox instructions from his erstwhile boss—during the construction of the Pentagon, Groves had once had him count every block of marble in the building—this one was all but incomprehensible. For better than half a day he sat in the luxurious DuPont boardroom, gilt-framed portraits of the company's former presidents staring down at him through a forest of crystal chandeliers, while a group of scientists from Chicago outlined the site requirements for a mysterious new factory. Matthias was a bright and outstanding young officer, a University of Wisconsin engineering instructor; he had supervised huge construction projects in the Tennessee Valley Authority and along the Delaware Aqueduct. But even with his technical background, the talk in Wilmington—the scientists were throwing around bewildering terms like *heavy water* and *uranium lattice*—was almost entirely beyond him. Worse, neither the scientists nor the DuPont engineers had mentioned what it was that this obviously enormous factory was expected to produce.

When he got back to Washington late that night, General Groves met his train at Union Station—odd in itself, Matthias thought, for someone as busy as the general.

"Well," said Groves, once they were inside his darkened car and out of earshot, "what did you think of the meeting?"

"I think," said Matthias without hesitation, "I'm going to need some special orientation. Maybe I should buy some Buck Rogers comic books."

Groves laughed, then slowly explained to the young colonel what his mission was all about. As he listened in the dark, Matthias became more and more certain that he had stepped into a science fiction novel. The Army, Groves told him, had been brought in to supervise the development of a radical new weapon that, if successful, might win the war. The factory that had been discussed with such animation but also with such maddening vagueness at Wilmington was expected to produce plutonium, an element that did not exist in nature but that, it was fervently hoped, could be generated in sufficient quantities to become a viable alternative to uranium as the explosive heart of the new bomb. But despite the best efforts of the scientists, plutonium was still almost nonexistent, and the technology for producing it was still in its infancy. In fact, the prototype for the huge nuclear reactors that would generate plutonium had been operated for the first time by the Chicago scientists only two weeks before. Despite their heartening success, the Chicago reactor had produced less than a single watt of energy, whereas the industrial versions would ultimately be designed to generate some 250,000 *kilo*watts—an almost unimaginable scale-up.

For the past two months, Groves had quietly but forcefully been assembling a team to create plutonium. The Chicago scientists—especially Eugene Wigner and John Wheeler—were obvious and essential members of that team. So was Franklin Matthias; Groves appointed the bewildered colonel the Army engineer in charge of constructing the plutonium works three weeks later. A third component of the team would be an enormous industrial firm with extensive experience in the design and construction of city-size factories. "As far as I was concerned," Groves explained, "there was only one firm in the country capable of handling all phases of the job.

"That firm," he said, "was DuPont."

Even before Groves had entered the picture, Arthur Compton had come to a similar conclusion. Himself a former industrial scientist, Compton thought it inconceivable that the Chicago group could handle the engineering and construction details involved in building a plutonium plant by themselves. On a scorching evening in June he had announced this conclusion to a group of seventy-five Met Lab researchers and administrators. "The effect," he wrote later, "was near rebellion."

Many of the men in the room had been pioneers in fission research and were bitterly angry at the idea of turning over their work to an outside firm. Many of the Europeans among them had had engineering training as part of their scientific curriculum (before turning to physics, Wigner had been a chemical engineer in Budapest) and felt themselves capable of overseeing the construction of the plant. "Just give us a hundred engineers and draftsmen," one of them said. "We'll build the place ourselves."

Groves had heard the same complaint when he visited the Met Lab on October 5 and again on October 15. With his emerging vision of the project's vastness and complexity, he brushed the scientists' proposal aside as "unacceptable" and even "absurd." Even Stone and Webster, the outstanding Boston firm that had been the fission project's first engineering subcontractor, was growing uneasy in the face of the project's mushrooming size and its increasing demand for sophisticated chemical knowledge.

Groves now saw that neither the scientists nor Stone and Webster were capable both of carrying out their extensive responsibilities (Stone and Webster was contracted to build the plant for Ernest Lawrence's electromagnetic method at Oak Ridge) and of taking on the construction of the plutonium plant. For that job the DuPont company, with its world-class size ($41 billion in assets, eleven major plants, and 121,000 employees) and its history of successful collaboration with the Army (Groves himself had worked with the company as recently as June in the building of a chemical warfare plant near Denver) seemed the ideal candidate. Kenneth Nichols had already brought the company in on a limited basis, contracting them to develop a chemical means of separating plutonium from the other radioactive by-products of the reactor process. Now Groves moved to involve DuPont in a much bigger way.

On October 30 he called Charles Stine, at thirty-six already a senior DuPont vice president and one of the company's top chemists. Groves had worked with Stine on a number of joint Army-DuPont projects and had found him the ideal liaison. A tough man, his opinions were respected by the company's top executives, and he had repeatedly displayed what the general called "unlimited nerve." At Groves's request, Stine agreed to visit Chicago and make an eyewitness evaluation of the plutonium process.

When he returned a week later his opinion was categorical: "The whole thing," he said, "seems beyond human capability." In Stine's view, none of the alternative pile designs offered much hope of success, and the feasibility of separating plutonium from the rest of the by-products seemed at best questionable. "I don't think there's a Chinaman's chance," Stine concluded, "of getting this thing done in five years."

Still, Groves persisted. He won an appointment with DuPont president Walter Carpenter, a distinguished, elegant executive whose bald head gleamed like a searchlight above his impeccable suits. Groves showed up in Wilmington on November 10. Carpenter was ready with an impressive list of reasons why DuPont should have nothing to do with the bomb project.

First of all, he said, the company was already overcommitted to war work. Second, the job Groves was offering was very dangerous—what if one of the reactors should explode? Third, he said, DuPont had no experience in this sort of thing. But the worst thing, in Carpenter's estimation, was that there was simply not enough time.

To Groves, all these arguments were hauntingly familiar. "You may be right," he responded, "but we have to go ahead anyway. It's very possible that Germany may soon produce its own fissionable material. If they do, and if they develop an atomic bomb, they'll have a weapon for which there's absolutely no defense. On the other hand, if we get the weapon first, then we'll have a way of shortening the war and saving tens of thousands of American lives."

It was a powerful appeal, but Carpenter remained noncommittal. In an afternoon meeting with the company's executive committee, Groves repeated his patriotic appeal. But the executive committee felt that these arguments ran counter to the strongly negative evaluation of the plutonium program in Chicago that they had heard from Stine and other DuPont scientists. Finally, there seemed to be nothing in it for DuPont. If the project failed, the company might go down with it, especially if there was a catastrophic explosion in one of the reactors. If the project succeeded, the company's name would forever be linked in the public's mind with a weapon of death and devastation. As the committee continued to debate, the balance seemed to swing away from Groves and the Army. Finally Carpenter spoke.

"However great the problems are, I think we really have no alternative but to go ahead. After all, we are an American company; we have a long history of contributing to the country's defense in times of emergency. Since the Germans are seeking to solve the same problem—and since, in the opinion of the government, DuPont's assistance is needed—we cannot refuse to accept the work."

In the end, Carpenter's emotional statement won the day. The members of the executive committee put their reservations aside and recommended to accept the job. Two days later DuPont's Board of Directors approved their recommendation without so much as looking at the voluminous information that Carpenter had provided them.

Although the approval relieved Groves's mind considerably, one major hitch still remained: he still had to negotiate with DuPont the precise terms of its entry. Here the general expected a tough battle. His suspicions were verified, he thought, when he appeared at the negotiating session in Wilmington and found a veritable army of lawyers and executives waiting for him.

"It seems I'm outnumbered here," he said to Carpenter. "Looks like the government's about to lose its shirt."

The executive smiled. "It's our thirty-five to your one. That makes us about even."

Actually, the grueling negotiations that Groves expected never materialized. The general was stunned when Carpenter summarily announced DuPont's terms. The company wanted no patents for anything that might develop from this work. All that would become government property. Second, DuPont wanted absolutely no profit. In fact, the only terms under which the company would accept the work would be a contract for a fixed fee. The fee: exactly one dollar.*

The general could scarcely believe his good fortune. He had made one of the project's most crucial acquisitions—the services of one of the world's largest and most successful companies—for virtually nothing.

With DuPont as an operating partner, he was now ready to secure a site for the plutonium plant. On December 15 he sent Franklin Matthias and DuPont engineers A.E.S. Hall and Gilbert Church on a two-week tour of the West and Northwest. They were hunting for a site that had hitherto existed only in the imaginations of the Chicago scientists. It had to be spacious (with at least 225 square miles of available land) and isolated (with no major town within twenty miles); and most important, it had to be an area that could supply not only a staggering 100,000 kilowatts of electric power but virtually unlimited pure water (minimally 25,000 gallons a minute) to cool the giant reactors.

Matthias and the DuPont engineers spent a week searching the high plains of Montana and Idaho but found no spot that satisfied all criteria. Then, two days before Christmas, they flew over the Sawtooth Mountains into western Washington's Columbia River Valley. Below them lay a vast stretch of scrub and sage desert, uninhabited except for a few scattered farming settlements. Neatly bisecting the valley, the majestic Columbia flowed broad and cold. "We were sold on it as soon as we saw it," Matthias said. "It had everything we were looking for."

Matthias immediately sent an enthusiastic report back to Groves. For the sake of thoroughness, the general insisted that the team continue to

---

*DuPont's largesse may have been due in part to its extremely robust financial condition. Thanks to its numerous wartime contracts, annual sales were zooming to $613 million, more than double the 1939 sales.

explore sites in California and Oregon. Even so, he tended to agree that Matthias, Hall, and Church had found the ideal spot. When they returned to Washington on New Year's Day, still convinced that the Columbia River Valley site was the best they'd seen, Groves set the wheels of acquisition in motion. In western Washington, in a six-hundred-square-mile area presided over by the tiny farm town of Hanford (one general store and one gas station) would rise the world's first plutonium factory, where humans would realize the ancient dream of transmuting elements and in doing so ultimately surpass nature herself.

Chapter Seventeen

To Major John H. Dudley, this assignment was an exercise in frustration. In October 1942 he had been suddenly whisked from his job with the Albuquerque District of the Army Corps of Engineers and sent to scour the American Southwest to search for a place where six scientists could retreat in isolation to form a secret and highly exclusive think tank. Although his orders were pointedly silent as to what the scientists were going to think about, Dudley had found from talking to them exactly what they had in mind: the design and assembly of a radical new bomb that could by itself bring about the end of the war.

Dudley had spent a month bouncing in a Jeep over thousands of miles of dirt road in five states until he found a spot that seemed to satisfy all the scientists' criteria. Jemez Springs, New Mexico, where he now stood with two scientists and an Army general named Groves, seemed perfect: it had a steep canyon to contain wayward explosions, a year-round stream to provide water, a usable access road, and an old resort that could be appropriated for housing.

But now, to Dudley's immense annoyance, one of the scientists was changing the criteria on the spot. The scientist—a thin, dreamy-looking fellow from the University of California—thought the access road was immaterial; all he had to be able to do, he said, was haul in a few howitzers. And he said he didn't like the canyon; it was too confining.

General Groves, who had flown in from Washington that morning expecting to confirm the choice of Jemez Springs, was clearly impatient. To him, this sudden change of criteria was one more disconcerting sign of the confused state of research on one of the most critical aspects of the project: the design and assembly of the bomb itself. Already he had seen signs that the scientists were taking design and assembly problems far too lightly; in fact, Ernest Lawrence had told him that once the fissionable material was produced, the bomb could be fabricated in three months by twenty men. That, thought the general, did not make sense.

Groves's instinct was correct. Research on the design of the bomb itself had in fact been relegated to the backwaters of the project. Arthur Compton and the Met Lab group had been far more interested in probing the nature of slow neutrons—those responsible for the controlled reaction in a uranium pile—than that of the fast neutrons that would theoretically precipitate the explosive reaction of a bomb. What research there was on fast neutrons had been scattered among nine universities and had produced very little helpful information. Even a special week-long conference that summer in Berkeley had failed to cast important new light on the bomb design's major mysteries. As late as July 28, Met Lab experimentalist John Manley was still complaining that "there is nothing very definite about the program for [fast neutron] research here in Chicago. Everyone is so interested with the slow neutron aspect of the work that it is hard to get the other aspects of the problem adequately considered."

On Groves's first visit to Chicago he had discussed the problem with Arthur Compton. They had agreed that a separate laboratory should be built to design and assemble the bomb and had made tentative plans to construct it adjacent to the uranium separation facilities at Oak Ridge. But during the two-day train ride to Berkeley, Groves had apparently begun to change his mind. Building the bomb lab next to the uranium facilities would present grave risks: if a test explosion got out of control, it might take the uranium facilities with it. It might be better, he began to think as the train rattled west, to put the bomb lab in a remote and isolated spot of its own.

In Berkeley, Groves met a physicist named J. Robert Oppenheimer who had apparently been thinking along the same lines. A frail, almost ethereal man with an unruly pompadour of black hair and a cigarette perpetually dangling from his fingers, Oppenheimer was introduced to Groves by Ernest Lawrence as someone knowledgeable on the theoretical aspects of bomb design. Although the general and the physicist seemed to have little in common—Oppenheimer was from a wealthy Jewish family in New York and had spent his entire working life in academia—Groves felt an inexplicable affinity for him. It may have been the physicist's manner; his obvious brilliance was offset by a surprising lack of academic pretension. It may have been their common love of the Southwest; both had found joy as teenagers in solitary horseback rides through the deserts and mountains. Or it may simply have been, as the scientist himself boasted years later, that the general had "a fatal weakness for good men." Whatever it was, Groves seems to have felt immediately and instinctively that in J. Robert Oppenheimer he had found a crucially important ally.

Oppenheimer had been pacing the sidelines of the project since its inception. As a student in the 1920s he had been attracted by atomic theory and its "beautiful, wonderful regularities"; now, thanks in great part to his long-standing friendship with Ernest Lawrence—they had spent many vacations together tramping about Oppenheimer's New Mexico ranch and were virtually inseparable partners at the Rad Lab—he had been brought closer to the center of the bomb effort. The year before, Lawrence had introduced him to Compton and the project's inner circle at a conference in Schenectady, saying that his friend had "important new ideas." Compton had immediately put him to work making theoretical calculations on the size of the bomb and eventually put him in charge of all the fast neutron research.

For Oppenheimer, this had the look of a career-making opportunity. Despite his general reputation for brilliance as a student at Harvard, at Cambridge, and at Gottingen and despite his growing influence as a teacher, his contributions as a working physicist (some two dozen papers on the nature of cosmic rays) had been relatively disappointing and had never won him the stature of an Arthur Compton, a Harold Urey, or an Ernest Lawrence. An important position in the bomb project might gain him entrance to the small and exclusive pantheon of great modern physicists. It was an opinion more than heartily shared by his ambitious wife, Kitty.

His chances seemed all the brighter when, during their first meeting on October 8, 1942, Groves and Oppenheimer found themselves in complete agreement on the need to move the proposed bomb lab away from what Oppenheimer called the Chicago "madhouse." Oppenheimer had been resigned to constructing the bomb lab at Oak Ridge but had rushed, with Groves's encouragement, to suggest several possible sites in the West—most of them in California, where they would be conveniently close to Oppenheimer's own bases, Berkeley and the California Institute of Technology in Pasadena. Groves agreed that these California sites should be investigated but decided that the search should cover the entire Southwest. From this meeting came the order to Major Dudley, issued several days later.

For his part, Groves may have had another reason for deciding to separate the bomb lab from Oak Ridge. Because the Met Lab would be running the scientific aspects of uranium separation at the Tennessee site, a bomb laboratory built there would tend to be seen as Chicago's domain.

This was probably less than desirable to Groves, who found many of the Chicago scientists unrealistic and unruly. Far better to isolate the bomb lab and put it under the aegis of a friendlier and less contentious research laboratory. Isolation would also have the advantage of improving safety and security; putting the bomb lab in the hands of another university would effectively reduce Chicago's power and influence yet at the same time place the operation more firmly under Groves's control.

The University of California fit perfectly into his scheme. Groves was already impressed by Ernest Lawrence's positive approach, by his strong and enthusiastic leadership, and by the harmony he seemed to create among the people in his laboratory. In Groves's mind Lawrence would have been the ideal director for the new bomb lab. But there was already heavy investment in the electromagnetic separation research in Berkeley, and Groves felt that Lawrence was needed there to see that process through to the construction stage. If a Berkeley man was to lead the bomb lab, J. Robert Oppenheimer just might be an interesting choice. Groves said later that even at their first meeting in October he was already "sizing Oppenheimer up" for the bomb lab job.

Groves and Oppenheimer met twice more in the following two weeks, once in Washington and once in a train compartment on the Twentieth Century Express. In those meetings Groves laid down conditions for the building and administration of the bomb lab. It would be built, as they had earlier agreed, in an isolated spot in the West, the precise location to be determined later. It would be administered not by Chicago but by the University of California. But most important, it would be under military control; Groves would make it an Army post, responsible to and under the jurisdiction of his own office. This meant that *all scientific personnel, including the director, would enlist in the Army and be commissioned as officers.* The director himself would have the rank of lieutenant colonel.

Although Oppenheimer had not yet been offered the job, he rushed to comply with the general's wishes. Even before Groves's appointment he had told Arthur Compton that he was "interested in obtaining an Army commission." Now, on his return to Berkeley in mid-October, he hurried to the Army installation at the Presidio in San Francisco (where young Lieutenant Groves had begun his family and his career) and took an enlistment physical. By all accounts, he stood ready to join the Army.

So it was as an incipient lieutenant colonel and an as-yet-unappointed director that Oppenheimer joined General Groves, Major Dudley, and University of California physicist Edwin McMillan at Jemez Springs that early November. The steep and cloistered canyon did not gibe with his breathless vision of a glorious, expansive setting from which he and his colleagues could draw inspiration to midwife the bomb. When Groves asked him if he knew of a better place, the physicist was quick to reply.

"I think I do," he said. "Let's go have a look at Los Alamos."*

Now Dudley was even more irritated. Oppenheimer had proposed Los Alamos — the site of an exclusive ranch school for boys — as if it were an original idea. Actually, the place had been suggested more than six months earlier by Percival C. Keith, a senior manager for the M.K. Kellogg Corporation who was supervising the industrial effort to produce barrier metal for Urey and Dunning's gaseous diffusion process. Keith had earlier sent two sons to the Los Alamos Ranch School and knew the area well.

Because of his suggestion, the site had already been surveyed by a military plane, and Dudley himself had made two trips there. But as far as Dudley was concerned, the site was unsuitable: the water supply, entirely dependent on the highly variable flow of Los Alamos Creek, was dangerously unreliable.

Swallowing his objections, Dudley drove the three men over the tortuous mountain road from Jemez Springs to Los Alamos. There they found a high, pine-rimmed mesa backed by the Jemez Mountains and an inspiring view out across the desert to the Sangre de Cristo Mountains in the distance. The brilliant reds and yellows of autumn leaves contrasted with the soft pastels that swept in huge patches across the desert floor. In a small clearing near the rustic main lodge a group of boys were playing soccer, still dressed in short pants despite the early snowfall.

Although Groves appreciated the scientists' need for expansive beauty, he himself examined the place with an engineer's eye. Basically, he liked what he saw. Because of the mountains in the background, the mesa was a cul-de-sac, meaning access could be controlled by the one entry road that twisted its way up from the desert. The road itself, he saw instantly, could be widened without much difficulty to accommodate the diesel trucks and heavy machinery that would stream into the place once the work got under way. A series of canyons below the plateau were perfect for containing explosives tests, and the Ranch School buildings, once the school was purchased, could provide immediate housing so that the project could start up at once. True, the water supply was not good, as Dudley had already reported, but since the lab population was not

---

*Accounts of this expedition vary according to the teller. McMillan, for example, remembered that the four men rode to Los Alamos on horseback; but this was corroborated by none of the others. The version retold here is Dudley's.

expected to rise above three hundred (including technical support for the six scientists), it would probably hold up.

All in all, Groves thought, the place was as good as they were going to find. He made up his mind over dinner in nearby Sante Fe and ordered the acquisition of the Ranch School and some fifty thousand acres of surrounding land; he moved, as Oppenheimer noted later, with "incredible dispatch."

Within two weeks the wheels of acquisition were fully in motion. The school's course was abbreviated to end in January. The military commander of the new post, Colonel J.M. Harman, delivered an impromptu commencement address and rushed the boys out the door.

There still remained the considerable problem of finding a director for the new laboratory. Oppenheimer, it was beginning to appear, had a number of troublesome liabilities. In the first place, he had had no administrative experience whatsoever. In the second, he was a theoretical physicist. Even though the design of the bomb still presented many unsolved theoretical problems, the actual fabrication of the weapon was seen as the domain of experimentalists. There Oppenheimer was remarkably weak. Even as a student he had, in the words of his Harvard adviser Percy Bridgman, been "not at home with the manipulations of the laboratory." Even his admiring colleague John Manley later noted ruefully that "*anyone* would have had more experimental experience than Oppenheimer."

There was also his worrisome medical history, which included a childhood bout with tuberculosis and serious attacks of near-suicidal depression. (Groves had seen the medical history taken at his enlistment physical, and it was enough to cause him more than mild concern.) There was his personality, which seemed to flip inexplicably back and forth between charming generosity (he had once given an expensive suitcase to a friend simply because she admired it) and an almost manic arrogance (at Gottingen, his tendency to completely dominate classroom discussion so annoyed his fellow students that they had gotten up a petition to silence him). There was his bothersome lack of stature in the community of physicists; if chosen to head the bomb lab, he would be the only scientific director in the project who did not have a Nobel Prize.

Even more serious in the minds of some was his political background. His wife, his former girlfriend, his brother, and his sister-in-law had all been members of the Communist Party, and his wife had formerly been married to one of the Party's American leaders. Although never a member himself, Oppenheimer had a history of fellow-traveling, of hosting

Party meetings and of contributing to Party causes. In fact, the FBI had been watching him for a number of years.

As Groves polled the project's scientific leaders, these points were brought up one by one. "The opposition [to Oppenheimer's appointment]," he said later, "was very strong." With Vannevar Bush and James Conant, with Ernest Lawrence and Arthur Compton, he went over the list of other physicists who might be both available and suitable for the job. "If you know a better man," he told Bush and Conant, "tell me who he is." A number of suggestions were made, including Edwin McMillan, who had married Lawrence's secretary and was the Rad Lab chief's favorite candidate; Cal Tech president Carl Anderson, who ironically turned the job down as too unimportant; and Anderson's Cal Tech colleague Wolfgang Panofsky. Groves found reason to reject them all. He was left, he said, with the feeling that Oppenheimer was "the best man, in fact the only man." In that feeling, he noted, "I stood almost alone."

In the face of opposition Groves pushed on with vigor and conviction that in retrospect seem almost puzzling. Given Oppenheimer's obvious liabilities, given the theoretical availability of a number of highly qualified physicists—not only McMillan, Anderson, and Panofsky but also West-inghouse's well-regarded Edward Condon and Columbia Nobel Laureate I.I. Rabi—why did Groves cling so stubbornly to his choice of Oppenheimer? Was it unshakable faith in his own intuition? Or was there a more substantial reason?

Rabi, who had long been a close friend and associate of Oppenheimer's, provided an important clue. "Oppenheimer," he said, "was brilliant, but he was not a strong character. He was indecisive, and definitely not a fighter. If he couldn't persuade you, he'd cave in, especially to group opposition. Groves, on the other hand, could provide him with strong backbone in the form of consistent policy."

At this early stage the policy that probably lay closest to Groves's heart was that Los Alamos be an entirely military laboratory. But he must have known that this policy would be roundly unpopular with the physicists. As Compton later wrote, "The experience of the scientists with military men was limited, and mutual confidence was not yet fully established. It had been suggested [by Groves] that the men in the more responsible research positions should be made members of the Army with officers' rank. The project leaders had given this suggestion careful consideration, *but had independently and unanimously returned a firm no.*" In other words, the leadership of the American physics community, which for the most part already regarded the Army with attitudes that ranged from wariness to outright hostility, stood virtually united against the further militarization of the bomb project.

Everyone, that is, except J. Robert Oppenheimer. Almost alone among the physicists, Oppenheimer enthusiastically and without hesitation agreed to the militarization of the bomb lab.* "I would have been glad to be an officer," he said later. "I thought maybe the others would." To Groves, Oppenheimer's unique compliance with what for him was one of the linchpins of bomb lab planning may have been the deciding, if not the overwhelming, consideration in determining that the physicist was "the best man, the only man" for the director's job.

But Oppenheimer's compliance, his minority-of-one status in being willing to join the military, soon came close to sinking the bomb lab before it was launched. Within weeks, it brought Groves to make one of the most important compromises of his career.

*Chicago's Samuel Allison also agreed in principle to militarization, although with somewhat more hesitation than Oppenheimer. Ironically, Allison later became one of the Army's most prominent and dedicated opponents.

Chapter Eighteen

Two men stood in line at the registration desk at New York's Biltmore Hotel, trying furiously to pretend that they did not know one another. Indeed, it would have been hard to imagine two more different physical types: the one in front, who was asking for the standard discount due an MIT professor, was short and slight with a prominent nose and a carriage that bristled with confidence. Though equally confident, the man behind was tall and hefty, wearing a slightly incongruous brush moustache and an ill-fitting business suit, the buttons of which were obviously strained to contain the bulk within.

Silently and separately the two men—physicist I.I. Rabi and General Leslie R. Groves—repaired to a room off one of the back corridors of the hotel. Waiting for them in the room were two more physicists: Robert Bacher, who was working with Rabi on a top-secret radar project at MIT's Radiation Laboratory, and J. Robert Oppenheimer, the not-quite-yet director of the bomb lab at Los Alamos, who lay stretched out on the bed with his head propped against the backboard.

The men were meeting this cold January day in 1943 to discuss the staffing of the new laboratory to be built in the New Mexico high desert. Oppenheimer was particularly hopeful that the meeting went well, for he was anxious to recruit Bacher—a specialist in neutron physics from Cornell whom he saw as the equal of Enrico Fermi—to head the lab's experimental department. Rabi had already declined an invitation, but his approval of the lab's basic planning was vitally important in recruiting other physicists, who tended to look to him for leadership.

But as Oppenheimer laid out the plans for the new lab, Bacher found himself growing increasingly disturbed. Somehow his Berkeley colleague seemed reluctant to talk about who would have final authority over the lab. "It took some time to get it out of him," Bacher recalled. "When we did, when we found out that the lab was to be military, with scientists taking commissions in the Army, we were horrified."

The argument raged on through the afternoon. If the lab were military, Bacher and Rabi contended, the work would be slowed down because of the need to submit everything through Army channels. Scientific decisions would be subject to the approval or veto of military officials, who could not possibly know enough physics to make correct evaluations. Security questions would tend to take precedence over matters that were purely scientific. Friction would arise between the commissioned scientists in the lab's top ranks and their civilian assistants below. Most important, in subjecting itself to military authority the lab would lose the intellectual autonomy so crucial to the effective solution of the bomb design's many problems.

Oppenheimer tended to wave these objections aside, certain that he would be able to persuade the other physicists that military authority was both necessary and unobjectionable. Groves, who had remained attentively silent throughout the argument, was apparently not so sure, but he was unwilling at this early stage to make any commitment that would reverse course. With matters at a virtual impasse, the meeting disbanded.

At the end of January, Oppenheimer resumed the dialogue at a Washington meeting with Rabi, Bacher, McMillan, and Alvarez. Rabi and Bacher remained adamant in their refusal to join a militarized laboratory; McMillan and Alvarez were equally negative. Oppenheimer argued as best he could but made no headway. With the score now four against one, and with Rabi threatening to persuade other physicists to stay away from the project, Oppenheimer reluctantly gave in.

In a February letter to James Conant (who had been an unwavering supporter of the militarization idea), he communicated Bacher and Rabi's demand that the lab be demilitarized. "I believe that the solidarity of the physicists is such," he wrote, "that if these conditions are not met we will not only fail to have the men from MIT with us, but that many men who have already planned to join the new laboratory will reconsider their commitments. . . ."

Groves realized that he had a considerable problem on his hands. If he remained inflexible in his commitment to a military laboratory, the lab would be severely crippled in its ability to recruit competent physicists. If he gave in to the scientists, he ran the risk not only of diminishing his own authority but, more important, of watching the new lab degenerate into an exclusive desert faculty club, where scientists could be tempted to follow their own research trails at the expense of a concentrated and focused effort to build an atomic bomb.

In the end, though, Groves apparently found it obvious that with no scientists, there would be no laboratory and no bomb. The time had come for compromise. On February 25, 1943, Groves and Conant sent a letter to Oppenheimer outlining their plan for the structure of the bomb lab. Until January 1, 1944, the lab would remain civilian. After that date, the entire scientific and engineering staff would be inducted into the Army and commissioned as officers. The lab's ultimate authority would be the Military Policy Committee, but Groves, as the Committee's executive officer, would be effectively in charge. Oppenheimer would be the scientific director, reporting directly to Groves and Conant. The letter ended with a call for the "closest cooperation" between scientific and military personnel.

The letter was a masterpiece: conciliatory and compromising, but firmly reminding who would be the lab's final authority. When Bacher and Rabi registered a favorable reaction, an important obstacle to the recruitment of physicists was removed.

But other problems remained. Unlike the labs at Chicago, Berkeley, and Columbia, which were already staffed, the Los Alamos scientific contingent would have to be built from the ground up. (By the end of 1942, Rabi and others had made it painfully obvious to Oppenheimer that the building of the bomb would require many more than six scientists.)

This would be anything but easy. First of all, among many notable physicists there was a lack of faith that the project would ever succeed. Even for those who were optimistic about the bomb project's chances, other areas of research seemed more urgent: radar work at MIT, for example, which was holding both Rabi and Alvarez, or the Navy's submarine research in San Diego, which was threatening to hold McMillan. Oppenheimer's lack of first-rank status among physicists became an ongoing headache. His initial approach to Bacher, for example, had to be made through the prominent German theoretician Hans Bethe. Perhaps stickiest of all, most university and department heads had already seen their ranks decimated by the demands of war research; they were loath to lose the few proven scientists who remained.

Oppenheimer plunged with unrestrained vigor against these considerable obstacles. Unfortunately, that vigor often made Oppenheimer himself a source of serious conflict. Flushed by his vision of a physics retreat in his beloved New Mexico mountains, he tended to wade into already established laboratories as if he were wielding the sword of scientific liberation. Nowhere was this more evident—and more resented—than at Princeton, where the acerbic Henry DeWolf Smythe (himself a project leader during the Lyman Briggs days) had built one of the best nuclear physics labs in the country. Smythe had already lost Eugene Wigner and John Wheeler to Arthur Compton, and now Oppenheimer, without bothering to so much as consult with him, was attempting to grab his last two top-flight men: Robert Wilson, who at twenty-eight was already leading Princeton's home-grown isotope-separation program, and Richard Feynman, an unorthodox young theoretician who had acquired a reputation as the most brilliant graduate student in the country. In the face of Oppenheimer's invasion, Smythe wrote howling letters of protest to Conant, who reacted with alarm. In a letter to Groves, Conant wrote that he was "not proposing to go ahead with the men Mr. Oppenheimer wants" until he and the general could talk again. "Both Dr. Bush and I are worried about . . . this whole scheme," Conant wrote. "We are wondering if we have found the right man to be the leader."

Concerned that Oppenheimer's excesses might scotch the whole recruiting program, Groves and Conant applied the brakes. In the wake of the Princeton uproar—which was repeated on a lesser scale at Harvard, at the University of Illinois, and at the Naval Subsurface Warfare Laboratory in San Diego—they worked out a set of mechanics for further recruitment attempts. First approaches would be made not by Oppenheimer but by Conant; and they would be made not to the physicists themselves but to the heads of the university department or government laboratory where the physicist was working. "Once we got the clearance from the top man in each organization who was likely to kick," Conant wrote, "then Oppenheimer would approach the man directly and try to sell him on the idea. If there was then reluctance, [Groves] or I or both of us would then write a letter to the man in question, telling him just how important it was for him to make this sacrifice for the war effort."

This approach, outlined in early January, did much to smooth out the recruiting process.* Wilson and Feynman were expropriated from Princeton, leaving Smythe to fume in silence as his lab was dismantled before his eyes. Thanks in part to Rabi's considerable influence, Hans Bethe signed on, and so did Robert Bacher, although the latter not until April and then only with the understanding that he would resign the day the lab went military. The mercurial Hungarian Edward Teller, who already had visions

---

*Still, even as late as March Oppenheimer was raising hackles at Columbia's Airborne Instrument Laboratory with his unsanctioned attempt to recruit physicist John Drewes, and at the Bureau of Standards, where he went after physicist Seth Neddermeyer without first consulting Lyman Briggs. And his efforts to secure Harvard's John van Vleck, who had already consulted on theoretical problems, were thwarted despite the intervention of Conant, who was Harvard's president!

of a "superbomb" that was powered by hydrogen fusion and exponentially more powerful than a fission bomb, was enlisted, as were two Stanford experimentalists, kindly Hans Staub and the aristocratic Swiss Felix Bloch. Rabi himself, although he never officially joined the project, ultimately became an important consultant, as did the Danish refugee Niels Bohr and the Hungarian computing genius John von Neumann.

But a number of top-ranked physicists—including Carl Anderson, Harvard's John van Vleck, the University of Wisconsin's Franz Kurie, Wolfgang Panofsky, and many others—were notable for their absence. In fact, of the thirty-three physicists listed by Oppenheimer as "leaders in their field," only fifteen came to Los Alamos, and one of those, Bloch, left in disappointment when he was not named head of the lab's Theoretical Division. Out of 165 scientists listed as "men of considerable ability and experience," the lab successfully recruited only thirty-five.

With a patchwork staff composed of a few indisputable masters (Bethe, for example, had written a radically inventive paper on the piercing of armor plate, using as a source only the *Encyclopaedia Britannica*), a director who was the unanimous choice of no one but Groves, a core of the director's former associates (in addition to Edwin McMillan and John Manley, the core included former Oppenheimer graduate students Phillip Morrison and Robert Serber), and a smattering of competent physicists from around the country, the laboratory at Los Alamos began the awesome task of designing and building the bomb that would end the war. But the successful completion of that task ultimately depended on a group that became the flesh of the new lab: a tribe of young physicists who, although obviously bright and apparently promising, were for the most part almost entirely unproven.

The average age of these Los Alamos physicists, who were expected to perform a job that many older and presumably wiser heads considered impossible, was twenty-five. Some of them had no stronger credentials than a bachelor's degree. A few had barely begun to shave.

Chapter Nineteen

Groves filled the rosters of Los Alamos with beardless youths, but for the jobs of building the gargantuan Hanford and Oak Ridge "fission factories" and of designing the project's otherworldly production machinery, he tended to seek out industrial veterans. DuPont's "Slim" Read, a cigar-biting rugged individualist who was a long-time cohort of the general's (and who shared with him an outspoken personality and an elaborate distaste for rule by committee) was already in place to help Franklin Matthias supervise the construction of the Hanford plutonium plant. The teetotaling and grimly efficient Edwin L. Jones—so unflappable that he had once accepted a Navy contract to build 212 Liberty ships, despite the fact that he had never built a boat in his life—would spearhead building the electromagnetic plant at Oak Ridge; it would then be turned over for operation to Tennessee Eastman's methodical general manager James E. White. As the war went on and the project grew even beyond Groves's expansive vision, scores more were added.

But perhaps the best of Groves's recruits—certainly the most volubly flamboyant—was a Texas engineer named Percival "Dobie" Keith. Keith's job was to find the Holy Grail of the gaseous diffusion method: a suitable metallic barrier. Blowsy and impetuous, Keith at forty-two had already acquired a dual reputation as one of the country's top chemical engineers and as one of industry's more eccentric figures. He had been kept in velvet pants and long curls until the age of eight and was now known for enlivening discussions of industrial plumbing with long and letter-perfect quotes from Dante's *Inferno*.

Keith and the company he worked for, M.K. Kellogg of Jersey City, New Jersey, were legacies from the days of the Briggs Uranium Committee. Groves had visited the company's barrier laboratory in Jersey City during his first tour and had been impressed by the Texan's energetic and authoritative style. Until that time, though, Keith and Kellogg's assignment had simply been to investigate the feasibility of various barrier materials.

But Groves could not afford the luxury of a leisurely research and development program—with its exhaustive testing and its demands for certainty—before going into production. A commitment to the gaseous diffusion method had been made in his report to Roosevelt; Groves had to assume the method would work. So the project had not only to find but also to start producing a suitable barrier material as quickly as humanly possible. This called for an enormous increase in Kellogg's role and an all-out, exclusive personal commitment from Percival Keith.

Over dinner in an expensive New York restaurant (Groves refused to eat the escargots), the general pressed Keith to make that commitment. But the engineer was not an easy convert. From his vantage point, the gaseous diffusion method looked like a combination of the labors of Hercules and *The War of the Worlds*. There was nothing like it in existence on earth. Its theories were entirely untested, and the requirements of its outlandish materials—especially the barrier—were unprecedented in industrial history. Why, he asked Groves, should he commit his time and energy to a process that looked like such a sorry bet?

"I understand your hesitation, Mr. Keith," the general said. "But you know, I didn't want my job, either. I was badly disappointed when they canceled my overseas assignment. But they told me, 'If you succeed, you can shorten the war.' What could I do but accept?"

Keith's resistance, based on the logic of peacetime industry, now fell to the perverse but compelling logic of wartime patriotism. With a handshake and a guarantee from Groves that the Army would not interfere with his handling of the job, Keith took the plunge.

To take the burden off Kellogg, Keith created a new arm of the company, an arm the only purpose of which would be to develop and produce the elusive barrier. The staff of the new company, known as Kellex, was an all-star team of top industrial engineers personally recruited by Keith himself; the company, created and financed for the purpose of producing the barrier, became a prototype of the modern task force.

By the spring of 1943 the most important players on Groves's team were essentially in place. But there was a problem at the top. Although General Somervell and General Styer had put Groves entirely in charge of the project and had given him all responsibility for its success, they had not bothered to relieve James Marshall, the Manhattan District's first commander, of *his* responsibilities. This created a hazy dual authority that was confusing to scientists and soldiers alike. It made the situation even more delicate that Groves and Marshall were personal friends.

But as far as Groves was concerned, the job came first, and he was rapidly developing a low opinion of Marshall's performance. "He was too deferential," Groves said later, "and he wasn't demanding enough of his subordinates. He did not have the drive and ability to push the project at the speed needed, and I found that my push was being slowed as it went through his hands."

In the face of these problems, both the working relationship and the friendship slowly disintegrated. Matters came to a head in the spring of 1943, when Marshall tried to hire six civilian engineers for the Manhattan District without first consulting Groves. When the general discovered the gambit and started to intercede, the normally quiet Marshall lost his temper. "He grabbed a plane from Syracuse," recalled a Groves staffer, "and was in Groves's office that afternoon. I could hear them in there, shouting at each other."

For Groves, the incident was the last straw. Within weeks he had quietly arranged for Marshall's transfer to the Engineer Replacement Center at Camp Sutton, North Carolina.

To replace Marshall as District Engineer, Groves chose Kenneth Nichols, the scholarly engineering professor whose mild, bespectacled countenance hid a personal toughness and a mind that, according to one physicist, "worked like a steel trap." "Nichols," Groves later said, "did a better job than Marshall from the day he took over."

It was now the early spring of 1943. The recruitment of DuPont and the assignment of Matthias to supervise plant construction in Hanford had brought the plutonium program out of the laboratory and onto a path toward industrial viability. The enlistment of the dynamic Keith and his Kellex team made the gaseous diffusion process look a bit more hopeful. The core staff of the bomb laboratory at Los Alamos was all but in place. The authority problem had been solved; with Marshall transferred Groves now stood in sole and unquestioned charge.

Its grim task outlined, its sites and funding secured, and its key posts manned, the Manhattan Engineer District was now ready to roll toward production. In the terrible race with the Nazis, Groves finally had the American effort fully organized and on the move.

Chapter Twenty

Franklin Matthias saw a cloud of dust rising from what seemed to be the other side of the world. Yellow and ominous, it roiled upward from the Washington desert, obscuring the horizon and darkening the bright spring sky. But this, Matthias knew, was not one of the ordinary dust storms that routinely scoured the Columbia River Basin. In fact, for him it was the herald of the war's most welcome invasion: the first squadron of an army of eleven thousand bulldozers, cranes, and tractors—many of them scavenged by Groves from the recently completed Al-Can Hiway—that would build the world's first and only plutonium factory.

The arrival of the heavy machinery meant the beginning of the construction of the huge nuclear reactors that would be the heart of the plutonium production process. Unfortunately, in April 1943 the design of those reactors had yet to be completed. In fact, as recently as February two competing designs—one cooled by helium and the other by water—were still in the running. Only in the middle of the month did DuPont's Crawford Greenewalt finally decide on the water-cooled pile. Because of this lag in design decisions, Matthias had to start the enormous task of excavation (25 million cubic yards of earth, enough to build four Pentagons) and construction (at least three mammoth reactor buildings 800 feet long, 65 feet wide, and 80 feet high) without the aid of as much as a single blueprint. "All we had," he said, "was a sort of conceptual plan. As DuPont figured out the dimensions, they sent them to us by telegram."

All through the spring the watchword, repeated time and time again in countless telephone calls from Groves, was *speed*. While DuPont engineers worked feverish double shifts to produce blueprints for the reactor and chemical separation buildings, Matthias's and Read's crews raced on, sometimes working at night by the red glow of parachute flares. By the end of the summer the sprawling tent and trailer city that had housed forty thousand workers (the trailer park, with some 480 units, may have been the largest in the world at the time) had given way to an enormous construction camp that boasted over eleven hundred buildings. For the rest of the summer and early fall, the hard yellow ground was rent by thousands of bulldozers and jackhammers, and the desert silence was shattered by the groaning of machinery and the cries of thousands of men. All the activity kept the entire six-hundred-square-mile reservation under a constant cloud of dust. Finally, on a cool day in mid-October, Matthias allowed himself a moment of quiet congratulation as he watched the driving of the stakes for the foundation of the first reactor building.

Getting to that point had not been easy. Just to secure the site for the Manhattan District, Groves and Matthias had had to fight off first the Quartermaster Corps, which wanted to use it for a million-acre warehouse, then the Navy, which saw the basin as a perfect site for a gunnery range, and finally the slings and arrows of the local farmers, who simply did not want to leave. They somehow had to recruit an army of forty thousand construction workers over the considerable objections of the War Manpower Commission, which growled that the needs of Seattle's Boeing and Kaiser Streel had to be satisfied first before they would turn men loose on a phantom project whose objective they were not even allowed to know— and then keep that army on the job despite the loneliness, the isolation, and the choking dust storms.

Groves had been able to stake a claim on the site in a quiet talk with his old friend E.B. Gregory, the commander of the Quartermaster Corps, and then by some less quiet but ultimately convincing discussions with the Navy. He had relentlessly moved the farmers out of the way by securing a series of court-ordered evictions and then had quieted them by paying high prices for their land and hiring many of them for the construction gangs. To attack the labor problem he had pulled a Donald Nelson–like bluff; he had threatened War Manpower Commission chairman Paul McNutt with a direct complaint to Roosevelt if he did not bend Commission policies in the Manhattan District's favor.

Although this tactic worked to get laborers to Hanford, it did nothing to keep them there. In fact, on some days more workers left the facility than entered. Groves and Matthias tried to meet the problem by steadily lowering skill standards; at one point they even considered beefing up the workforce with Italian prisoners of war. But nothing quite worked—labor problems plagued Hanford throughout the war.

Still, these problems paled before the Hanford project's most pressing need for most of 1943. By ignoring standard production procedures and pushing buildings through in anticipation of blueprints, Groves and

Matthias were able to at least start to put up the shells of the monolithic reactor buildings. But without the reactors that went inside them, the buildings—and indeed the entire plutonium process—were nothing but empty hulls, silent and gutless monuments to a failed approach and, quite possibly, to a nonexistent bomb.

Yet the designs for the reactors lagged maddeningly behind schedule. That lag was the direct result of one of the project's most disturbing failures to communicate, a failure that involved the anonymous engineers at DuPont and the highly visible rebel faction at Chicago's Metallurgical Laboratory. The resulting conflict threatened to explode into a scientific civil war.

Groves had known that the restaurant, with its fashionable location in Chicago's Loop District and its army of waiters and wine stewards, was expensive, but the check—seventy-five dollars for lunch for four people—must have made him gulp. For the habitually thrifty general, it was one thing to spend $400 million of the government's money on a weapon; if the weapon actually shortened the draining war, it would save far more than it cost. But it was quite another thing to spend more than 10 percent of his own monthly salary on a single meal.

Still, he sighed, if the lunch had its intended effect, the money would be more than well spent. For the guest of honor, flanked by Arthur Compton and by Army liaison officer Major A.V. Peterson, was Eugene Wigner, and the purpose of the lunch was to woo the brilliant Hungarian physicist back into the Manhattan District fold.

Beginning in the fall of 1942, when Groves had brought DuPont into the project, Wigner's politeness had begun to wane. He was one of the pioneers of the American project, and was perhaps the central figure in the design of the huge reactors that would produce plutonium, now that Szilard was increasingly isolated from the top ranks. A competent engineer with an impressively broad knowledge of chemistry, Wigner was convinced that he and his group at Chicago could easily supervise the design and construction of the plutonium plant to be built at Hanford. Both DuPont and the Army, he believed, were superfluous—their unwieldy presence could do nothing but slow progress.

There was more to Chicago's anti-DuPont rebellion than Wigner's injured pride. The Met Lab scientists had discovered a significant difference in salary between themselves and the DuPont engineers; some of the latter were making more money than the Chicago physicists who were training them. More important, many of the Met Lab scientists saw the entry of DuPont as the beginning of a battle for control of the plutonium project. This battle, they suspected, would eventually become a struggle to dominate the nuclear industry in the postwar world.

The Chicago scientists had been among the first to realize that the discovery of fission could revolutionize the way the world got its energy, and many saw bright futures for themselves in the new and growing industry to which they soon gave an appropriately futuristic name: nucleonics. DuPont, many felt, was attempting to muscle in and establish a monopoly over the infant industry. Not even DuPont's surrender of all its patent rights to the government could convince them otherwise.

Probably fueled by this suspicion, the Chicago rebellion bubbled to the surface at least twice during 1943. In February, Wigner, angered by what he saw as DuPont's consistent failure to consult him on the design of the Hanford reactors, threatened to resign. Talking furiously, Compton had persuaded him to stay on, while Groves—who always considered the Hungarian an "honorable man"—pressed Walter Carpenter to make sure that the unhappy physicist was thereafter included in the design process. In March, when Wigner was invited to Wilmington for a series of conferences, the situation seemed to improve. But Wigner's dissatisfaction surfaced again in July. In a stormy meeting with Compton on the twenty-third, he insisted that DuPont be replaced as the contractor for the pilot plant. "We just can't work with them," he said.

Groves himself had exacerbated the tension by attempting to resolve what he called "the scientist problem" with an iron fist. In June he solicited a letter from President Roosevelt that pointedly reminded the physicists that Groves was in charge and that exhorted them to be "equal to the challenge" posed by the Germans. The letter was an utter failure: how, the physicists wanted to know, could they be expected to be "equal to the challenge" when they were obviously being stripped of all authority? With the still-essential laboratory in an ugly mood, Groves tried a softer approach. He attempted a reconciliation by courting Wigner and his group with a series of VIP luncheons, designed, the general said, "so they would understand my feelings as to their importance in the picture," and also "to make them feel more friendly to me." Probably more helpful than these luncheons was his August appointment of a committee of scientists and engineers under MIT's W.K. Lewis to review progress and, more than incidentally, to hear out the physicists' complaints vis-à-vis DuPont and the Army.

After their souls were unburdened and they were included in the design phase of the reactors, the Chicago rebellion simmered down. But the truth of the situation remained evident: the Met Lab had been undermined, inexorably replaced by the Army and its temporary ally DuPont as the central authority in American nuclear physics. From that point on, Chicago's role in the project would decline precipitously. Realizing that they had been shunted to the sidelines and that the glowing future they saw for themselves in the postwar nuclear picture was steadily growing dimmer, the Met Lab physicists remained in what Compton called "a state of tension" throughout the war. In the final stages of the war and once again in peacetime, that tension erupted, changing Groves's life in the process.

For Hanford and for the plutonium process, 1943 had not been a very good year. Delayed by the acquisition struggle, further delayed by labor problems, and severely threatened by the Chicago rebellion, progress had been slow and disappointing. Earlier, Compton had blithely predicted that the production of plutonium during 1943 was 99 percent assured, and even the cautious Lewis Committee had concluded that the plutonium process might yet provide the "earliest achievement" of the production of material for the bomb. But 1944 dawned with the reactor buildings only beginning to go up and with still no final designs for the uranium piles to go inside.

The specter of German capability was still hanging over Groves's head; far too much precious time had gone by with far too few results. Hopefully, Groves thought, some of the time that had been lost in the deserts of Washington could be made up in the mountains of Tennessee.

Chapter Twenty-One

It looked, Colonel Kenneth Nichols would have agreed, like a good place for an explosion. The 825 acres of Bear Creek Valley at the southwestern edge of the Oak Ridge, Tennessee, complex were bounded on both sides by wooded ridges that rose a thousand feet from the valley floor. These ridges could probably contain any disastrous explosion that might occur in the plant to be built there, the plant that would house the enormous U-235-producing Calutrons of Ernest O. Lawrence.

Bear Creek Valley became Lawrence's personal fiefdom, but the whole of Oak Ridge became the domain of Colonel Nichols. A mild-mannered, bespectacled man, his scholarly look was no accident; he had graduated fifth in his class from West Point, had studied at Berlin's renowned Technische Hochschule, and had earned a Ph.D. in experimental mechanics from Iowa State University. But Nichols could also be tough and demanding, with drive and energy that belied his professorial appearance.

Between Groves and Nichols there was no love lost. Nichols had worked in the Syracuse District under James Marshall, and Groves knew that he admired Marshall greatly. Perhaps because of this, the general seemed to go out of his way to remind Nichols who was in charge. More than once, he kept the MED's District Engineer waiting for hours on a hard wooden bench outside his office; from time to time he would playfully pop his head out the door to say, "Now, where's Nichols?" This treatment later led Nichols to characterize his boss as "the biggest son of a bitch I ever met."

But despite their personal distaste for one another, their working relationship was based on mutual respect. For his part, Nichols admired Groves's determination, the effective simplicity of his administrative organization, and his almost mysterious ability to get things done. To Groves, Nichols was all but invaluable: he was a trained professional soldier with an engineer's eye for practical results, but his academic credentials gave him a certain snob value among the scientists. "I knew the Chicago scientists liked Nichols better than they did me," Groves would say, "so I had him do most of the routine dealings with Compton and his people."

As District Engineer, it was Nichols's job to supervise the construction and operation of the uranium production facilities at Oak Ridge. In that regard, Groves and Bush had made a bold decision: to simultaneously—and expensively—pursue two distinct methods for separating out the fissionable but maddeningly elusive U-235 isotope. One was the gaseous diffusion method, now being flogged full-bore by Dunning at Columbia and Keith at Kellex; and the other was the electromagnetic method, the favorite child of Ernest Lawrence.

In early 1943, Lawrence's method looked to almost everyone like the surest and swiftest horse in the race. The fact that a working prototype for the method already existed—Berkeley's potent 184-inch Calutron—gave it a clear head start over both gaseous diffusion and plutonium, neither of which could claim to have a functioning pilot.* By the end of 1942 the Berkeley team, driven incessantly by the autocratic Lawrence, had already determined the approximate size and shape of a production-model Calutron, as well as the power requirements of its huge magnets. In the swell of optimism created by growing stacks of solid data, the fact that as yet not one production-model Calutron had been built—of several *hundred* that would eventually be needed—seemed little more than a minor and purely temporary annoyance.

In light of this optimism, Groves set a typically demanding schedule. He wanted the electromagnetic plant (known, for reasons neither Groves nor Lawrence could ever determine, as Y-12) built and the first of its five "racetracks" installed by July 1, 1943. Each racetrack would contain as many as ninety-six Calutrons. To the Stone and Webster engineers, the schedule was "impossible." To Groves, to Nichols, and to Ernest Lawrence, it was a challenge that had to be met.

Thus, Nichols was more than gratified when Stone and Webster broke ground for the first Alpha building on February 18. Over the next three months, as spring rains turned the entire Oak Ridge complex into a slushy bog of red mud, 1,585 railroad cards delivered 13,000 windows, 5 million bricks, and 38 million board feet of lumber. In April, construction

---

*Possibly for safety reasons, Groves had ordered the Staggs Field pile, where Fermi had first demonstrated the self-sustaining chain reaction in uranium, moved to a new site in the Argonne Forest south of Chicago. It was not fully operational until March 1943.

began on a new building to house the second-stage plant, one that would take partially purified U-235 from the first stage and run it through another series of racetracks to purify it still further. (By ordering the building of this stage, Groves overruled Lawrence himself, who thought the additional process unnecessary.)

In late May, Lawrence climbed the ridge overlooking Bear Creek Valley. Even this archetypal big thinker was taken aback by the magnitude of the operation spread out below him. "It sobers you up," he told his people in Berkeley. "It makes you realize that whether we want to or not, we've got to make things go . . ."

By late summer the ground was strewn with hundreds of thousands of crates and boxes that held the mechanical guts of the two buildings. In the welter of pipes and valves, pumps and cables, and especially vacuum tubes—one of the scientists had estimated that the plant would ultimately swallow every vacuum tube the country could produce—one item stood out: the coils of the enormous magnets that would be the heart of the system, built by Allis-Chalmers of Milwaukee with forty-seven thousand tons of silver borrowed, incredibly enough, from the U.S. Treasury.

By October, Groves was pleased to note that the Alpha building was nearly complete and that the first magnetic coils were in place and ready for testing. But over the next two months the start-up operation was plagued by a series of delays. The system was found to be short-circuiting with such regularity that resistance in the coils remained far below operating levels. The steel vacuum tanks in which the U-235 was to be collected were leaking badly. And somehow the tremendous forces generated by the magnets were actually pulling the fourteen-ton tanks loose from their welds, so that they were "walking" as much as three inches away from one another.

Within a few weeks the leaks were sealed and the tanks were held in place by newly installed steel straps. Still, the Alpha system stubbornly refused to develop the reliable ion beam necessary to actually separate the uranium isotopes. By mid-December the entire operation had all but ground to a halt, and the once-heady morale of the Oak Ridge team and of Lawrence's Berkeley laboratory disappeared.

Groves reacted to the critical stoppage with characteristic speed and directness. On December 15 he arrived in Oak Ridge to meet with on-site engineers and review the problem himself. A grim band of engineers accompanied Groves to the Alpha building, where the twenty-four-square-foot magnets lay infuriatingly quiet.

Groves immediately ordered one of the magnets opened up for inspection. When the engineers protested that this would cost at least fifty thousand dollars and weeks of delay (the magnets would have to be sent back to Allis-Chalmers in Milwaukee for rewinding), Groves simply repeated the order. Reluctantly, the engineers obeyed. Groves's practiced eye saw immediately that the coils were badly designed; the silver bands that composed them had been wound too tightly together. Worse, the oil that lubricated the system had not been properly filtered, and the result was an engineer's nightmare: a grimy scale of dirt, rust, and even iron filings had completely incapacitated the coils. "It was," Groves recalled, "just pitiful."

Quietly furious, the general kept repeating the word "unforgivable." He blamed the engineers who had designed the magnets so badly, the Allis-Chalmers technicians who had failed to incorporate proper oil filters into the design, and Ernest Lawrence for not telling him that a Berkeley Calutron had once been crippled by the same problem. He also blamed himself for not personally inspecting the equipment before it was installed.

In the end Groves ordered the magnets sent back to Allis-Chalmers for cleaning and rewinding. A special pickling plant was set up to ensure that every piece of pipe in the oil system was thoroughly cleaned before installation. As a coup de grace, Groves fired Stone and Webster's managing engineer at Oak Ridge.

Still, it was more than a month before the magnets in the first Alpha building were reassembled and tested. In the furious race with the Germans, in which the fate of civilization itself seemed to hang on a single day, the delay seemed a near-tragedy. The electromagnetic method, so proudly hailed by Lawrence and so hopefully held up by Groves as the shortest route to the bomb, had not only lost its decisive edge; there were now doubts as to whether it would work at all.

Nine miles away, in a nearly flat valley formed by the confluence of Poplar Creek and the Clinch River, the homestead of Tennessee pioneer William Gallaher was being relentlessly replaced by the world's largest single factory building. Known as K-25, the two-million-square-foot edifice—which was actually up to fifty-four four-story buildings under a single roof—was intended to house the production facility for the gaseous diffusion method, the approach that of the three seemed the most straightforward in principle but that was the most demanding to execute. In fact, the requirements for gaseous diffusion's technology were so rigorous and impossibly exact that some of the project's more somber scientists considered it the method most likely to fail.

Its most damnably difficult problem lay at the very heart of the gaseous diffusion system: the production of an adequate material for the barrier. The scientists were searching for a substance with a combination of properties never seen on earth—a microporous metal with holes absolutely uniform in size but so minuscule as to allow no more than a few molecules of gas to pass at a time. The material had to be malleable enough to be cast into huge sheets and flexible enough to allow those sheets to be rolled into a tubular shape; and the metal had to be able to resist the onslaughts of uranium hexafluoride, one of the most corrosive of all gases.

By the fall of 1943, scientific personnel in at least three laboratories were sweating and swearing their way through tedious trial-and-error experiments, trying desperately to develop a metal alloy that would fit this unlikely prescription. At Bell Laboratories, sharp-tongued, ultraconservative Alabaman Foster Nix was testing a material made of a compressed nickel powder. At Kellex, Clarence Johnson—a quiet Canadian who had financed his college education by working as a fur trapper—was doing an administrator's job by day, then clearing his desk to experiment at night on a promising but untried nickel derivative. At Columbia's Schermerhorn Laboratory, fiery young chemist Edward Adler was working with Englishman Edward Norris, who may have had the most incongruous job training of anyone in the project. Norris was an interior decorator who, while in the process of reinventing the spray gun, had developed an ultrafine metal mesh that coincidentally had many of the characteristics of the barrier now being sought so frantically. Norris and Adler were further refining the antique of possible barrier materials, the nickel alloy that had been the first product to show signs of suitability.

Each of the three possible barriers had its problems. The Norris-Adler barrier, although it did an acceptable job of separating isotopes, seemed too brittle and fragile to survive the rigors of mass production. Nix's compressed nickel powder seemed to have better production characteristics, but its ability to separate isotopes was marginal at best. Johnson's nickel-derivative barrier, a relatively new entry that attempted to combine the best features of the other two, lagged far behind the others in development.

Compounding these purely scientific difficulties was the difficult and puzzling attitude of Harold Urey. Nominally the head of all research and development for the gaseous diffusion process, the Nobel Prize winner seemed curiously determined to lead his program into self-destruction. Through the summer of 1943, as the barrier problem stubbornly resisted solution, Urey grew increasingly convinced that gaseous diffusion would never work. As his pessimism grew, so, it seemed, did the emotionality that Groves had noticed earlier. Always energetic and high-strung, Urey now appeared to be headed for a nervous breakdown. During meetings, his hands trembled so violently that he could barely hold a glass of water. His relationship with the more practical Dunning, never sound to begin with, disintegrated still further until they were, according to Groves, "fighting like cats and dogs."

By August, Urey was convinced that the only hope for gaseous diffusion lay in an all-out push to develop the Norris-Adler barrier. He devoted the following six weeks to a last-gasp effort to make the Norris-Adler barrier work. But tests continued to show that the metallic nickel barrier was erratic in performance and that during processing it had a disturbing tendency to develop pinholes and cracks. In the meantime, Percival Keith was becoming more and more certain that the Norris-Adler barrier could never be mass produced and was increasingly interested in the promising new material being developed by Clarence Johnson.

The first showdown between Urey and Keith came at an October 20 meeting in New York. Urey stubbornly insisted that the Norris-Adler barrier was gaseous diffusion's only hope; any change in emphasis, he feared, would destroy his laboratory's already precarious morale. Then Keith emerged to champion the Johnson material, which he thought should at least be pursued as a promising alternative.

Unable to reach an agreement, the two leaders brought their argument to Groves. The general, who had already researched the problem through the District's New York office, took a stance typical of his approach to the bomb effort as a whole: if two methods looked almost equally promising, pursue them both until one of them showed a clear superiority. So on November 5 he ordered that the Norris-Adler barrier be pushed to the hilt and that the District continue to actively pursue the Johnson material as a form of insurance.

What for Groves was a simple compromise, an almost mandatory hedging of his bets, was for Urey the last straw. At his wits' end, he wrote an angry and frustrated letter to Groves, saying that if the barrier search were expanded to include the Johnson material at this relatively late date, the gaseous diffusion method would never be ready for use during the war. That being the case, Urey said, it would be better simply to scrap the entire effort rather than spend hundreds of millions of dollars more on a method that now looked singularly futile.

Urey's distraught overreaction created a new set of problems for Groves. Here was the leader of one of the project's most important research programs telling him that further pursuit of the program would be a waste of time. If he overruled Urey, he would be challenging a Nobel Prize winner and one of the project's three or four most respected scientists. If he went so far as to replace him, he ran the risk of provoking the other project scientists into another rebellion. On the other hand, if he agreed with Urey and left him in charge, his pessimism might seriously impair the work of Dunning and Keith and in general destroy the already fragile morale of the Columbia laboratory. If Urey and Columbia went down, they would very likely take the gaseous diffusion method with them.

As usual, Groves did not hesitate. Unintimidated by titles and reputations, he tended to judge people by their performance, and Urey's performance was becoming dangerously erratic. Urey would simply have to get out of the way. Since he could not ship him to the South Pacific, Groves did the next best thing: he sent the scientist on a "fact-finding" mission to England, hoping that it would keep him away "a good long time." When the overwrought Urey came back only a week later, the general packed him off on a fishing trip to his native Montana. Nothing if not persistent, Urey returned to New York the next day.

Groves saw that the scientist was leaving him no way out. Urey would simply have to be replaced. Adroitly careful not to remove his title and thereby foment another scientist insurrection, he quietly brought in Laughlin Currie, a chemist from Union Carbide. A charming and tactful southerner, Currie took charge of matters at Columbia smoothly and diplomatically, remaining all the while exquisitely deferential to Urey, whom Groves had kicked upstairs to a nominally more exalted position. At the same time, Currie quietly gathered the reins of the gaseous diffusion program, skillfully coordinated the efforts at Columbia, and gradually restored the laboratory's morale.

Urey, however, was not fooled. Knowing that he had been neatly displaced from his seat at the center of the project leadership, he fussed and fumed for the duration of the war. Despite all his efforts to avoid it, Groves had made another high-profile enemy.

Although Groves's only partially successful resolution of the Urey crisis helped put the gaseous diffusion program back on track, at the end of 1943 the barrier problem remained unsolved. While Norris, Adler, Johnson, Nix, and dozens of other scientists worked double shifts in their laboratories, the behemoth K-25 building at Oak Ridge lay empty, a half-finished, yawning shell waiting to be filled by hundreds of square miles of material that did not yet exist.

To the scientists at Los Alamos, who were charged with building a bomb from fissionable material that no one seemed able to produce, the news from Oak Ridge and Hanford would have been upsetting indeed had they known it. But because Groves had compartmentalized the project, there was very little transmission of news from one facility to another. In the intial stages, at least, this policy must have saved the Los Alamos staff a load of discouragement. For during the stumbling start-up phases in 1943, Los Alamos was beset by serious problems of its own.

Chapter Twenty-Two

The party was a typical Oppenheimer affair. His ample home, which overlooked San Francisco Bay from the heights of Berkeley's Eagle Hill, was gaily lit and crowded with the smorgasbord of scientists, writers, and doting students who constituted the physicist's eclectic band of friends. The martinis, made very dry and with a ceremonial Oppenheimer flourish, were flowing, and the rooms were loud with cheerful talk of wartime adventure.

But two of the guests were not in a festive mood. John Manley, Oppenheimer's experimentalist partner in fast neutron research, and Robert Wilson, recently recruited from Princeton, had just come from Los Alamos. They were, in Wilson's words, "scared to death." The new lab was in its first stages of organization, but instead of an orderly setup process, with schedules in place and responsibilities assigned, Wilson and Manley had found frantic and leaderless chaos. Since almost no housing was ready, the scientists had had to stay in dude ranches in the Santa Fe area and drive forty miles over rugged mountain roads just to get to the site each day. There was no food available, and the only communication with the outside world was over a U.S. Forest Service telephone line whose crackling static obscured all conversation. Laboratories were unfinished and equipment unassembled. Worst of all, no one seemed to be in charge.

Now, at the Berkeley party, Manley and Wilson unburdened themselves to the lab's new director. "We got into a terrible argument," Wilson later recalled. "We just went after Oppie unrelentingly with all these practical problems that we were trying to make him understand. . . . After a certain stage, Oppenheimer became extremely angry. He began to use vile language, asking why we were telling him of these insignificant problems, that it was none of our business. . . ."

Oppenheimer's explosion left Manley and Wilson deeply disturbed. "We were frightened," Wilson said, "because if this was the leader, and the leader was going to have a tantrum to resolve a problem, then how was anything going to be sorted? So we withdrew, John and I, and we discussed some more, and we decided that we would take more initiative and not look for so much leadership from Oppie."

Manley and Wilson were not the only ones with reservations about Oppenheimer's ability to lead. Rabi, who had stepped in to undertake much of the bomb lab's early planning, had already suggested bolstering Oppenheimer with a nine-man Governing Board. Hans Bethe discreetly offered his wife Rose to do the initial planning for the housing of the scientists, an offer that Oppenheimer gratefully accepted. Manley, who had helped make the first sketches of the bomb's physical plant, in the wake of the Eagle Hill battle returned to that task with new dedication and increased precision.

From their first meeting, Groves, too, had been concerned about Oppenheimer's lack of administrative experience. In organizing Los Alamos the general had carefully kept ultimate authority for the lab for himself, bypassing the rest of the MED organization and making Oppenheimer directly responsible to him alone. In the spring of 1943, as the laboratory creaked and groaned to a start, the general moved to surround Oppenheimer—who was still clinging to his vague, semipoetic vision of a high-altitude scientific Shangri-La—with a matrix of hard-nosed, get-things-done administrators. To handle the actual operation of the laboratory, Groves brought in Edward Condon, a respected physicist who had headed an important research division at Westinghouse. To direct the ongoing recruiting effort, an effort that grew with each new and unexpected increase in the bomb lab's workload, Groves himself recruited Samuel Arnold, the Dean of Men at Brown University. Concerned about Oppenheimer's choice of twenty-six-year-old Joseph Kennedy to lead the crucial Metallurgy Division, Groves enlisted Charles Thomas, who had vast industrial experience as a chemist for Monsanto and who would, he thought, lend weight and support to Oppenheimer's youngsters.

Perhaps the most important of Groves's early moves to bolster Oppenheimer was the enlistment of William Parsons. A crisp, starch Navy captain with a receding hairline and a no-nonsense air, "Deke" Parsons came recommended by General Styer as the best man in the military for supervising weapons design. Groves, who had met Parsons while working on antiaircraft development in the 1930s, agreed so enthusiastically that he appointed him the lab's associate director, overruling Oppenheimer, who had preferred the Met Lab's Samuel Allison. In conferring the assignment on Parsons, Groves made it clear that the captain would operate as Oppenheimer's virtual coequal. The two men were given Los

Alamos's only full-fledged houses, complete with its only full-fledged bathtubs; and they were the only lab personnel guarded around the clock by MPs. "Parsons," acknowledged one scientist, "ran his own show."

Groves had felt from the beginning that Parsons would fit in well with the scientists, and events seemed to prove him right. As a Navy man, Parsons seemed somehow exempt from the scientists' animosity toward all things military, despite his private evaluation of the technical group as "a bunch of crabs." His cool, almost mechanical approach to problems and his eagerness to learn—"He read physics texts at night," recalled one scientist, "the way someone else would read detective stories"—won him the respect of the physicists, while his wife's gracious charm soon endeared them both to the doyens of Los Alamos's elitist social circles. Groves took full advantage of Parsons's "insider" position—a position that the general himself never enjoyed—monitoring the activities of the scientists through the captain's lengthy reports and frequent phone calls.

Parsons's Ordnance Division was charged with the most critical task of all from the military point of view: how to turn the scientists' theories and the industrialists' fissionable material into a real and functioning weapon. Specifically, Parsons's group was to design the bomb's firing mechanism. If the weapon were to explode, two pieces of plutonium or U-235 would have to be fired together to initiate the chain reaction that would end in an explosion. In 1943, Parsons assumed, like most of the project leaders, that the two pieces could be merged simply by firing one half at the other, rifle-style. Because this "gun bomb" was based on conventional and established technology, the path to success seemed relatively straightforward.

But a radical new idea for detonation was stirring interest in high project circles in Washington. Originally discussed by James Conant and Cal Tech physicist Richard Tolman, who had been appointed Groves's personal scientific advisers, the idea involved using high explosives to violently compress a spherical shell of material into an explosive critical mass. ("I think," wrote Tolman in one of the project's outstanding underestimations, "that this would be an easy thing to do.") To the consistently practical Groves, the idea was especially intriguing because it required less fissionable material than the relatively wasteful gun design. In the end, Groves thought, this would make for a quicker and cheaper bomb.

The new idea, known as "implosion," was presented by Bureau of Standards physicist Seth Neddermeyer during a series of April organizing conferences at Los Alamos. But Neddermeyer's intense eyes and incipient beard gave him the look of a dangerous desert prophet; and he was further handicapped by his muddy, mumbling style and his outsider status in a laboratory that even in its early stages was dominated by a Berkeley-Cornell axis. Few of the physicists paid him any attention, and Oppenheimer gave him only eight men to begin the pursuit of implosion, despite the fact that he was under mandate from Groves to explore as many detonation processes as possible. Not until late October 1943 did Oppenheimer move, again under Groves's prodding, to give the method "high priority," and even then neither Neddermeyer nor Oppenheimer seemed willing to push implosion to the limit.

In the meantime, Oppenheimer was having problems of his own. In the midst of a summer water shortage that had left only a foot and a half in the lab's tanks ("If there had been a fire," Bacher said, "we would have been in big trouble"), in the midst of a chaotic deluge of incoming equipment, manpower, and construction materials, Oppenheimer found himself sinking under the weight of administrative detail. Edward Condon, who had argued heatedly with Groves over security regulations, left. The overwhelmed Oppenheimer now suffered a complete loss of confidence, despairing openly to Bacher. "He told me," Bacher said, "that he just couldn't do the job. I told him he was the only one who *could* do it."

Oppenheimer's despair was exacerbated by the fragility of his status with the security people. After his appointment to direct the lab, the FBI had loudly insisted that Groves examine their lengthy and elaborate file on him. Groves read every page but remained unswayed in his conviction about Oppenheimer's loyalty. On July 20 he wrote to Nichols, "It is desired that clearance be issued for the employment of J. Robert Oppenheimer without delay, irrespective of the information which you have regarding Mr. Oppenheimer. He is absolutely essential to the project."

But Groves's confidence was not shared by his own security officers. In the Berkeley office Boris Pash, an energetic, exuberant White Russian refugee who spoke several languages and roundly hated all things Communist, was convinced that Oppenheimer was passing secrets to the Soviets. He now pursued the physicist with a determination that bordered on mania. In June, Pash's suspicions seemed to be borne out, for Oppenheimer surreptitiously took time off from a recruiting trip to Berkeley to visit his former lover Jean Tatlock, who was still thought to be active in Bay Area Communist Party affairs. Then in August, Oppenheimer paid a surprise visit to the MED security office in Berkeley, where he casually let drop a tantalizing spy story. It seemed, Oppenheimer said, that a known San Francisco Soviet operative named

George Eltenton had been seeking information on the project through an unidentified Berkeley intermediary. Although he apparently knew who the intermediary was and although he was questioned intermittently for months by Pash, by security officer Lyle Johnson, and then by MED security chief John Lansdale, Oppenheimer steadfastly refused to give the man's name and thereby implicate him in a spy scandal that, for some reason, Oppenheimer himself was concocting. "I think it would be a mistake," he told the frustrated Pash. "To go any further would be to involve people who ought not to be involved in this."

Finally, under increasing pressure from Pash, Lansdale, and Los Alamos security officer Peer de Silva, Groves stepped in to resolve the matter himself. During a December visit to Los Alamos, he asked Oppenheimer point-blank to reveal the identity of Eltenton's mysterious and long-sought "intermediary."

"General," Oppenheimer said, reverting at once to his quasi-military posture, "if you order me to tell you this, I will tell you."

"In that case," Groves replied, "it's an order."

Reluctantly Oppenheimer revealed the name: a Berkeley English professor named Haakon Chevalier, who, it turned out, was one of Oppenheimer's closest friends. The physicist's revelation ultimately ruined Chevalier's career—he was fired from his University of California teaching post and virtually forced into exile in Paris—but it quite possibly saved his own. Newly armed with Chevalier's name, Groves had the leverage he needed to restrain Pash, de Silva, and Lansdale.

Still, the three remained unconvinced of Oppenheimer's desirability as director of the exquisitely sensitive bomb lab. "If General Groves had not considered him so vital to the project," Lansdale concluded, "he simply would not have been employed."

Actually, Oppenheimer was only part of a much broader security problem at Los Alamos, a problem that would once again bring the military and scientific communities to the point of open conflict.

In making the compromises necessary to recruit physicists, Groves had struck an interesting bargain with Oppenheimer. In exchange for airtight external security, to be established and enforced by the Army, the Los Alamos scientists would be free to develop their own means for assuring security inside the lab. Groves himself suggested that each scientist find two others who would guarantee his loyalty, thus establishing a sort of round robin of mutual assurances.

The scientists accepted Groves's suggestion, and the round-robin system worked almost perfectly. For its part, the lab leadership labored mightily to keep up its end of the security bargain. Oppenheimer continually reminded Edward Teller and other members of the foreign contingent not to speak German in the presence of people they did not know, and Robert Bacher complained loudly to the Governing Board about revealing conversations, secret information left unattended on black-boards, and vital documents left carelessly scattered about on office desktops. The Board even suggested that it would be "inadvisable" for scientists to discuss secret material with their wives.

But with these attempts at self-policing, the scientists' agreement with the military on security policy seemed to come to an end. From the beginning Groves had insisted on compartmentalization, meaning that most of the scientists would be privy only to enough vital information to allow them to do their own jobs, while the "big picture"—including, in some cases, the bomb itself—would be revealed only to the administrative elite. This meant in theory that a scientist working on calculating the bomb's projected explosive force might have to fill out an application to get the results of the experiments that even in 1943 were already rattling the walls of Little Pajarito Canyon. It also meant, as far as Groves was concerned, as little communication as possible between scientists at Los Alamos and those at other labs, particularly Chicago.

To the scientists, accustomed to the intellectual freeflow of academia, the compartmentalization policy was anathema. At an early Governing Board meeting, Bethe suggested the establishment of a Colloquium—a sort of free-form seminar open to all lab scientists in which problem areas could be discussed openly and new ideas generated and cross-fertilized. To Groves the Colloquium violated the spirit of compartmentalization. But by the time he could object, the seminar was already established, and its freewheeling debates—usually capped by a dead-on summary from Oppenheimer himself—became one of the cornerstones of Los Alamos scientific society. "To abandon the idea," Groves wrote later, "would have been a breach of faith, and would have shown that Oppenheimer was a mere puppet in my hands." To preserve the illusion of scientific indepen-dence from the military, Groves allowed the Colloquium to continue. To compensate for this loosening of the internal reins, Groves moved to isolate Los Alamos even further from the rest of the world. The post was fenced in in its entirety, and the fence itself was heavily guarded by an around-the-clock mounted patrol.

Although the fence kept the Los Alamos scientists in, it did not keep them happy. In the fall of 1943 another security problem arose, one that threatened to erupt into open warfare between the physicists and the Army. In September two scientists came to Oppenheimer and angrily protested that their mail had been opened. Oppenheimer went first to post commander Whitney Ashbridge, who unequivocally denied that the letters had been opened locally. When Oppenheimer took the matter to Groves, the general immediately investigated. His investigation eventually exonerated Ashbridge and the Los Alamos security office.

But the two angry scientists had inadvertently given Groves what appeared to be a good idea. "Open censorship," he wrote to Oppenheimer, "would be desirable from a security standpoint, and it would dispel any apprehension over what anyone might believe to be a clandestine and unwarranted invasion of their privacy." The younger scientists on the post, particularly Joseph Kennedy, objected strenuously, and for a few uncomfortable weeks it seemed there would be open rebellion. But ultimately the calmer heads on the Governing Board prevailed, and censorship was instituted over the objections of the younger scientists. It remained a sore point, though, and it became even sorer when high-spirited Richard Feynman, then an irreverent twenty-two, had his wife send him an envelope full of Pepto-Bismol. When opened, it followed the law of gravity and spilled all over the Army censor's lap. After this and a series of similar stunts, the battle lines between the Army and the younger scientists grew ever clearer, with Groves, Oppenheimer, and the Governing Board struggling to maintain an armed truce.

For Groves, for the Manhattan District in general, 1943 had not been an auspicious year. The gaseous diffusion method still lacked a suitable barrier, and the construction of the plutonium factory at Hanford was seriously delayed. At Oak Ridge, Lawrence's huge Calutrons, the single best hope for producing fissionable material before the war's end, lay broken, silent, and so far useless. The Los Alamos scientists were still struggling with weighty technical problems (critical mass had not yet been established, and the implosion program was struggling), with manpower shortages, and with crises in leadership. Security restrictions had already alienated important factions at Los Alamos, and Wigner's group at Chicago had come close to perpetrating an outright antimilitary revolution.

Still, Groves did not lose confidence. The Johnson nickel-powder barrier was showing promise, and DuPont's engineers were finally beginning to catch up with Matthias's builders. The delay at Oak Ridge caused by the faulty magnets was drawing to an end. The Los Alamos physicists had at least been able to establish the bomb's ultimate feasibility, and by the end of the year Oppenheimer seemed to have solved his security problems and was grasping the reins of leadership with less hesitation.

Through a series of adroit compromises and power shifts, Groves had subdued opposing factions at Los Alamos and Chicago into a sort of restless calm. All things considered, Groves's private estimate of the project's chances for success had risen from an initial 60 percent to well over 95.

But time was the critical factor. The scientists continued to assume that the Germans had a formidable lead and that the Manhattan District, despite its political commitment and military muscle, was still playing a catch-up game. In fact, this assumption so imbued the scientists' thinking that when rumors of an advanced German test swept through the physics community in early 1944, the Chicago contingent began making plans to evacuate the city—perhaps the first atomic bomb scare in history.

But Groves was not interested in assumptions, rumors, or bomb scares. Where the Germans were concerned, he wanted facts.

Chapter Twenty-Three

The waiting room of Santa Fe's Union Station was nearly empty. In different areas of the room, several men paced about, their obvious nervousness belying their equally obvious attempts to look inconspicuous. But physicist Luis Alvarez knew all the men, and he knew that each knew all the others. All were scientists, and all were part of Oppenheimer's group at Los Alamos except Alvarez himself, who was then at the Met Lab in Chicago. All had elaborate instructions not to talk to anyone, especially not to one another. All were waiting for General Leslie R. Groves.

Alvarez himself had never met Groves, but he knew that the general liked to use train stations as impromptu meeting rooms, often scheduling as many as half a dozen quick conferences during the time it took him to change trains.

Now the Superchief pulled in from Los Angeles, and General Groves, who always had compartment 101 reserved for him, stepped down. Wasting no time, he walked quickly into the waiting room and over to the bench where Alvarez was sitting. Groves paid the other scientists no attention but addressed himself to Alvarez in a soft, calm voice.

"Doctor," he said, "I need to find out how far along the Germans are. I need to find out if they're really building a reactor. Any ideas?"

Alvarez thought for a moment. "Well," he said, "we could sample their air for radioactivity. If there's a working reactor in Germany, it should be emitting radioactive krypton when the uranium slugs are dissolved. Now, there are some people at General Electric in Cleveland who've developed a system for filtering and trapping rare gases like krypton. So if we can fit their system into an airplane—"

"Fine," interrupted Groves. "That's going to be your job. When you have it ready, let me know."

Before Alvarez could speak the general had stood up and, without so much as a "good-bye" or a "nice to meet you," gone on to the next scientist.

But his brief meeting with Alvarez had important implications. For the first time, the Manhattan District was actively assessing the enemy's progress. Originally a purely scientific program for physicists, chemists, and engineers, the District was now about to become a training ground for high-tech spies.

From the very beginning the bomb project had been seen as a life-and-death race with the Germans; in fact, the Manhattan District raison d'être had been to deter a German atomic bomb by developing an American bomb first. Ever since communication with Germany ceased in the wake of the invasion of Poland in 1939, disquieting rumors of German dedication and progress had crossed the Atlantic.

In the fall of 1939 Dutch physicist Peter Debye, accused of being insufficiently enthusiastic about National Socialism, had been fired from his post as director of Berlin's Kaiser Wilhelm Institute. Debye had fled to the United States, bringing with him upsetting news of a top-secret nuclear physics program at the Institute, a program that in his absence would be directed by the great Werner Heisenberg, one of the giants of modern theoretical physics. Then in 1941 Heisenberg had visited Copenhagen, where he had had a long and curious conversation with Danish Nobel Laureate Niels Bohr. Heinsenberg's coy circumlocutions in response to Bohr's questions about the state of German bomb physics had left Bohr deeply worried, and on a subsequent trip to the United States he had communicated his concern to his friends in the American physics community. Then, late in 1943 *The New York Times* had loudly quoted an ominous broadcast from Radio Berlin: "It is not far from the point," the broadcast thundered, "when mankind can and will blow up half the globe."

But harder evidence of German interest in an atomic bomb came from Norway. There, on a crystal lake near the town of Rjukan, the Norwegian company Norsk Hydro operated what at the time was the world's largest facility for the production of heavy water. Heavy water, originally discovered by Harold Urey, was thought to be of use in separating uranium isotopes and in moderating the reaction in a self-sustaining pile. After the Nazi takeover of Norway, the Norsk Hydro plant began shipping as many as 120 kilograms of heavy water a month directly to the Kaiser Wilhelm Institute in Berlin. A daring winter raid on the Norsk Hydro plant by British ski troops had temporarily disrupted regular shipments, but the implications seemed clear: the Germans must indeed be working feverishly on an atomic bomb of their own.

Alarmed by the mounting evidence, Hans Bethe and Edward Teller wrote to Oppenheimer. "It is possible," they said, "that the Germans will have by the end of the year enough material accumulated to make a large number of atomic bombs, which they will then release at the same time on England, Russia, and this country. . . . There would be little hope," they concluded, "for any counter-action."

In the face of this dire prediction, it became obvious to Groves that an intense effort was needed to gather intelligence on the secret German project. But the Army G-2 branch, which was then handling all foreign intelligence activities, did not have the necessary scientific expertise to make such an effort. In fact, as John Lansdale noted later, "there was a total lack of awareness [on the part of G-2] of the need for 'scientific intelligence.'" When Groves made this point to General George C. Marshall in the fall of 1943, the Chief of Staff said, "Is there any reason why you can't handle this yourself?" So in addition to his manifold other duties, Groves was now summarily put in charge of U.S. intelligence on atomic physics. The assignment, he said, "hit me like a bolt from the blue."

Despite his lack of experience in intelligence work, Groves moved into the intelligence arena with his customary speed and confidence. His Santa Fe meeting with Luis Alvarez was one of the first steps the Manhattan District took to actively spy behind German lines. To complement Alvarez's search for traces of radioactivity in the skies over Germany, Groves asked Franklin Matthias to develop a description of a hypothetical German isotope-separation facility. In December 1943 he sent young Princetonian Robert Furman to London to coordinate with the British in searching German territory for such a plant: "an enormous factory," as Matthias described it, "with heavy rail activity, where lots of material went in and almost nothing came out."

But to Groves and to a few of the top scientists, it was not enough merely to search for a German reactor. They soon began to consider a counterattack, and even entertained notions of infiltration, assassination, and mass murder. In late 1943, it was suggested to Groves that one way to disrupt German progress would be to simply assassinate the leading German physicists. Groves took this suggestion seriously enough to have General Styer propose it to General Marshall. Later, Styer transmitted Marshall's reply: "Tell Groves," the Chief of Staff said, "to take care of his own dirty work."

At the same time, a small group of top Manhattan District scientists were considering an even more drastic and sweeping scheme. Robert Oppenheimer, Edward Teller, and Enrico Fermi were fascinated by the notion of wiping out huge segments of the German population by poisoning their food supply with radioactive strontium. In May, Oppenheimer proposed the idea to both Groves and Conant, who were apparently interested enough to suggest further discussion and planning among the scientific elite. If the poisoning project were brought to successful fruition, the number of German casualties would far surpass anything expected from an atomic weapon: "We should not attempt a plan," Oppenheimer wrote, "unless we can poison food sufficient to kill half a million men."

There is no evidence that either of these schemes ever went beyond the stage of initial discussions. But in early 1944 U.S. reconnaissance planes were flying low over Germany, on missions so dangerous that many pilots recommended scrapping them altogether, to search the air for traces of radioactive krypton and the ground for signs of huge and mysterious factories that consumed trainloads of material but produced nothing. But despite months of dogged and dangerous surveillance, nothing turned up.

Where, Groves was beginning to wonder, was the vaunted German bomb?

If Groves was vitally interested in the potential nuclear threat posed by America's enemies, he was no less interested in the danger posed by her friends. The Russian physicist Pyotr Kapitza—a free spirit who had once had himself photographed lying under the wheels of a car "to see what I would look like if I were being run over"—had been studying and working in England since 1921. In 1934 he was invited back to his homeland, ostensibly to be honored for his election to the Soviet Academy of Science. After he arrived in Moscow, Stalin's police refused to let him leave the country. His many friends in the Western scientific community believed he had been commandeered to head the Russian program in nuclear physics.

Groves was worried about Kapitza's celebrated talent and energy; at Cambridge he had been the favored protégé of the renowned Ernest Rutherford. The general assigned Captain T.O. Jones of the Counterintelligence Corps to keep his eyes open for hints of a Soviet nuclear bomb project. By late 1943, Jones had dug up a number of unnerving clues. The Central Institute of Roentgenology, Radium, and Oncology in Kharkov was conducting an energetic series of experiments on X-rays and radiation. The summer session of the Soviet Academy of Science had reported the results of a full year's work with a huge new cyclotron in Leningrad. The Academy also hailed the work of two young physicists, K. Peterzhak and G. Florov, who were said to be on the verge of using neutrons to split the uranium atom.

But perhaps the most disturbing item came from Kapitza himself. Apparently fully reintegrated as a Soviet patriot, the physicist had issued a cryptic declaration that in effect drew an iron curtain over the state of Soviet nuclear physics: "The conditions of wartime secrecy," he said, "prevent us from dealing more concretely with the scientific work being carried on in our country."

There was dangerous atomic competition on both sides of the wartime fence. In the case of Germany, the competition came from an out-and-out, undisguised enemy; in the case of the Soviet Union, it came from an enemy dressed for the war dance in the gown of an ally. But in both cases the threat, dire as it seemed to be, could only be met in the simplest and most straightforward way: by winning in America the great race for the bomb.

If that race was to be won, Groves knew, the victory would begin in his own office.

Chapter Twenty-Four

Every morning by 7:00 A.M., General Leslie Groves climbed into his green Dodge sedan, pulled out of his garage, turned left down Washington's Thirty-Sixth Street Northwest, and headed for work. This middle-class street was modest; Groves's own house at number 3508 was a decidedly unspectacular two-story yellow brick. A few doors down, he stopped to pick up his secretary, a slight, fast-talking blonde named Anne Wilson who had known the general most of her life and was a close friend of the family. As they drove through the morning traffic, they lapsed into a comfortable prework routine: Anne read the newspaper aloud and always in the same order; for only after a tour of the sports pages and a thorough reading of Mary Haworth's mail ("Advice to the lovelorn," Anne later recalled; "The general was always very curious, in an innocent sort of way, about other peoples' love lives") would he allow her to go on to the more serious business on page one. If it were a Monday, Groves might in return fill her ear with an account of the previous day's tennis; he was known to play as many as seven sets on a single Sunday afternoon. On other days it would be a report on his latest diet — "He was running the project," Anne remembered, "on 1,000 calories a day."

Once they arrived in Foggy Bottom, however, and passed through the guarded doors of the new War Department Building, they were immediately enveloped in the building's atmosphere, a combination of wartime bustle and spy-novel mystery. A young officer who asked the whereabouts of the offices of the Manhattan Engineer District would get in response only a blank stare from the building's guards or perhaps, if he were lucky, a "wait a minute, why don't you try the fifth floor? There's an office up there that's busy as hell, but that no one knows anything about."

The office, in Rooms 5120 and 5121, was indeed that of the MED. It was a simple, unimpressive place on the inside; its six small rooms were furnished with government-issue green carpet, gray steel files, and utilitarian oak desks. The only concessions to luxury were a large, oak-paneled conference room and one leather sofa, and even these had been accepted by the District's boss—who confessed to a personal horror of large and fancy organizations—as an inevitable result of necessary expansion. In fact, for the first year of its existence Groves had run the megalithic MED, which would come to employ over a quarter of a million people, from only two small rooms.

It was no accident that Rooms 5120 and 5121 were the mysteries of the War Department Building. Keeping the bomb project secret was considered so important—not only by Groves but by President Roosevelt himself—that the doors were locked and dead-bolted, and the ventilating ducts were acoustically sealed. Had the Germans or Soviets been able to place a spy in a cleaning woman's job, that spy would have come up empty-handed, for the general ordered all papers—even desk calendars—to be locked up every night in one of the office's three-combination safes. Written communications were either put entirely into a complex and mystifying numerical code or obscured by coded references to important aspects of the project. (Thus uranium was "23," plutonium "39," the bomb "the gadget," and Hanford, Oak Ridge, and Los Alamos "W," "X," and "Y.") Only Groves was allowed to keep a diary, and it was so elliptical as to thoroughly frustrate an entire generation of historians. Telephone conversations were purposely garbled; Groves identified project VIPs only as "Mr. You-Know-Who," even in front of his own daughter.

Of the several dozen people who eventually worked in Rooms 5120 and 5121, only Groves and his executive officer Jean O'Leary were allowed comprehensive knowledge of the entire program. (O'Leary, a pretty widow, survived her boss's revolving-door policy on secretaries by being just as fast with a verbal dart as he was.) Most of the staff, especially the secretaries and stenographers, officially had no knowledge that the object of their labors was the most spectacularly devastating of all weapons. Still, there was much whispered speculation in off-hours bars, and one enter-prising aide was able to deduce the nature of the project by going to the library encyclopedia and looking up the word *uranium*. Few of Groves's staffers went that far, though: wartime secrecy was in general a serious proposition, and for those inclined to take it lightly, a sign in the office reminded, in the guise of a Daily Prayer, "O Lord! Help me to keep my big mouth shut!" As if this were not enough, it was known—or at least rumored—that Groves had no compunction about sending overly talkative MED employees to long-term assignments in the South Pacific.

There were compensations, however, for the tight security and the long hours. During the workday a steady stream of fascinating visitors came through the office. There was Oppenheimer, with his intellectual sex appeal and dreamy charm, for whom everyone's work was "the most important thing in the whole project"; Groves's grandfatherly scientific adviser Richard Tolman, whose sweet personality could suddenly give way to a surprising torrent of profanity ("He must have been a stevedore at some time in his career," Groves commented); and delegates from the British mission, including the dashing Sir Charles Hambro, impeccably British with his brush moustache and Savile Row suits, and the dourly mysterious Sir James Chadwick, the discoverer of the neutron, who was fast becoming one of Groves's closest friends. There was the balloonlike General Styer, perhaps the only man in Washington who earned the right to call Groves "Fats"; and Edgar Sengier, the urbane Belgian financier who never made his way back to Groves's office without kissing the hand of every secretary in his path.

To help keep things in perspective, there were signs: THINKING SCIENTIFICALLY SHOULD NOT DIMINISH ONE'S ABILITY TO ACT INTELLIGENTLY was a personal favorite of the general's, but it stayed tactfully hidden in Jean O'Leary's desk. And there were even songs. One anonymous staffer composed and circulated one that might have been called "The Song of Security," to be sung (if at all) to the tune of "Genevieve, Sweet Genevieve":

> *Oh LRG, oh LRG*
> *We want you to know that we love thee*
> *We'll stay with you on secrecy*
> *Though all the rest may turn away*
> *Though all the world may toot your horn*
> *We'll deny you were ever born*
> *Oh secrecy, oh secrecy*
> *All our crimes we'll charge to thee.*

Primarily and predominantly, though, Rooms 5120 and 5121 were about hard work. Groves himself set the tone; after a sunrise breakfast in the War Department cafeteria, he was at his desk by 7:30. Any officer or office worker who arrived later than 8:15 ran the risk of a Groves scolding, which usually amounted to a cold, gray-eyed stare or, for chronic offenders, days of silent treatment.

A typical morning might find him meeting in his office with a parade of dignitaries both scientific and statesmanly; Tolman and the acerbic James Conant became virtual fixtures in the office, as did Chadwick and the British emissaries Hambro and Sir John Winant. Or he might be trekking to the Pentagon offices of Secretary of War Henry Stimson and his assistants, Harvey Bundy and George Harrison.

Lunch was a sandwich brought from home, generously supplemented by the rock candies he kept stored in a private safe. Afternoon brought another of the seemingly endless series of meetings and conferences, dictation, the reading of reports from others, and the painstaking, multidraft composition of his own reports. At 6:15 P.M. came the daily telephone call from Grace advising him of that evening's dinner menu. Usually the general chose to eat at the nearby Allies Inn cafeteria so that he could stay close to work, but if the featured entrée at home was minced clam chowder, a favorite dish that he mysteriously called "stew," he might jump into the Dodge and make the fifteen-minute drive home. On these occasions, the cry "It's stew!" would circulate like a hot wind through the office, signifying that Groves's staffers would have a rare full hour for dinner.

After dinner, the general and O'Leary would return to the office, where Groves spent the evening in a small telegraph room sending urgent secret cables to Oak Ridge, Hanford, and Los Alamos. Usually it was long after midnight before he made the weary drive back to Thirty-Sixth Street.

Throughout his long working day, Groves's most constant companion was the telephone. Because he tried to keep written communication to a strict minimum for security reasons, hundreds of calls a day might go through his phone lines. Groves sometimes talked as often as five times a day each to Oppenheimer at Los Alamos, to Nichols at Oak Ridge, and to Matthias at Hanford. In addition, there were calls to and from his staff officers at other key project locations: Major Arthur Peterson at the Met Lab; Major Harry Fidler at Berkeley; Lieutenant Colonel James Stowers in New York; and the varied (and harried) military commanders at Los Alamos. There were calls to Arthur Compton at Chicago, to Laughlin Currie at Columbia, to Ernest Lawrence and administrative officer Robert Underhill at Berkeley. There were calls to Percival Keith at Kellex in New York, to K. T. Keller at Chrysler Corporation in Detroit, to Oak Ridge architect Edwin L. Jones, and to dozens of contractors, subcontractors, and sub-subcontractors. There were Washington calls to Stimson, to Bundy and Harrison, to Undersecretary of War Robert Patterson; to the Selective Service Board, the War Production Board, and the War Manpower Commission; to Vannevar Bush and James Conant, to Generals Styer and Somervell, and even on occasion to Senator Harry S Truman.

In fact, by 1944 Groves had spent so much time on the telephone that he was beginning to suffer from an unusual form of physical fallout: his elbows, which he used to brace himself on his desk while talking, were scraped so raw that they bled. Although the general himself hardly noticed, his concerned secretaries attacked the problem by placing cotton padding between his elbows and the desktop. Groves rubbed and scraped right through them. Not until someone in the office outfitted him with a telephone operator's headset did the bleeding finally stop.

Yet although the office was the center of the Manhattan District, Groves spent only about a third of his time there. The rest of the time he traveled to the project's outposts, making as many as six trips a month. This gave others the impression that the general was restless omnipresence, ready always to concentrate on spots where trouble came up. ("He could sense impending difficulty," Richard Tolman once said, "quicker than a bird dog can sniff out a covey of quail on a cold morning.")

Initially he traveled entirely by train, as if to set an example for the top scientists, whom he had restricted from flying for reasons of safety and security. Later in the war, however, as the job heated up and time became more than ever the all-important factor, he was given a DC-3 that had formerly been reserved for the use of the Secretary of War. (The plane bumped awkwardly around the country, stopping for fuel every few hundred miles. "As the hours go by on one of those planes," Groves told one officer, "the meaner I get—and I'm mean enough as it is.") But whether traveling by plane or by train, Groves always wore civilian clothes and kept a pistol under his coat to protect the top-secret documents that he invariably carried in a plain brown envelope. (The envelope never left his side. He held it in his hand on long airplane rides and kept it under his seat in Pullman cars. During nighttime train rides, he tied the door of his compartment shut so that he would hear any would-be intruders enter.)

Everywhere he went, project personnel noted his prodigious memory ("He never took a note," marveled I.I. Rabi—"he kept the whole of that enormous project in his head"); his unflappability ("Whenever things got tough," said one staffer, "he just stuck a piece of candy in his mouth and chewed away"); and his grasp of often-bewildering nuclear science ("The scientists were amazed," said Franklin Matthias, "that he could absorb all that technical theory, then express it in terms anyone could understand"). At Hanford, where Matthias always had a bowl of fresh local cherries ready to satisfy his boss's congenital sweet tooth, he once interrupted an inspection tour to personally rewrite a safety sign that he considered unclear. At Oak Ridge he would don the mandatory white coveralls and give the mammoth K-25 building a close-up inspection, touring its two million square feet of floor space by bicycle. At Los Alamos he nosed about the Tech Area, noting everything from potential fire hazards in the parking lot to the cleanliness of laboratory equipment.

He drove everyone incessantly, from Nobel Prize winners like Lawrence and Compton to the harried stenographers in his own office. To many of his subordinates he seemed ruthless and tyrannical, and the stiff bluntness of his approach won him few friends. ("It can't be helped," Groves shrugged. "Anyone who has been in any organization knows that the first privilege is to criticize the commander, and that criticism can get awfully sharp.") He set construction and production schedules that seemed impossible to the MED's enormous stable of contractors, then harassed and bullied the contracting companies' officials until they met the schedules out of sheer resentment.

He seemed to enjoy reminding people—brutally, if necessary—that he was the man in charge. He often kept Los Alamos's military commanders waiting for hours in the summer heat while he ran minor errands or chit-chatted aimlessly with Robert Bacher or one of the other scientists. On one New Year's Eve he kept everyone in Oppenheimer's office, including Oppenheimer himself, working until almost the stroke of midnight. ("He just likes to remind us," smiled Oppenheimer to his secretary, "that there's a war on.")

Yet at other times he could be light-handed, courteous, and even charming. Entering the home of one Los Alamos scientist, he asked the man's wife if he could take off his shoes, which were encrusted with mud from the unpaved sidewalks, and leave them outside so as not to track up the floor. "The request," according to one observer, "forever endeared him to that suffering housewife." When Oppenheimer's secretary Priscilla Green married Los Alamos physicist Robert Duffield, Groves went out of his way to congratulate the young couple. "He was as gracious and as charming as he could be," remembered Mrs. Duffield. "In fact, his charm came as such a surprise that it made me mad at him all over again."

When neither gruffness nor courtesy paid off ("Sometimes," remembered one Los Alamos scientist, "he tried *too* hard to be hail-fellow-well-met"), he knew when to back away. He knew, as Los Alamos physicist Harold Agnew put it, "when to lean on the scientists and when to leave them alone." At Los Alamos he dealt almost exclusively with Oppenheimer, using him as a sort of membrane to pressure the other scientists by psychological osmosis; and he used Nichols in much the same way to ride herd on the scientists at Chicago.

In retrospect, most people who knew Groves well agreed that he drove no one harder than himself. Ernest Lawrence, himself a nearly tireless worker, recalled one all-night plane ride with the general. "I finally had to stop working at about three A.M. and get some sleep," he told another physicist. "When I woke up the next morning he was still there, working away. I never knew anyone with such an incredible capacity for work." Indeed, during the entire course of the project Groves seemed hardly to sleep, apart from quick naps on his office couch ("He could drop down for ten minutes," said one secretary, "and come out totally refreshed, ready to go all night") and occasional catnaps in the back seat of an Army Buick, speeding over the twisting, bumpy roads from Los Alamos to Santa Fe at over eighty miles per hour.

Eventually the strain that Groves refused to show in his demeanor overtook the one thing he could never entirely control: his body. Throughout the war he struggled furiously with his weight, undertaking with his wife's tutelage a grim series of ever-more-restrictive diets. After one particularly long period of self-denial he managed to reduce to a wartime low of 217 pounds, but within a few months his appetite overtook him, and he was back to his more typical 250-plus.

The combination of the overweight and the unimaginable stress of running the bomb project eventually took its toll, exacerbated no doubt by Groves's absolute refusal to show any doubt about the project's ultimate success. On several visits to Oak Ridge he complained of severe pains in his chest and arms. On those occasions Oak Ridge hospital director Dr. Charles Rea, who became one of Groves's most trusted personal physicians, had him secretly confined overnight for observation. Although the pains generally subsided the following day, Dr. Rea was convinced that the general was afflicted with atherosclerosis and privately opined that he had suffered at least one heart attack. The episodes were not revealed to anyone outside Groves's family until long after the war was over, and they were never revealed publicly.

As long as the bomb was not yet made, Groves simply had no time for heart attacks.

Chapter Twenty-Five

It was late in the evening of January 16, 1944, and Groves was stranded in Cincinnati. His memorization of the schedules of every railroad that served Oak Ridge now did him little good; the afternoon train that he and chemist George Felbeck had taken from Knoxville arrived late in Cincinnati and missed its connection to Decatur, Illinois. There could be no waiting until morning for the next train; Percival Keith and a roomful of scientists and engineers were expecting him in Decatur to announce what for many of them would be the most important decision of the war.

For the last several months, Keith and the engineers at Decatur's Houdaille-Hershey Company had been operating in a state of high tension. Almost a year earlier, in April 1943, Houdaille-Hershey—a company normally dedicated to the metal plating of automobile bumpers—had gulped, taken a deep breath, and contracted with Groves to manufacture several hundred square miles of nickel barrier for the gaseous diffusion process. Harold Urey had given them a model of the barrier material, the strange nickel compound designed by the even stranger partnership of a chemist and an interior decorator. Assuming that the Norris-Adler barrier was what they were actually going to manufacture, Houdaille-Hershey had hurried, driven incessantly by Groves, to build and outfit a brand-new $5 million plant in nearby Garfield.

But even as the plant was being constructed, Houdaille-Hershey engineers were getting disturbing news from New York. Keith, the head of the barrier show, was wondering if the Norris-Adler barrier would work. Keith suspected that the material designed by Clarence Johnson was a better bet. Now, with the new Garfield plant almost ready to start producing the Norris-Adler barrier, the obstinate Texan was insisting that that material be scrapped in favor of Johnson's. This would mean completely gutting the millions of dollars' worth of machinery already installed at Garfield and replacing it with all-new equipment, a project that would cost months of the one commodity Groves could not buy: time.

Harold Urey, who continued to champion the Norris-Adler barrier from his upstairs room at Columbia, was beside himself. As far as he was concerned, the continued effort to develop the gaseous diffusion method was itself dangerous, a diversion of the project's resources that was both uncertain and unwise. But to scrap the already developed Norris-Adler barrier and replace it with the essentially unproven Johnson material seemed reckless to the point of madness. Acknowledging the dilemma, Groves had ridden both horses at once, saying that equal time, money, and attention should be invested in the Norris-Adler and Johnson barriers. In the spring of 1943 this had seemed a wise hedging of bets; but in the winter of 1944, with the Germans growing ever more desperate, it looked like dangerous fence-straddling.

Groves knew that there was no time now to construct a second factory to indulge Keith: he would simply have to choose between the two barrier materials. Either way, it would be a shot in the dark. There was still no guarantee from the laboratory that the Johnson barrier would work—only a few hopeful experiments and the instinctive faith of "Dobie" Keith. Even if the Johnson barrier could be made to work on the scale demanded by the K-25 plant, the sudden switch and the gutting of the Garfield factory would mean that the gaseous diffusion method might not produce bomb-grade U-235 until sometime in 1946. By then, the war might well be over.

But Groves had something up his sleeve. Recently he and the project's scientific leaders had wondered whether it was really necessary that the K-25 plant for gaseous diffusion produce uranium fully enriched to weapons grade. Could they, instead, use the gaseous diffusion method to put out a lower grade of U-235, then feed this only partially enriched fuel into Lawrence's Y-12 electromagnetic plant for further enrichment? If it worked, it would take a great deal of the strain off the K-25 plant, which would no longer have to meet purification standards that were impossibly high. If it worked, it would at least mean that K-25 would make a real contribution to the bomb effort, that the $150 million spent on it was not in vain. And if it worked, America might even have an atomic bomb in time.

All these factors must have been on Groves's mind as he detrained, hours late, at the Cincinnati station. He had no time to fume. Striding immediately to the phone, the general called the Cincinnati office of the Army Corps of Engineers and asked for a car and driver to take Felbeck and himself the two hundred miles to Decatur. At midnight the Army car arrived at the station. "Now," said Groves, getting in next to the driver, "I'm going to talk to you all night long, just to make sure you stay awake."

Nine hours later, his eyes bleary and his ears ringing with the general's nonstop commentary, the driver delivered the two men to their destination. Carrying a bag full of coffee and sweet rolls, Groves and Felbeck marched into a small office at the Houdaille-Hershey factory in Decatur. The two men were unshaven; they had not slept all night.

No one in the room seemed to care. Keith and four Houdaille-Hershey engineers leaned forward in their seats as Groves made the announcement they had all been waiting to hear. His decision was unequivocal: the Norris-Adler barrier would be scrapped. The machinery in the Garfield factory would be ripped out and replaced as soon as humanly possible with equipment that would manufacture the Johnson barrier.

Groves had taken a tremendous gamble. If the Johnson barrier failed, it could mean not only the death of the gaseous diffusion method but a greatly increased chance that the bomb would not be ready during the war. Yet the next day the general was back in Washington playing tennis as if nothing had happened. "How can you do that?" asked Groves's staffer Joseph Volpe, who knew about the barrier decision and its costly implications and who may well have entertained visions of Groves as a latter-day Nero, fiddling with a tennis racket while Washington burned around him.

"The time to worry about a decision is before you make it" was Groves's unbothered reply. "Once it's done, it's done. All you can do is forget about it and move on to the next thing."

In Groves's mind the "next thing" was the Y-12 electromagnetic plant at Oak Ridge. His decision to scrap the Norris-Adler barrier and lower purification standards for the gaseous diffusion process may have reduced the strain on the K-25 plant, but it also meant that Lawrence's monster magnets would have to carry an even greater burden. In essence, instead of doing only half the purification job, they would now be doing as much as 90 percent of the work. Making the Y-12 burden even weightier, Oppenheimer's men at Los Alamos had thoroughly revised their estimates of the bomb's critical mass and were now calling for almost three times as much finished U-235.

Yet the Y-12 racetracks, now more than ever the star of the uranium show, continued to be dishearteningly temperamental. During the first half of 1944, Lawrence pushed frantically to get all nine tracks into a semblance of operation. But trouble kept interfering: insulators cracked, vacuum seals broke, chemical tanks corroded, and ion beam sources mysteriously quit working. Any one of these tiny failures could, and did, shut down an entire track for days. (In one case a track remained out of service for almost a week while mystified operators scurried madly to find the source of the breakdown. When some shreds of fur and a tail were found in a vacuum line, the source became known: a mouse had somehow found its way into the sealed line and blocked it.) Worst of all, the huge magnets were actually driving up to 90 percent of the U-235 atoms so deep into the stainless-steel skins of the receiving tanks that it was almost impossible to recover them.

All these problems combined to make Y-12 an almost constant source of headache and disappointment. By early spring of 1944, the entire plant had produced only a few hundred grams of U-235, and that was enriched to a maximum of only 12 percent—far less than the 90-plus that Groves and the scientists had estimated would be necessary for a bomb. A partially enriched "starter" U-235 provided by K-25 could be expected to boost this figure, but K-25 was many months away from producing anything. Clearly, the electromagnetic method—and with it the entire U-235 production enterprise at Oak Ridge—was in deep trouble.

Some way, Groves thought, would have to be found to give Y-12 a quick boost, preferably a shot of partially enriched U-235. But by what miracle could he pull off such a trick? Fortunately, there was a production method under way that could possibly provide that miracle, or at least provide it more quickly than the stalled gaseous diffusion method. Ever since 1941, Phillip Abelson had been working independently at the Naval Research Laboratory, trying to use liquid thermal diffusion to squeeze U-235 from raw uranium.

Isolated from the MED but aware of its efforts, Abelson had kept his Berkeley friends apprised of his progress. In March 1944, young Joseph Kennedy suggested to Oppenheimer that Abelson's method might be just what was needed to provide Y-12 with partially enriched "starter" U-235. Oppenheimer passed the suggestion on to Groves, who was immediately interested.*

Actually, the liquid thermal diffusion method was a ball that Groves had prematurely dropped. The Naval Research Lab had been one of the first stops on his first tour just after taking over the MED in the fall of 1942. He had been much impressed by Abelson's quiet competence but less so by what he had seen as the arrogant unfriendliness of project director Ross

*Historians of the Manhattan District, including Groves himself, have invariably credited Oppenheimer with originating the idea. In fact, the suggestion was Kennedy's. See telegram, Oppenheimer to Conant, March 4, 1944, Oppenheimer Correspondence, Library of Congress.

Gunn. Technically, the method had looked frighteningly expensive, and Groves, who was then thinking in terms of producing fully enriched U-235, had considered the liquid thermal diffusion method incapable of that.

But, Groves thought, if liquid thermal diffusion now had to produce only partially enriched uranium, it was a good deal more attractive. Cooperating with Navy officials, he deliberately moved to begin building a liquid thermal diffusion plant at Oak Ridge. Calling in the H.K. Ferguson Company of Cleveland, he gave them a gruff mandate: there was no time to design anything new, he said; the company was to build an exact copy of the Navy pilot plant in Philadelphia. He assigned supervision of the project to Lieutenant Colonel Mark Fox and gave him a typical Groves schedule to meet: four months from groundbreaking to finished plant; production was to start an incredible seventy-five days after driving the first stake.

Fox and the Ferguson Company responded by making a heroic effort. In early July construction started at Oak Ridge on the "Fox Farm's" main "barn"—an enormous black monolith 525 feet long, 82 feet wide, and 75 feet high. By mid-September—only sixty-nine days after the construction start—the plant's first production columns went into operation. Hundreds of technicians scurried about amid clouds of vapor and the ear-shattering whistles of escaping steam. By the end of October the thrumming plant had produced 10.5 pounds of slightly enriched uranium, and by November, 171.8. With K-25 still several months away from its first production, the "Fox Farm" helped save the day.

Meanwhile, the bugs in the Y-12 process were slowly being worked out. Clarence Larson, a determined chemist from the College of the Pacific and an old friend of Lawrence's, devised a way to copper-plate the insides of the receiving tanks, borrowing generators and ripping copper sinks out of Oak Ridge's lavatories to do the job. With Larson's method, many of the atoms that had previously been lost in the stainless-steel skins of the tanks could be recovered by removing the copper plating and washing it in chemicals. At the same time, insulator failures and operator inexperience were also slowly being overcome. To boost morale and accelerate operating procedures, Groves brought in Lieutenant Colonel John Ruhoff, an experienced chemical engineer who had been working in the MED's New York office. The general himself mercilessly drove officials of Tennessee Eastman, the company in charge of the Y-12 operations, telling them that they should "work until they fell into their graves just as the war was over."

The combination of technical innovation, time, and pressure from Groves seemed to work. By the end of 1944 all nine Alpha tracks were in operation, as were the three updated tracks in the new Beta building, where the second series of electromagnetic racetracks was housed. By the end of the year, Kenneth Nichols could finally report to Groves that after a year of false starts, fuel production for the atomic bomb was increasing steadily.

It was the laborer's first day on his new Oak Ridge job, and he boarded the bus in an advanced state of confusion. "Please, sir," he begged the bus driver, bending down to show his identification badge, "look at my badge and tell me where I want to go."

The laborer's dilemma was symbolic of life in Oak Ridge's new frontier. By the beginning of 1944 the series of quiet, rolling hills had become a sprawling boom town; its population would ultimately reach some seventy-five thousand, making it the fifth largest city in Tennessee. It had something of the flavor of a Klondike outpost combined with a South Bronx housing project. Apple orchards and pine groves were rapidly converted into housing developments; Stone and Webster put up semipermanent prefab houses known as Cemestos at the startling rate of one every thirty minutes. Seventeen cafeterias served over forty thousand meals a day; some of the food was supplied by the community's own cattle and chicken ranches. The single grocery store struggled in vain to serve ten thousand customers. "I started stocking my shelves in 1943," the store's manager later lamented, "and didn't get them completely filled until 1946." (The beleaguered store eventually gave way to the world's first shopping center.) The transit system, whose eight hundred overstuffed buses carried sweating passengers over three hundred miles of roads, was the ninth largest in the United States. The population of the hastily built school topped eight thousand; the hospital boasted 337 beds. Houses of worship competed for or shared space with movie theaters, so that on Sundays the marquee of the Oak Ridge Cinema read, NOW SHOWING: METHODIST CHURCH.

Working conditions in this brave new world can best be described as bizarre. This was especially true for the twenty-two thousand who worked inside the Y-12 buildings. Anyone who worked with radioactive materials had to wear white coveralls, a cap, and a gas-masklike respirator and had to wash their hands on an hourly basis, then coat them with a protective oil. Those who worked near the gigantic ten-thousand-ton magnets constantly found hammers and screwdrivers plucked from their hands or their hairdos suddenly rearranged as the magnets indiscriminately stripped them of hairpins. Operators spent twelve-hour shifts turning a single knob or writing down the readings of a single dial without having the slightest idea of what the knob was controlling or what the dial was measuring. Still, the "ignorant" operators ultimately became better at their jobs than the scientists who trained them; for while the scientists couldn't resist the temptation to experiment with the controls, the operators stuck rigorously and efficiently to their assigned tasks.

Security was breathlessly tight, as it was everywhere in the vast project. The entire nine-thousand-acre complex was surrounded by an unscalable barbed-wire fence and patrolled by MPs on horseback. No one was allowed to talk about their job or the nature of the plant, leading to speculations that Oak Ridge was fabricating everything from poison gas to suitcases for Eleanor Roosevelt. Even the wives of the top scientists were kept in the dark: "All I knew about what went on at Oak Ridge," said Ernest Lawrence's wife Molly, "was that *uranium* was a dirty word." One scientist found a neat solution to his wife's curiosity. "You have your choice," he told his inquisitive mate. "I can tell you, but then you won't be able to breathe a word to anyone. Or I can not tell you, and that will leave you free to guess about it with your friends." The woman thought it over, then decided to stay blissfully ignorant — the right to know was apparently less important to her than the freedom to speculate.

To be sure, there were compensations for all the strangeness and the enforced silence. The pay was more than most of the workers had ever made, certainly more than anything available at local factories, and there was the added incentive of "helping out the boys" in Europe and the Pacific. And once the long workday was over, it was nearly impossible to be bored. There was the homegrown newspaper the Oak Ridge *Journal*, a bowling league with over a hundred teams, libraries, little theater groups, and clubs ranging from the Civic Music Group to the Rabbit Breeders' Association. At the weekly dances, determined young women arrived wearing mud-covered hip boots under their dresses, then removed the boots in favor of dancing shoes.

Still, despite the best efforts of the Roane-Anderson Company, which managed the town of Oak Ridge and which came to be known as "the best whipping boy the Army every had," many workers found themselves ill suited to boom-town living. One laborer, finally disgusted by the inconveniences, the secrecy, and the eternal red mud, quit his job in the end, and his parting statement undoubtedly reflected the opinion of many of his cohorts: "Whatever the government's building in there," he said, "they'd be better off to just go out and buy it."

Chapter Twenty-Six

For much of 1944, it seemed that all Groves and the government were buying at Hanford was trouble. Throughout the year the plutonium project was plagued by a series of crippling problems. Despite Groves's accommodation with Paul McNutt and the War Manpower Commission, labor remained in critically short supply; in fact, a February report from DuPont complained of shortages of 850 laborers, 350 carpenters, 200 rod-setters, 125 pipe-fitters, 31 welders, 133 electricians, and 60 millwrights—and these for only one of the facility's six major installations. The pipe-fitter shortage, a constant irritation throughout the construction phase, was solved when Groves shanghaied hundreds of plumbers from the Army ranks and brought them wholesale to Hanford, where, according to one of them, "the pay is better, the work is easier, and no one's shooting at me."

Still, both Groves and Matthias were kept frantically busy trying to keep Hanford's manpower in full force. Much of the problem was due to living and working conditions: the constant and demoralizing dust storms, the summer heat, which sometimes reached as much as 130 degrees, and the mysterious nature of the job. Many newly recruited workers quit on arrival once they discovered that they were not to be told the real objective of their work. The facility, especially the construction camp, had the rowdy, free-wheeling ambience of an 1850s gold-mining settlement, replete with drunken brawls, knife fights, and overstuffed jails. Some drunks and pugilists got out of jail almost as soon as they were thrown in since DuPont's sole concern was to get men back to work as quickly as possible. Other offenders never reached jail at all; sweating MPs piled revelers into the front end of a paddy wagon only to have spectators cheerfully pull their pickled friends out of the back.

Through all the pandemonium, Colonel Matthias and his staff bustled about in "The Dachshund," an old Buick sedan that had been sawn in half, then stretched into the mottled semblance of a staff car.

Eventually, their attempts to provide workers with some niceties began to pay off. In the huge trailer encampment, where the resident population reached twelve thousand, lawns, vegetable gardens, and even picket fences sprouted, softening the trailer city's metallic bleakness. An enormous tent doubled as a church and recreation hall, and a thirty-thousand-square-foot auditorium played host to circuses and dance bands. There were nine baseball diamonds; by May 1944, 250,000 people had watched Hanford intramural baseball, an attendance record that rivaled that of some major league teams. And there were several movie theaters, 144 horseshoe courts, and 150 pinball machines. For the bachelors there was a surplus of women that ran more than two to one.

In the raucous boom-town atmosphere, as busloads of arriving workers stared uneasily at equally full busloads of those who were leaving, Groves and Matthias somehow managed to keep construction speeding ahead. Even before the shell of the first pile building, known as 100-B, was completed, workers began the enormously painstaking task of building the steel and concrete walls that would enclose the reactors themselves. By May 1944, the graphite blocks that would hold tens of thousands of uranium slugs were being meticulously laid into place, using plumb lines and guide wires to ensure placement errors of no more than .0005 inch. A few miles away, workers were already sealing in the ghostly concrete galleries of building 221-T, the first of three subfacilities in which, if all went well, the plutonium would finally be separated from the uranium that spawned it.

Everywhere the first concern was the protection of human beings from the virulent and deadly effects of radiation. Precautions were particularly vital because radiation, new enough to the scientific world but almost unheard of in industry, was at best poorly understood. Some scientists dismissed the problem entirely, saying that the neutron-absorbing cadmium rods that were an essential feature of pile design would be sufficient to keep the reactors from irradiating their surroundings. But for Groves, who would be held accountable in the event of a life-threatening accident, these assurances were not enough.

With safety in mind, John Wheeler and the DuPont engineers placed the three gargantuan pile buildings at a minimum of three miles from one another and had designed the piles themselves so that they would be shielded by thousands of tons of concrete, steel plate, and a covering of a specially developed high-density pressed wood. The separation buildings, where the entire plutonium retrieval process would take place in a radiation bath, were designed so that the deadly plutonium and uranium would remain not only untouched by human hands but unseen by human eyes. For the first time in history, an enormous factory would be run entirely by remote control: plutonium and uranium would be handled by a series of specially designed mechanical "hands," ranging from huge cranes to tiny pincers, and from above, hundreds of operators would conduct and monitor the process with the help of another brand-new technology: television.

But not even these extreme precautions were enough for Groves. Experiments at Chicago had indicated that a burst of radiation from the reactors' exhaust stacks could spread as far as forty miles. To study this alarming possibility in situ, the general brought in a University of Washington meteorologist, who promptly built an experimental smoke-stack that towered three hundred feet above the desert. The radiologist then made painstaking observations for weeks as to what direction a radiation cloud might take. To ensure that no radioactive waste leaked into the Columbia River, Groves ordered all underground disposal pits sur-rounded by walls of concrete two feet thick. (Years later, even those armored pits were found inadequate, as measurable amounts of radiation were detected in the river.) When his former boss General T. M. Robins warned him that "you will incur the everlasting enmity of the entire Northwest if you harm a single scale on a single salmon," he built an entire fish laboratory to study the problem.

By the second week in September, with safety precautions in place, Matthias and the DuPont engineers could breathe a sigh of relief. The 100-B pile building had been completed the month before, and an on-site DuPont factory was now producing at a rate of hundreds per day the tens of thousands of uranium slugs needed to fuel the reactor. Everything was ready for the beginning of the plutonium process's most crucial test: the loading of the slugs into their graphite receptacles and the slow mounting of the self-sustaining chain reaction by which plutonium would be produced. If it worked, Groves and the MED scientists would have not only accomplished a major piece of alchemy—the production of plutonium from U-235 was, after all, transmutation of elements in line with the ancient dreams of Paracelsus—but would have generated an elegant manmade fuel for the atomic bomb. If it didn't, Groves joked to Matthias, "you might as well jump right in the middle of it. It'll save you a lot of trouble."

To Enrico Fermi, who almost two years earlier had armed the first experimental reactor in a squash court under the University of Chicago grandstands, fell the honor of loading the huge Hanford pile. On Septem-ber 13, he and Arthur Compton arrived from Chicago. Together with Franklin Matthias and DuPont executives Roger Williams and Crawford

Greenewalt, they drove to the 100-B building. At 5:43 P.M., Fermi calmly and quietly plugged an aluminum-coated uranium can into a hole in a smoothly polished block of black graphite. But celebration would have been premature: it would take a full two weeks and the loading of hundreds more slugs before the pile reached critical size and a reaction began.

Just after midnight on September 27, with more than nine hundred slugs already loaded, Fermi gave the order to begin withdrawing the cadmium control rods that were keeping the nuclear reaction in check. Over the next two hours, as the rods were slowly withdrawn, operators watched the overall power outlay of the enormous pile reach levels unrecorded in history. But even this output was only a tiny fraction of the capacity for which the reactor was designed and which would be necessary even to contemplate the production of plutonium in quantities sufficient for a bomb. To reach that level—the level where success might actually be at hand—much more power would be needed.

But at three o'clock in the morning, operators noticed something strange. The power output of the pile, which had been climbing steadily, now registered a slight drop. Bemused and then alarmed, the operators watched as the power dropped by 50 percent in only an hour. Surely, they thought, something was wrong with their instruments. They frantically checked every switch and dial on the complicated control board, but the power continued to decline. By 6:30 the dials registering power had dropped to zero. Without ever coming near its capacity, the pile had mysteriously shut itself down.

Matthias, who had been rousted from bed in the interim, put in an emergency call to Groves, who was visiting the Radiation Lab in Berkeley. The general reacted with a calm order: "I don't want anyone from Chicago going out there unless they talk to me first," he said. "This is Hanford's baby; let them solve it."

Already the Hanford scientists were methodically advancing theories to explain the reactor's puzzling failure. Perhaps one of the cooling tubes, they speculated, was leaking water into the pile. Or perhaps the cooling water itself was somehow absorbing an inordinate amount of neutrons, thereby robbing the reaction of its ammunition. But measurements over the next two days showed that neither of these two factors was to blame. In the meantime, the pile inexplicably began to recover on its own. By the evening of the twenty-eighth, it had reached its previous high. Then over the next few hours, just as the operators were beginning to sigh in relief, the pile mysteriously shut itself down again.

Amid the general tongue-clicking and brain-wracking, John

Wheeler remained cool. While in Chicago, Wheeler had spent much time trying to anticipate problems that might shut the reactor down. Principal among them was the possibility that the pile might be "poisoned" by fission products created during the intermediate phases of the reaction. Specifically, Wheeler thought, some radioactive gas might be produced during the reaction that was just long-lived enough to absorb enough neutrons to kill the reaction. Once the unstable gas had decayed into a less "poisonous" element, the neutron count—and thus the power of the reactor—would go back up.

Wheeler's theory, it turned out, exactly fit the profile of the shutdown. In one day he and Fermi identified the "poison": a radioactive isotope of the gas xenon. But it was one thing to find the cause of the problem and quite another to fix it. If the creation of radioactive xenon was an integral feature of the reaction itself, then the whole process—and the entire vast plutonium program—might be useless.

It was possible, however, that a solution was at hand, a solution that had been incorporated by DuPont engineers into the design of the reactor. Earlier, DuPont's George Graves, a tough, hard-bitten engineer whose lifetime of experience had given him a healthy regard for the unexpected, had proposed that the reactor design feature room for an extra set of five hundred cells and uranium slugs so that the power capacity of the reactor could be increased if necessary. It had been a seat-of-the-pants judgment; Graves could not enumerate the situations under which extra power might be needed, but instinct told him that it was vital to build in such a safety factor, if only to allow for a margin of error.

Graves's idea had not been a hit in Chicago. Confident in their calculations of the reactor's fuel needs, Compton, Wigner, and even Fermi had scoffed at what they thought of as DuPont's exaggerated conservatism. Among the leading Chicago scientists, only Wheeler had thought Graves was right. Groves agreed with the "conservatives," and over the objections of the rest of the Chicago group he had approved the extra cells and slugs despite the fact that they effectively increased the amount of uranium needed for full capacity by 25 percent and, of course, greatly increased the reactor's cost. Still, Groves had reasoned, spending the extra money could well amount to purchasing an insurance policy against the reactor's failure.

Now, in the face of the alarming shutdown, Groves ordered the insurance policy invoked. Slowly over the next two months, all 2,004 of the reactor's cells—including the extra five hundred built in by the "conservative" George Graves—were loaded with uranium slugs. By mid-

December the extra fuel was giving the pile the power it needed to overcome the xenon poisoning. By Christmas Day, two of the Hanford piles were operating at full capacity.

After more than two years of planning and effort, of theories and countertheories, of hopes dashed and hopes revitalized, plutonium production was at last under way. The stubbornness of George Graves had, in Groves's words, been "the salvation of the entire project."

But although Hanford was beginning to produce plutonium, production in bomb-size quantities was still by no means assured. Even if the bomb itself still had to be built and tested. The latter was Los Alamos's job, a job beset by hundreds of mind-numbing technical difficulties. Yet as 1944 rolled relentlessly on, the Los Alamos scientists found themselves all too often distracted by problems of daily living in Oppenheimer's Shangri-La, problems that often seemed as devilish and frustrating as those that hampered the building of the bomb itself.

Chapter Twenty-Seven

At first glance, Gerald R. Tyler looked like anything but a competent engineering officer. Big and pot-bellied, he seemed at constant war with his own uniform: his shirt bulged at the middle until it looked like his shirttails would escape his pants, and the force of gravity seemed to pull the knot of his tie inexorably down from his collar. Yet Tyler came highly recommended by the Army Corps of Engineers; he had just finished an important assignment on the construction of the Al-Can Hiway. As a commander he had a reputation for no-nonsense firmness mixed with a shrewd understanding of people's motives.

He would need both qualities in abundance in his new job. Groves had told Tyler that as of November 1944 he would become the commanding officer of the military post at Los Alamos. Now, on a bright autumn day in Washington, Groves gave the bemused Tyler an extraordinary preview of his new assignment.

"The scientists detest the uniform," the general said matter-of-factly. "They'll make your life a hell on earth and will do everything they can to embarrass you. When you start talking to them about accountability, they'll scream that you are a fascist and that you're trying to regiment them.

"Your job," the general went on, "will be to run the post. Try to satisfy these temperamental people. Don't allow living conditions, family problems, or anything else to take their minds off their work."

Groves's grim speech was based on a year and a half of experience in dealing with the Los Alamos scientists, experience that came as close to outright combat as anything the general saw during the war. Almost from the beginning, the scientists and the soldiers had squared off against one another; indeed, as Luis Alvarez put it, "It was as if we were from two hostile tribes." In general, the scientists' attitude toward the Army engineers, whom they variously called "creeps" or "plumbers," was laced with feelings of superiority, intellectual and otherwise. "The scientists," said Priscilla Duffield, "felt they were an elite group. They didn't consider the military helpful; anything the soldiers had done to get the post started could have been done better by a scientist."

Much of this derision was focused on Groves. "The prevailing view," said Alvarez, "was that the general was a busybody who should have gone off and built a dam and not messed around in physics. If it were not for him throwing roadblocks in the way, the scientists thought, things would move along a lot faster." "As an absentee landlord," wrote Bernice Brode, wife of Los Alamos physicist Robert Brode, "General Groves got the blame for everything that went wrong."

To those who had only superficial contact with the general—which was almost everyone in the Tech Area except Oppenheimer, Rabi, and division heads like Bacher and Bethe—he seemed inflexible and uncomfortable to the point of boorishness. Indeed, the general did nothing to soften this impression: instead of saying good morning when entering Oppenheimer's office, for example, he would look at the dirt on the doorjamb and ask, "Doesn't anyone wash their hands around here?" Even when he was in a conciliatory mood, the scientists often heard a hollow, clinking sound in his efforts at amiability. "He would be on his best behavior," said one officer, "trying to charm someone, but in the end something sarcastic would always come out. He wasn't even aware that he did it."

The scientists' antimilitary stance was not based solely on prejudice and personality. Many had come from academic communities, where wartime privations were discussed but not deeply felt; for them, the isolation, the sacrifice, and the choking dust of Los Alamos came as a distinct shock. To the younger scientists, the security, with its censorship, phone tapping, and manipulations, rankled. Rossi Lomanitz, a Berkeley physicist who was thought by some MED officials to have "questionable" political ideas, was mysteriously denied a draft deferment and inducted into the Army instead of being brought to Los Alamos with the rest of his Berkeley colleagues. There were chronic food and water shortages, and meat, when available, did not always meet academic standards. In fact, the wife of one scientist actually flung a hamburger patty at Tyler's predecessor, screaming, "Dog meat!" There were no sidewalks, no cooking gas, and few bathtubs. The walls in the houses and dormitories were as thin as paper, and the coal-burning stoves, known as "Black Beauties," were all but unusable.

But these problems paled in comparison to the problems of the young scientists who were suddenly railroaded into the Special Engineering

Detachment (SED). Early in 1943, physicist John Manley had been concerned that some of the younger scientists might not be able to get draft deferments; this could seriously deplete the Los Alamos work force. "Would it be possible," Manley wrote Oppenheimer, "for them to be inducted into the army and then assigned to us?"

As manpower requirements doubled in 1943 and again in 1944, Groves became increasingly attracted to the idea. By mid-1944 the general could see no alternative: the Special Engineering Detachment was inaugurated. "We sent all those draft-age physicists from Los Alamos to the induction center," recalled one Groves assistant. "When they came out the other side, we were there waiting to take them right back to Los Alamos." But the SEDs, as these physicists came to be called, were now working at Army pay, which was only a fraction of their civilian salaries. Also, as one MED colonel noted, "they were working their brains out all week in the Tech Area, and then we were taking them out on weekends and drilling their asses off. Naturally, there was some resentment."

If the SEDs had abundant reason to complain, the nonscientific soldiers at Los Alamos had resentments of their own. Many had originally signed up for overseas duty and were bitterly unhappy at being assigned to an isolated and seemingly unimportant Stateside post. The sight of healthy young men their own age escaping service altogether and being paid what seemed an executive wage (up to six hundred dollars a month for some) only increased their bitterness. Scientists were allowed housing for their wives and families; soldiers were not. Promotions for soldiers came slowly, and furloughs were often canceled for unexplained "security reasons." In medical emergencies, scientists were hospitalized on the post, while soldiers had to be driven over forty miles of tortuous roads to hospitals in Santa Fe.

To make matters worse, Groves had ordered the Army officers and enlisted men to treat the scientists—whom they called "longhairs," "eggheads," and "Tech Area jerks"—with the softest of kid gloves. "We had many small benefits courtesy of the Army," recalled Bernice Brode. "Soldiers cut and stacked wood outside our houses for our fireplaces and 'Black Beauties.' Soldiers came with trucks and work gangs to collect garbage and trash, and to fix plumbing or anything else. At Christmas they went into the woods and mountains and cut trees of every size for us to choose. Heating was taken care of by the Army, which seemed like easy living for those of us used to stoking our home furnaces." In addition, mounted MPs were ordered to surrender their horses to the scientists for recreational riding, then were expected to clean and rub down the tired animals after the scientists returned.

"The civilians were getting things you couldn't get at any other installation," recalled Ralph Carlisle Smith, who as the post's patent officer was the only military man who worked daily in the Tech Area. "Steaks, roast beef, all the butter they wanted. In fact, when [radiologist] Stafford Warren would come from Oak Ridge, he would take pounds of butter, wrap it in dry ice, and sneak it out in his baggage.

"Everyone talked about how terrible life was at Los Alamos," Smith concluded. "But I don't think anyone in the United States had it as good."

But the pressure of confinement, close contact, and essential differences in outlook inevitably created conflict between the military and the scientists; and the weight of that conflict was borne not as much by Groves and Oppenheimer as by the various officers who served as Los Alamos's military commanders. The first of these was Lieutenant Colonel J.M. Harman, whom one Los Alamite described as "a funny little fat man who seemed to feel that the job was beyond him." Harman and Oppenheimer, who had overlapping responsibilities for getting the post built, clashed early and often, and at the end of the spring of 1943 Groves replaced Harman with an Oppenheimer favorite: Lieutenant Colonel Whitney Ashbridge.

A Philadelphia patrician and MIT graduate who as a boy had attended Los Alamos Ranch School, Ashbridge's mainline sensibilities were more in tune with Oppenheimer's. Cool and correct, his uniform always briskly starched, Ashbridge was the picture of an officer and a gentleman. But Ashbridge's crusty courtesies were like whispers in the shouting matches that increasingly characterized relations between the scientific and military camps. After eighteen months of shrieking complaints followed by ineffectual mediation, Ashbridge's body gave up: on a trip back from Washington he collapsed at the Amarillo airport, the victim of a severe heart attack.

After Ashbridge's "surrender," Groves passed the ball to Gerald Tyler. The sloppy-looking but tough-minded colonel soon let it be known who was in charge. At a town council meeting when presented with a list of the scientists' demands, Tyler announced that he would entertain only "requests." Furthermore, he said coolly, "The first man, woman, or child who throws hamburger on my desk will go straight through my screen window." The colonel's firmness, coupled with a well-developed sense of fair play and a saving sense of humor, seemed to help turn things around. Although conflicts between the soldiers and scientists continued to bubble under the surface, they appeared somehow less serious. Indeed, a War Department analysis later concluded that the soldier-scientist conflict created tension that actually helped speed up the scientific work and that the success of the Los Alamos scientists occurred in great part "not in spite of, but *because* of these conflicts." Personally, Groves seemed to agree. "There were more stories told about me than you could shake a stick at," he said. "You can't be fussy and worry about it. Actually, you build morale that way."

If Groves's efforts at morale-building seem curiously backhanded, the reverse seems true of Oppenheimer. In the midst of Los Alamos's unexpectedly explosive growth (the lab, originally intended for six quiet thinkers, had by midspring a technical staff of 908, with new scientists arriving at the rate of one every day), in the midst of the dust and confusion raised by the furious construction of new labs and dormitories ("If Oppenheimer needed a new building," recalled Ralph Carlisle Smith, "all he had to do was call Groves; the foundations would be poured in three days, and the building would be up in two weeks"), Oppenheimer came alive. Gone was the effete dreamer, the leisurely theorist who was never awake before midday. For the most part the arrogance and snobbery that had earned him the enmity of so many of his colleagues were kept under control. The new Oppenheimer scurried to his office long before the 7:30 whistle sounded and seemed for the most part to have left his acid tongue in retirement.

During the working day he roamed the Tech Area, often accompanied by a retinue that included Bethe, the umbrella-toting Rabi, and the hawk-nosed Robert Serber; he stuck his head into laboratories encouraging, listening, cajoling, and in general illuminating the work with his highly personal style of intellectual cheerleading. In individual conferences, at division meetings, and at the free-wheeling Colloquia, his ability to grasp an exceedingly complicated technical problem, to summarize it clearly, and then to offer directions toward its solution dazzled and inspired even those scientists who were aware of the more unfortunate aspects of his personality. "It was a stroke of genius on Groves's part to appoint Oppenheimer as Director," enthused Rabi. "He did a fantastic job."

At the same time, Oppenheimer and Groves enjoyed a working relationship that, in light of the great differences in their personalities and outlook, was almost amazingly smooth and free of conflict. No one who was close to them recalls ever hearing them argue. This surprising accommodation may have grown partly out of mutual manipulation and partly out of mutual gratitude. Groves was grateful to have a sympathetic scientist to pass on the more unpalatable of his decrees, and Oppenheimer was grateful for the opportunity to compensate for an essentially undistinguished career as a physicist by shining as a physics administrator. In any case and for whatever reason, the two cooperated beautifully on everything from sweeping decisions on laboratory policy to the changing of a flat tire on a crippled Army sedan.

But it took more than cooperation at the top to solve the technical problems involved in designing and assembling the bomb. Here, as Oppenheimer himself said, the lab had "a bear by the tail." Indeed, the field was so new, the problems so unimaginably complex, and its requisite measurements so exasperatingly precise (to give only one example, the time elapsing between the fission of a U-235 nucleus and the subsequent emission of neutrons was on the order of one one-*billionth* of a second) that at first there were neither the experimental techniques nor the appropriate equipment to begin solving the problems.* Critical materials were so scarce as to be almost nonexistent: until the spring of 1944, Los Alamos scientists were working with no more than two grams of U-235 from Lawrence's Berkeley Calutron and under 200 micrograms of plutonium manufactured in a prototype pile at Oak Ridge and carried by Glen Seaborg to Los Alamos in a suitcase. (So rare and valuable was the plutonium that even physicist Robert Wilson, a gentle soul who later became a leader of the scientists' pacifist movement, picked up Seaborg's sample in Santa Fe with a rifle next to him on the front seat.)

Exacerbating the basic scientific problems were difficulties that arose out of the sheer newness of Los Alamos itself. Despite the bravest efforts of Groves and his contractor, the M.E. Sundt Company, construction inevitably lagged behind the scientists' needs for new facilities. Dust was everywhere, which was particularly irritating for those scientists charged with keeping the minute samples of uranium and plutonium antiseptically clean. The lab's power plant was subject to capricious surges that not only disrupted laboratory experiments but kept all Tech Area clocks running either madly ahead or hopelessly behind.

The complexity of the situation, the Rube Goldberg nature of the facilities, and perhaps most important, the terrible sense of urgency caused by the war itself brought out the best and most ingenious in the Los Alamos scientists, so that by late spring of 1944 Oppenheimer could report considerable and heartening progress. The physicists under Bacher and Bethe were coaxing the elusive neutron into giving up its secrets, while the chemists under Joseph Kennedy, Cyril Smith, and Charles Thomas had

---

*Although the idea of an explosive fission bomb was based entirely on the use of fast neutrons (as opposed to the slow neutrons used in the manufacture of plutonium), as late as 1943 no one had developed a detector capable of tracking fast neutrons.

succeeded in purifying plutonium to such an extent that even the demanding Groves found their program "fully up to expectations."

Still, at the beginning of the summer of 1944 the things that were known were greatly outnumbered by questions that remained stubbornly unanswered. Of the remaining puzzles, undoubtedly the most important was critical mass—the amount of fissionable material necessary to generate a nuclear explosion. Without an answer substantially more precise than that given him by the Chicago scientists the year before, Groves had little idea how much uranium or plutonium would have to be produced and thus only an imprecise notion as to when a bomb might actually be ready. Raw estimates of U-235 for critical mass tripled in early 1943 and were later doubled again after new measurements brought an important correction in Oppenheimer's earlier calculations. As time went on, Bethe and his theoreticians—who posted a DO NOT ERASE sign on their blackboards so that months of calculations would not be wiped out by a thoughtless pass of a janitor's eraser—brought more and more brainpower to bear on the crucial subject. But in February 1944, when Bethe's group could estimate nothing more precise than between eight and eighty kilograms of U-235 (with no estimate at all hazarded for plutonium), Groves was forced to report to Roosevelt that the vital figure remained essentially unknown.

It was assumed by everyone involved that as more and more fissionable material became available for study, the figures for critical mass would grow more and more precise. Thus an eventual, timely solution to the problem was fully expected. But in the summer of 1944 a new problem arose from an almost entirely *un*expected quarter. The problem threatened to render Groves's massive investment in the plutonium process completely useless. As it was, it threw Groves, Oppenheimer, and the Los Alamos laboratory into a paroxysm of hasty reorganization.

Chapter Twenty-Eight

Emilio Segrè was perplexed. The handsome Italian physicist, a colleague and great friend of Enrico Fermi, was one of the discoverers of plutonium, and he felt he knew the element and its bizarre properties as well as anyone in the world. (Hard as glass under some conditions, plutonium was as soft as plastic under others; even stranger, it actually contracted when heated.) But in midsummer of 1944, as he conducted tests on a tiny sample from the prototype pile at Clinton, Segrè found something that seemed to stand his knowledge on its head. His tests showed that the sample contained unmistakable traces of a new plutonium isotope whose atomic weight, at 240, was one unit greater than the Pu-239 with which he and everyone else had been working.*

The discovery was chilling. If Pu-240 emitted alpha particles on its own, Pu-239 would be "contaminated" by an excess of unattached neutrons. Because a gun-type bomb—a sort of adaptation of a reliable standard model then in wide use in other bombs—would be triggered by a mechanism that was relatively slow-moving, the plutonium would detonate in advance of the trigger, rendering the bomb a harmless fizzle. Only in an implosion bomb—in which, theoretically at least, the mechanics were so fast that the explosion would take place before the contaminating isotope had time to cause predetonation—could the crippling effects of Pu-240 be overcome. Segrè's next round of tests confirmed his worst fear: Pu-240 was indeed an emitter of alpha particles. The chances of using plutonium successfully in a gun-type weapon were now virtually zero.

Had the implosion bomb actually received the sort of attention at Los Alamos that Groves had called for, Segrè's discovery might not have been so upsetting. But like the fast-neutron work earlier in the project,

*Although Segrè later maintained that the discovery of Pu-240 was unexpected, it had in fact been predicted by Seaborg over a year earlier.

implosion had remained essentially a back-burner item. At a Governing Board meeting in October 1943, with Groves conspicuously in attendance, Oppenheimer had exhorted the other lab leaders to give implosion research the "highest priority." But months went by with little change. By February 1944, five months after his "high priority" speech, Oppenheimer had put only five additional men into the implosion program. Neddermeyer continued to work in an isolated canyon, rattling the walls with his explosive tests, slowly and methodically trying to find the best candidate for detonating an atomic "implosion." But he was still very much the outsider, the isolated lone wolf.

Obviously, Neddermeyer needed help. With this in mind, Groves recruited George Kistiakowsky, a Harvard chemist whom many scientists considered the nation's number-one expert on high explosives. A high-spirited White Russian refugee, his parents had fought against the Bolsheviks. (When someone innocently made him a present of a book with a red cover, he flung it angrily across the room, declaring that he would not look at a book that had Communist colors.) Kistiakowsky thought that the atomic bomb in general and the implosion bomb in particular were "probably a waste of time." He felt that his work at the NDRC laboratory in Bruceton, Pennsylvania, preparing explosives for the D-Day invasion of Normandy, was far more important. In fact, he was such a reluctant recruit that Groves and Conant, the latter his nominal boss at both the NDRC and at Harvard, virtually had to order him to Los Alamos.

What he saw there left Kistiakowsky singularly unimpressed. "It puzzles me," he wrote to Conant after his first inspection of Neddermeyer's implosion unit, "that a project which is supposed to be so hot . . . does not rate more personnel." He immediately pressed Oppenheimer for more men; and by May 1, the implosion division had been beefed up to 110. Still, in the wake of the crisis brought on by Segrè's discovery of Pu-240, even this was not enough. The manpower resources of Los Alamos were already stretched to the limit, and it was growing increasingly difficult for Groves or Arnold simply to wave a wand and bring in a fresh batch of young scientists from outside. Somewhere inside the laboratory itself, something would have to give.

It fell to Groves to determine the next move. On July 17 he met in Chicago with Oppenheimer, Fermi, Compton, Conant, and others. After a heated discussion that lasted all day, the general made his decision: the effort to make a gun bomb from plutonium, which had occupied Los Alamos scientists for over a year, would have to be abandoned. In its place, a great portion of the laboratory's energy and resources would be thrown into a furious crash program to make implosion work.

His mandate clear, Oppenheimer shook the lab with a violent reorganization, creating an entire new division, X Division, to attack the implosion problem. Neddermeyer was moved aside, replaced by the still-reluctant but far more dynamic Kistiakowsky. After the Russian's permanent transfer to Los Alamos in June, things began to happen. Some of the lab's top talent, including Luis Alvarez and Harvard's Kenneth Bainbridge, moved over to take important places on Kistiakowsky's team. Pushing relentlessly for more men, the Russian soon commandeered four hundred of the overworked, underpaid SEDs. With two hundred more scientists from other divisions, Kistiakowsky's division was ready to attack the implosion problem head-on.

But it was very nearly too little, too late. Oppenheimer's initial inattention had delayed the implosion push by as much as five months. Groves himself was responsible for a further delay when he allowed a full month to elapse between Segrè's discovery and the Chicago meeting. To make matters worse, Neddermeyer's summary replacement and Kistiakowsky's independent approach annoyed a number of influential Los Alamites, most notably Deke Parsons, Kistiakowsky's nominal boss.

So Kistiakowsky launched himself at the implosion bomb with an alienated commander, a patchwork division of men, and a nearly impossible schedule. (Groves had promised an implosion weapon would be ready in the spring of 1945.) The technical problems, he knew, were immense, and the technology for solving them was still all but nonexistent. Somehow the Russian and his men would have to not only bring order out of chaos but, in a scientific sense, create something from nothing. In effect, they were being asked to accomplish the impossible. They had eight months in which to do it.

At the same time, Kistiakowsky and his Los Alamos colleagues had to carefully avoid revealing what had become World War II's most important secret.

Chapter Twenty-Nine

On a typically muggy August Sunday in Washington, John Lansdale invited some of the officers in his security section for a casual dinner party at his home. While Lansdale mixed drinks in the kitchen, one of the officers turned on the antiquated console radio in the living room. The room was immediately filled with the booming voice of CBS correspondent Arthur Hale, broadcasting his popular news-gossip show, "Confidentially Yours," on WKBU in Harrisburg, Pennsylvania. At first the officer paid little attention to the broadcast, but soon a single word penetrated his Sunday consciousness and put him back to work. The word, new to the radio commentator, was carefully pronounced, syllable by syllable: *uranium.*

His attention now riveted, the officer listened with growing alarm to the rest of the broadcast. The "Columbia Project," trumpeted Hale, was "investigating the energy of the atom." Experts agreed that "a blast based on this energy could destroy everything for a square mile." Researchers were "staggered," and the fruits of the project would certainly "alter the destiny of the world." Horrified, the officer quickly sought out Lansdale in the kitchen. Speaking in a voice barely above a whisper, he repeated the text of Hale's broadcast nearly word for word.

"I think," the officer concluded, "we've got a problem."

Lansdale agreed. Within an hour the irascible Virginia Military Institute graduate and lawyer quietly broke up the dinner party and gathered his men in his office at the War Department building. Groves was informed, and the wheels of investigation immediately whirred into motion. Two days later a frightened Arthur Hale found himself side by side with WKBU manager James Moss in a War Department conference room being grilled by John Lansdale. In another room, Richard Tolman was carefully interrogating Herbert Bernstein, an Illinois Institute of Technology chemistry professor who, although unconnected with the Manhattan

175

District, was current enough on the state of nuclear research to provide Hale with the information in his broadcast. When the interrogations were finished, both Lansdale and Tolman were satisfied that the slip had been inadvertent and that neither Hale nor Bernstein knew more about the bomb project than what Hale had revealed.

Still, to Groves the Hale broadcast was a flagrant violation of MED security. He had previously warned every radio station manager in the country not to discuss anything to do with uranium, nuclear physics, or atomic bombs; that warning had obviously been ignored by both Hale and Moss. Calling the three men into his office, Groves made his point softly but with exquisite clarity. "Gentlemen," he said, "I'm convinced that you meant no harm. But I'm also convinced that all three of you are entirely lacking in good judgment, moral principles, and patriotic Americanism. If anything like this happens again, I'll have you in court."

Chastened, the three men returned to their jobs and expunged the word *uranium* from their vocabularies for the rest of the war. But the incident reflects the monumental task faced by Lansdale and William Consodine, the two officers charged by Groves with maintaining airtight projectwide security. To perform the massive job of keeping the project secret, Lansdale had organized a corps of over three hundred security agents, recruiting his men with a special eye for former attorneys, reporters, and IRS investigators. Known as "creeps," these operatives scoured the country, constantly on the alert for violations of the project's intricate and labyrinthine security regulations.

The job was as heartbreaking as the regulations were elaborate. Millions of pages of top-secret documents—including some twelve hundred *miles* of blueprints—had to be disguised in indecipherable codes, then stored in safes with as many as three separate combinations. Every office in the project featured bright red "burn boxes" in which coded documents were meticulously burned after they were read. Newspapers, magazines, and radio stations were asked to voluntarily censor anything having to do with nuclear physics and atomic bomb research, with no explanation other than a cryptic "when the story breaks, you'll get all the information."

As far as Groves and Lansdale were concerned, the greatest security threats came not from outside the project but from inside. By virtue of their academic training, most of the scientists were enthusiastically open in their conversations, a tendency that to Groves's wartime mentality seemed extremely dangerous. Thus enormous precautions were taken to keep the scientists and their conversations entirely under wraps. Code names were devised for all top personnel: Arthur Compton became "Mr. Comas,"

Enrico Fermi "Mr. Farmer," and Eugene Wigner "Mr. Wagner." (When Ernest Lawrence's shirts came back from the Oak Ridge laundry bearing tags with the name "E. Lawson," his wife lamented, "Oh, Ernest, they've sent you someone else's shirts." Not until after the war was Lawrence free to explain that "Lawson" had been his code name.)

The scientists were mercilessly tailed and their bodies jealously guarded. Oppenheimer's Los Alamos "chauffeur" was actually counterintelligence agent Andrew Walker, who was assigned to keep an eye out for any untoward contacts by the physicist. When Niels Bohr crossed a New York street against red lights—standard practice for this archetypically absent-minded professor—six Manhattan District "creeps" jaywalked with him. Edward Teller became so amused by the transcontinental shadowing that he finally suggested to the agent who had been tailing him that the two of them give up what had become a pointless subterfuge and travel together. Enrico Fermi went Teller one better and established a close friendship with his Italian-American bodyguard.

None of these high-jinks dissuaded Groves in the least. In fact, the general was so adamant in his insistence on personal surveillance that he even had *himself* followed—to ensure that no one else was following him! So great was his interest in counterespionage that he once smoked what he called a "doped cigarette" (almost certainly marijuana) proffered him by Jean O'Leary to see if the drug could induce him to reveal secrets. (The cigarette, he noted, had "no effect whatsoever. But Mrs. O'Leary told me that the reason for this was that I did not inhale.")

Despite Groves's extraordinary precautions, security slips were inevitable. Even before the general took over the MED, *New York Times* science reporter William Laurence had written two major articles on nuclear fission, both of which had mentioned the possibility of developing an extremely powerful bomb. In 1944 *Cleveland Press* reporter Jack Raper published an article called "Forbidden City" in which Los Alamos was identified as a secret government lab where "tremendous explosions" had been heard. (Groves was ready to draft Raper and send him to the South Pacific until he was advised that the columnist was in his sixties. "Intelligence," wrote the general, "has its problems.")

When Science Service, Inc., sponsored a nationwide scientific essay contest, seventeen-year-old Clifford Swartz of Niagara Falls, New York, wrote a stirring contribution on atomic power, mentioning, to Groves's horror, that both General Electric and Westinghouse were working to isolate U-235. His fellow winner Beatrice Meirowitz of New York City devoted her entire essay to U-235, saying that "it is a weapon that could end the war quickly, but we know the Nazi scientists are working on it too." Even Walt Disney seemed to be in on the secret: in the fall of 1940 he published a two-part story in which Mickey Mouse and his friend Goofy pursue a mysterious Dr. Einmus, who had discovered a power locked up in radium atoms that could, in Goofy's immortal words, "blow us to bits."

More serious security threats were the constant incursions of curious congressmen. In late 1943 Representative Albert Engel of Michigan asked Undersecretary of War Robert Patterson for permission to visit Oak Ridge. When Patterson promptly turned him down, Engel wrote angrily, "It seems rather strange that while every day 360,000 workers are allowed to go to these plants, I, a member of Congress and a member of the subcommittee which has the responsibility of handling these tremendous expenditures, is not even permitted to see what is going on." Worried by Engel's threat to take the problem to open debate on the house floor, Groves arranged a meeting in which Secretary of War Stimson, General Marshall, and Vannevar Bush revealed the nature of the program to a trio of congressional leaders in exchange for a pledge to keep themselves and other congressmen quiet. This strategy worked well. When an investigator for Senator Truman's Military Expenditures Committee showed up unannounced at Hanford, Franklin Matthias stalled him and put in a frantic call to Groves. The general quickly called Truman, who, true to their earlier agreement, immediately called his watchdog off.

In fact, the only truly serious threats to MED security came from a quarter over which Groves had little control. Ever since 1942, American scientists in the Manhattan District had been cooperating closely with the British, particularly on the gaseous diffusion progress. In a Met Lab meeting on January 9, 1944, Groves gave a talk to a delegation of Canadian scientists who formed part of the British mission. Because of a complex diplomatic agreement that had been reached by Roosevelt and Churchill a few months earlier, Groves was forced to allow the British to do their own security checking on their own scientists. Apparently, the British were not as thorough as Groves would have wished, for two members of the delegation in that Chicago meeting room—Englishman Alan Nunn May and Italian Bruno Pontecorvo—were at that very moment actively spying for the Soviet Union.

Even worse was the case of Klaus Fuchs. German born and raised, this quiet physicist was the son of a dedicated Communist and had himself led a Communist cell in Quebec. Fuchs slipped through the cursory British security check and became one of the high-ranking members of the British mission. As such he had been invited into the closed inner circles of Theoretical Division research at Los Alamos.

In March 1944, carrying a tennis ball as a covert badge of identification, he showed up on a Lower East Side street corner for his first meeting with a tiny Soviet messenger whom he knew only as "Raymond." Over the next two years Fuchs had at least six more meetings with the courier, whose real name, Harry Gold, later made the most negative kind of history. At their meetings Fuchs turned over sheafs of information on Los Alamos, on bomb progress, and on several breakthrough discoveries in the development of implosion. Back at Los Alamos his colleagues admired the precision and cool logic of his physics — "Some of the most beautiful work I ever saw," commented one. But another co-worker noted sourly that the quiet Britisher seemed to be "all ears and no mouth."

In the meantime, Groves and his men were keeping their eyes open for signs of a massive and concentrated effort to build an atomic bomb in Germany. But there was a puzzling dearth of clues. Reconnaissance planes fitted with Alvarez's krypton detection system flew numerous missions over Germany's dangerous skies but found no traces of the radiation that might reveal a German Oak Ridge or a Hanford. Similarly, Matthias's hypothetical plant, with "lots of material going in and almost nothing coming out," had failed to appear. Perhaps most telling of all, Furman and Major Tony Calvert, operating from the joint British-American intelligence office in London, reviewed hundreds of aerial photographs of the Nazi-controlled radium mine in Joachimstal, Czechoslovakia, where an enormous pile of uranium-bearing pitchblende tailings lay mysteriously untouched. "Those piles," said Furman, "just stood there all through the war." All the information led to one conclusion: "The Germans," said Furman, "weren't actively interested in the bomb. In fact, our information led us to believe that their chances of having one were only about one in ten."

Although increasingly convinced that the German threat was a chimera, Groves wanted confirmation. In late 1943, as the American Fifth Army prepared to move into Italy, the general prepared to move with them. Under the code name ALSOS — Greek for "Groves" — he dispatched a mission of thirteen soldiers under Boris Pash and six scientists under Dutch physicist Samuel Goudsmit to see if anything could be found from Italian sources. Six months later Pash and his men interviewed two captured Italian physicists. But the two were either uninformed or unwilling to talk about any German experimentation in search of an atomic bomb.

By then Eisenhower was preparing the great D-Day invasion of Normandy. (Groves warned the Allied commander that the Germans might put down a radioactive barrier across the Norman beachhead. Thus some of the first Allied troops to hit the beach on D-Day were carrying Geiger counters.) Once a foothold was established on the continent, Pash, Goudsmit, and the ALSOS mission hurried to join the invading army. When Eisenhower's men pushed into Strasbourg, France, an ALSOS jeep with Pash aboard moved in, under withering enemy fire, with the first Allied tanks. After the city was taken, Goudsmit joined the mission. Working by candlelight in a University of Strasbourg medical laboratory while the Germans shelled the city from across the Rhine, Goudsmit and his colleagues soon found a treasure cache: a bundle of memos, notes, and documents left behind by a team of German nuclear physicists who had worked there but who had fled in the face of the Allied advance. The documents confirmed the conclusions reached earlier by Groves and Furman: the Germans had been unable to separate U-235 from U-238, and their work on a prototype plutonium-producing pile was only in the earliest experimental stages. "In short," Goudsmit concluded, "they were about as far as we had been in 1940." Weeks later, American soldiers found the shell of the only German pile in a cave near the quaint mountain village of Haigerloch. The pile had never operated. There was no German bomb.

Chapter Thirty

From Groves's point of view, the findings of the ALSOS mission were interesting but largely irrelevant. First, they only confirmed a conclusion at which he, Furman, and Calvert had arrived months earlier: that the Germans were not pushing hard to develop an atomic bomb. But more important in the minds of Groves and the MED planners, *Germany had ceased to be a potential target for an American bomb at least a year and a half earlier.* In a Military Policy Committee meeting on May 5, 1943, Groves had discussed the first use of the bomb with Bush, Conant, Styer, and Purnell. Germany was the obvious first choice as a target, the planners acknowledged, but what if the bomb turned out to be a dud? If the Germans recovered it, they would have a living, ticking model for a bomb of their own.

This was a risk that Groves and the Committee felt they could not take. Realizing this, their attention turned immediately to Japan. Since the Japanese nuclear enterprise was thought to be far less advanced than either the American or the German, there was far less risk that they would be able to profit from a salvaged dud. Even so, Groves and his colleagues were cautious. The first target, they decided, should be a harbor in which a Japanese fleet was concentrated; the water in that port should be deep enough to prevent easy salvage should the bomb fail to go off. Tokyo, with its relatively shallow harbor, was rejected for that reason. The bomb's first target, Groves and the Committee decided, would be the Japanese port Truk.

Only once during the war did Groves have reason to reconsider his decision not to drop an atomic bomb on Germany. In the winter of 1944, the Nazis launched a desperate counterattack against the invading Allied forces. The Battle of the Bulge, as it was called, wore on, looking increasingly like a stalemate and threatening to upset Allied schedules for ending the war. President Roosevelt was growing impatient. On December

30, 1944, he called Groves and Secretary of War Stimson to the White House. (It was the general's first and only face-to-face meeting with the President.) There, during a discussion that lasted an hour and a half ("The outer office was going wild," Groves remembered. "We only had a fifteen-minute appointment"), Roosevelt asked Groves point-blank if the bomb could be used against Germany.

This made the general uneasy. "It would be very difficult," he told Roosevelt, "for us to change our plans." First of all, Groves explained, no bombs were expected to be ready for at least another eight months, by which time, even given setbacks, the war in Europe would almost certainly be decided. The second inhibiting factor was the chance of a dangerously revealing dud. Third, Groves said, the bomb would be much more effective against Japan than against Germany, where building construction was much more solid. Finally, the only plane capable of carrying the bomb was the B-29, which was not available in the European theater. Even if brought to Germany and protected by a strong "umbrella" of fighter planes, Groves reasoned, the B-29 would face heavier resistance there than in Japan because "it would have been a new phenomenon in the German skies, and the Nazis were always eager to bring down any new Allied plane."

Groves's arguments were to no avail. Roosevelt insisted that in the event of a stalemate use of the bomb against Germany should be reconsidered, saying to Groves that he was "perfectly prepared" to drop the bomb on the Nazis. "I told him," Groves said, "that if this should become his decision, we could and would do it." With that Roosevelt closed the meeting.

The subject never came up again. When the Battle of the Bulge was won in early 1945, victory over Germany became a matter of time. Figuratively, the bomb returned to the post it had occupied in Groves's planning for over a year and a half: on a shelf clearly and exclusively marked JAPAN.

During that time Groves had carefully avoided revealing both the absence of an all-out German bomb project and his decision not to use the bomb in Europe to Manhattan District scientists, even to those on the level of Compton, Lawrence, and Oppenheimer. Instinctively, Groves probably felt that as a motivating factor the threat of a German atomic bomb was too good to lose. As far as many of the scientists were concerned, Germany was the principal enemy and the threat of a German atomic bomb was the raison d'être of the entire American nuclear effort. It may well have occurred to Groves that if the German threat were eliminated, so might be many of the physicists, who from the beginning had viewed the bomb as a deterrent and not as an offensive weapon and who, with Germany out of the picture, might simply resign. This was a risk Groves could not afford to take, for the resignation of key scientists would not only lead to crippling delays; it might deal a fatal blow to the entire fission project.

As it was, the absence of a German threat revealed by the ALSOS group soon moved a significant contingent of the Chicago scientists—led by the already disaffected Leo Szilard—to look at the bomb in a new light. Their conclusions and their subsequent actions generated one of the most bitter of all the Manhattan District internecine conflicts: the battle over how the bomb would be used.

Part Four

THE FINAL PUSH

Chapter Thirty-One

On a cold and windy day in early February 1945, Colonel Franklin Matthias placed a small vial in a double-heavy metal container, then wrapped the container in a special leakproof plastic lining. He closed the container and put it in a $14'' \times 14'' \times 20''$ wooden box. Carrying the box by a self-contained handle ("It looked," Matthias recalled, "like an ordinary piece of luggage"), he boarded a train from Portland, Oregon, to Los Angeles. On arrival at Union Station, he was met by a MED officer who was to board another train to take the box and its contents on the rest of its journey.

"Do you have a sleeping compartment?" Matthias asked the officer.

"No, sir," came the reply. "I couldn't get one. I had to take an upper berth."

"Well," said Matthias, "maybe you should try again. What you're carrying here is worth three hundred and sixty-three million dollars."

The young officer blanched, then took off at a dead run. Alternately wheedling and threatening the stationmaster, he finally wangled a private compartment. Nervously, he took the box and its precious contents from Matthias and boarded the train.

Suspended inside the box was a vial containing a jellylike nitrate of plutonium, the first produced by the mammoth Hanford plant. Its destination was the bomb lab at Los Alamos.

About a month later, two armed couriers in civilian clothes left Oak Ridge in an innocuous Chevrolet sedan with Tennessee license plates. Between them in the front seat rested a special suitcase in which had been packed a container of uranium tetrafluoride. Driving slowly, almost breathlessly, the couriers reached Knoxville just in time to catch the 12:50 Southland Express for Chicago. The next morning they were met at the Chicago station by security men from Major Arthur Peterson's MED office. Taking the suitcase from the Knoxville couriers, the Chicago security men boarded the Santa Fe Chief. Twenty-six hours later, they pulled into a nearly deserted siding in Lamy, New Mexico. An unmarked car from Los Alamos was waiting to meet them. The suitcase, and with it the Y-12 plant's first U-235, was on its way home.

These two dramatic deliveries marked the culmination of almost three years' work and the spending of some two billion dollars. The tiny containers represented the collective sweat and ingenuity not only of Groves, his officers, his contractors, and the project scientists but also of over two hundred thousand engineers, technicians, plumbers, pipefitters, electricians, welders, and common laborers. But the trick, the production of fissionable material—which Robert Bacher later called "by far the most difficult aspect of the project"—had been turned, and had been turned, amazingly enough, almost in accordance with Groves's "impossible" schedule.

At Hanford, the resolution of the xenon poisoning crisis had cleared the way for production of plutonium on a steadily accelerating basis. So smooth was this acceleration that in May 1945 the quantities were five times greater than they had been only a month before. Within weeks of Matthias's first shipment, regularly scheduled biweekly caravans of army ambulances ("We thought they would provoke the fewest questions," Matthias later said) and unmarked radio patrol cars were plying a rout from Hanford through Boise, Idaho, and Fort Douglas, Utah, carrying ever-increasing quantities of plutonium nitrate to Los Alamos.

At Oak Ridge, victory had come much harder. By March 1, 1945, the Fox Farm was steaming out slightly enriched U-235 in quantities that were double those of all previous months combined; this enabled Y-12 to generate enough highly enriched U-235 to begin the Los Alamos shipments. But important as they were to Oppenheimer and the anxious Los Alamos scientists, the quantities of U-235 were mere driblets compared with what was actually needed to make a bomb. If the uranium bomb were to become a reality, Groves knew, the immensely problematic K-25 plant would simply have to come through.

But it was precisely at K-25 that trouble seemed always to loom. For the most part, *trouble* continued to be a synonym for *barrier*. The general's decision to go ahead with the Johnson nickel-powder barrier did not smooth things out. First of all, the Houdaille-Hershey plant in Garfield had to be completely retooled to produce the Johnson barrier—despite the fact that as of the fall of 1944 production equipment for the newer material had yet to be fully designed. To make matters even more confusing, experiments with the Johnson barrier continued to show disappointingly poor performance, while the rejected Norris-Adler material suddenly began to show signs of improvement.

Groves might have been tempted to reverse course once again, to return to the Norris-Adler barrier and race to get it into production. But if he were tempted, the general did not show it. Instead, he plunged ahead with the Johnson barrier, confident that his team could make it work. For that team Groves brought together every available mind in every available laboratory: Laughlin Currie, Edward Mack, and John Dunning at Columbia; the Englishman Hugh Taylor at Princeton; Percival Keith and Clarence Johnson at Kellex; George Felbeck and Frazier Goff at Union Carbide; and Don Devor and Frank Fisher at Houdaille-Hershey.

The barrier effort was thus far-flung and desperately in need of coordination. Realizing this, Groves formed a centralized group with representatives from each of the companies and laboratories. Code-named K-1, the group had its headquarters on the fourteenth floor of the Woolworth Building in New York. But even with the K-1 group as a unifying force, the barrier team was dangerously close to being overlarge and underdirected. Groves, however, held the balance firmly in his own hands: when a bewildered Currie asked the general to whom he should report, Groves replied instantly, "Me. That's who."

Under the joint attack orchestrated by Groves and the K-1 group, the barrier problem gradually and grudgingly began to give way. By January 1945 the refitted Garfield plant was steadily producing enough usable barrier material to begin actually testing at Oak Ridge. Still, a number of stubborn problems remained. The K-25 plant needed thousands of valves that were utterly leakproof and resistant to the highly corrosive uranium hexafluoride. In addition, these valves would have to stand a combination of pressure, temperature, and vibration unprecedented in the history of industry—and all this without a drop of oil, for when combined with any lubricant, the uranium gas became dangerously explosive. No valve existed that could even remotely satisfy these torturous criteria.

At about the same time, it was determined that over five hundred miles of piping would have to be plated with nickel, the only metal known to be impervious to uranium hexafluoride. (The first thought had been to make the K-25 pipes out of solid nickel, but that idea had to be discarded when it was found that that would require more nickel than was produced in the entire free world.) Unfortunately, no usable nickel-plating process existed in industry, and even if it had, the scientists were convinced that a mere plating would never stand up to the wildly corrosive uranium gas.

At Kellex, the self-reliant J. C. Hobbs attacked the valve problem.

Independent and cantankerous—he had quit several companies when executives refused to go along with his radical design ideas—Hobbs had the reputation of being one of the country's most ingenious (and expensive) designers. But as far as Groves was concerned, Hobbs earned his pay and more. In late 1944, he came up with an engineering miracle: a design for a perfectly symmetrical metal valve that was thin enough to effect heat transfer and that had a free-floating, tubular seat that dangled in the middle of the apparatus and thus was not affected by the tremendous vibrations expected once the K-25 cascades rumbled into action.

To handle the development of a nickel-plating process, Groves reached once again into his own past. While working as a lieutenant in Services of Supply in the 1930s, Groves had looked for a cheaper, faster way to make searchlight mirrors, which up to then had been ground out laboriously by hand. His search had turned up a Swiss inventor named Blasius Bart, who had developed a way to mass-produce mirrors by electroplating surfaces with a reflective metal coating. Bart had since retired, but his son Sieg was still working his trade at the Swiss and Gorham Silver Company in Bellevue, New Jersey. Groves sent Keith to recruit the quiet young man. Remembering the favorable impression Groves had made on him as a teenager, Bart readily agreed to take a stab at electroplating steel pipes with nickel.

For months Bart and his assistants tried without success to develop a process that would leave the nickel plate absolutely smooth and uniform; even the slightest irregularity would foul the gigantic barrier cascades that were the heart of the gaseous diffusion process. Finally they came up with a way to rotate the pipe itself during plating so that every tiny imperfection in the steel surface would be filled with a perfectly smooth, polished coat of heavy nickel.

At Groves's insistence, Bart converted his tiny shop into a full-scale production facility, bringing in four hundred workers from Harlem and driving them through three shifts, twenty-four hours a day, seven days a week. By the end of 1944, production of the nickel-plated pipes was precisely on schedule. The MED had performed another miracle.

With the almost simultaneous solution of the barrier, valve, and plating problems, Union Carbide moved in more than nine thousand workers and operators in a frantic push to get the K-25 plant finally and firmly on-line. Conditions during the installation of the hundreds of miles of pipes and the hundreds of acres of barrier were extreme. Because even the tiniest amount of dirt or foreign matter could contaminate the entire process, installation had to be done in an atmosphere more antiseptic than that of a hospital operating room. Workers labored in head-to-toe white coveralls and lintless gloves, breathing air that was specially filtered to remove dust. The floor of the huge plant was dotted with man-size inflatable canvas balloons, inside which workers performed welding and other "dirty" operations. Once the piping and barrier tubes were installed, the entire system had to be painstakingly checked for leaks, for even one tiny pinhole in the miles of valves and piping could incapacitate the whole enormous factory.

Finally, on January 20, 1945, the Union Carbide operators pumped uranium hexafluoride through the first series of completed cascades. The K-25 plant, built at a cost of almost $200 million with the cooperation of three universities, six major industrial firms, and more than fifty thousand workers, was at long last in operation. Now, in the eerie semidarkness of the world's largest building (light entered the two-million-square-foot structure only through a series of tiny windows at the very top of the four-story walls, while the floor space was so enormous that inspectors had to patrol it by motor scooter) the production of semienriched U-235 was finally under way. As winter turned to spring, more and more cascades were put into operation. The fully charged, operated plant emitted a strange, high-pitched buzzing sound.

In April 1945, when Groves brought an awed Secretary of War Stimson for his first visit to a MED installation, the plant was producing a material enriched to 1.1 percent U-235, rich enough to profitably feed hundreds of waiting Calutrons at the Y-12 building. At the end of the tour Stimson, who at seventy-eight was in failing health and who had confided to Groves that he had stayed in office primarily to "devote all my time to this particular project," now found himself "immensely cheered and braced up." The K-25 plant, undoubtedly the greatest of Groves's many gambles, was finally paying off.

Chapter Thirty-Two

"Waiting for a call from on high," wrote Jean O'Leary in the office diary. Indeed, on the morning of April 25, 1944, everyone in Groves's office, even the usually unflappable O'Leary, seemed atypically agitated and full of expectation—everyone, that is, except the boss himself. "They won't call for another half an hour," he told his astonished executive officer. "I'm going out for a haircut."

The "they" to whom Groves so nonchalantly referred was the White House staff of the new President of the United States. Thirteen days before, President Roosevelt, who had led the nation for an unprecedented thirteen years, had died at his Warm Springs, Georgia, retreat. The news had come as a terrible blow to a nation that, love him or not, had grown used to, perhaps even dependent on, his firm leadership and his elegant style.

It must have been a particular shock to Groves. From the time he had approved Groves's quadrupling of the project's budget, Roosevelt, although not actively involved on a day-to-day basis, had been totally committed and consistently supportive. From now on, the MED would have to deal with Harry Truman. It was bad enough, Groves must have thought, that the new President was a nuclear neophyte and an unknown quantity as a leader. Worse, and far more worrisome, was the fact that Truman had a long history of bitter clashes with Groves himself. Before the war, when Groves had been supervising military construction, Truman and his Committee on Military Spending had dogged his every step. Under Truman's leadership, the Committee had continued to nip at the general's ankles during the course of the MED, trying to get him to include Congress in the atomic secret. Groves's early refusals had generated a series of acrimonious disagreements between the general and the senator. In truth, Groves seems to have had little respect for Truman, whom he saw as a petty politician, a product of a semishady Kansas City political machine, and an essentially accidental President.

But accidentally or not, Truman was now in the White House and, from Groves's point of view, a fact of life. On April 25, freshly shorn and shaved, the general made ready to face that fact of life in the flesh. Would the project now lose the support in highest places that had helped keep it alive in the early, doubtful days? Would Truman, either out of ignorance, personal animosity, or political weakness, slow the wheels of the MED just as the desperate pursuit of the bomb was beginning to pay off? Groves had to wonder.

The call from the White House came at noon. Groves rushed to the Pentagon to meet Stimson. To his surprise, General George Marshall, who was expected to join the briefing team, had decided not to come. "Mr. Stimson and I agreed," Groves wrote, "that General Marshall's decision might have been influenced by the possibility that the meeting would be very unpleasant." Marshall had also thought it unwise for Stimson and Groves to appear together in the presence of the White House reporters, so he assigned a lieutenant colonel from his own staff to usher Groves into the President's office through a back door.

While Stimson went into the White House through the front entrance, Groves was led through a series of underground passageways to an office adjacent to the President's. Soon he was summoned into Truman's presence, where he found the Secretary of War already waiting. Truman was reading a short memo that Stimson had prepared. The memo began ominously: "Within four months," it said, "we shall in all probability have completed the most terrible weapon known in human history, one bomb of which could destroy a whole city. . . ."

Stimson interrupted the President to introduce Groves. It was an important moment: from Truman's reaction Groves would be able to get a feel for the President's attitude, both toward him personally and toward the project as a whole. The reaction came at once: Truman brushed aside Stimson's introduction, saying, "I've known General Groves for years." To Groves's great surprise and amusement, he then launched into an impromptu eulogy about the general's outstanding ability. "A typical politician's remark," Groves later sniffed, but undoubtedly Truman's positive attitude left him greatly cheered and more than a little relieved.

Stimson then handed the President a copy of Groves's report on the state of the project, which had been boiled down to some twenty-five pages and distilled into lay language. But the President was impatient. "I don't like reading long reports," he complained. Only after Stimson explained that the report had been condensed "to a degree that we couldn't possibly duplicate verbally" did Truman grudgingly read it. When he had finished, Groves braced himself for the storm of negativity that he expected from his old antagonist. But the President had surprisingly little to say. "I'm all in favor of it" was his only comment. "I hope you'll be successful."

For Groves, the meeting now had the look of triumph. Truman had not only waved aside his former diagreements with the general; he was bestowing on him a renewed presidential seal of approval for the bomb itself. Groves and Stimson, it appeared, could now be assured that Roosevelt's policy of energetic support would continue under the new President. Even more important, it was implicit in Truman's unquestioning approval of Groves's report that the new President would leave the management of the project—and perhaps even the military deployment of the bomb itself—to the knowledgeable professionals. At that juncture that meant the Military Policy Committee, in particular Groves himself.

The meeting was over. But for Groves, making a graceful exit turned out to be an unexpected problem. The general had failed to note the door by which he had been ushered in. Now, turning to Truman in confusion, he said, "Mr. President, how on earth do I get out of here?"

In light of the bitter conflicts that dogged the rest of his tenure as head of the MED, the question might be read as a predictive sign. For now, though, Truman had given Groves the green light to continue planning for the birth of the bomb. But the birth, currently in the hands of the scientific midwives at Los Alamos, was proving slow and difficult, a delivery beset with agonizing labor pains.

Chapter Thirty-Three

They called it "twisting the dragon's tail," the most nervewracking and dangerous of all Los Alamos experiments. Canadian physicist Louis Slotin would arrange a series of uranium slugs into a sort of lopsided cube, leaving a small hole in the center. He would then place a slug of uranium hydride on a system of metal tracks, dropping the slug gingerly but as quickly as possible through the hole. For a split second, if the slug passed through the "tunnel," the entire configuration would become critical, generating some twenty million watts of nuclear energy. If for some reason the slug stuck in the tunnel, the room and everyone in it would be showered with lethal radiation.

Knowing this, nervous physicists in adjoining labs took long hikes in the mountains whenever it was known that Slotin was working. But the brash and excitable Canadian seemed somehow calmed by the experiment, as did his boss. Oppenheimer sometimes made a special point to be there during the exercise, to chat quietly with the young physicist who had become his special favorite.*

Slotin's bizarre experiment was one of many signs that the Los Alamos scientists were beginnning to reach some of their long-sought goals. By "twisting the dragon's tail," Slotin was getting ever more precise figures for critical mass, the sine qua non of atomic bomb research. Over the heated objections of Compton and Nichols, Groves and Oppenheimer had moved Enrico Fermi from Chicago to Los Alamos. There the Italian had built a small reactor, known as the "Water Boiler," by which he was able to verify earlier calculations of the probable critical mass for a

*While performing the experiment after the war, Slotin's screwdriver slipped, allowing the uranium slug to stick in the tunnel. Slotin threw his body over the assembly to shield the six other scientists in the room from the deadly radiation, undoubtedly saving their lives in the process. Slotin himself died a week later in terrible pain.

plutonium bomb. Greatly relieved, Groves could now confidently establish production schedules at Hanford and Oak Ridge, where plutonium and uranium-235 were being pushed out in ever-increasing quantities.

In the Chemistry and Metallurgy Division, two hundred young scientists in coveralls and rubber gloves labored away behind protective walls, trying to purify the Hanford plutonium without actually touching it. The new manmade element was devilishly difficult to work with; it perversely changed through no less than five different states depending on its temperature, and it mercilessly corroded the metal cubicles in which it was melted. Worse, the inhalation of even a tiny amount of the substance could cause lung or bone cancer. Only by holding the plutonium with long, awkward tongs could the work be done at all. Still, the young scientists under Joseph Kennedy and Cyril Smith managed to work through the difficulties, and by the end of the spring of 1945 they were finally purifying plutonium to the nearly perfect specifications necessary for a bomb.

Work on the uranium gun bomb, which had been turned over to Harvard-trained naval commander Francis Birch, was going smoothly. The mechanism, based on existing designs, was straightforward enough, and once U-235 began to arrive in quantity Birch and his team made the minute modifications necessary to eventually produce a finished weapon. With the path toward the uranium bomb cleared and the final specifications set, Birch's division exuded confidence.

If the gun bomb looked like a sure thing, the implosion program continued to seem a desperate and last-minute bad bet. Although they did not say so to the Los Alamos staffers, Groves and Conant privately agreed that they would be lucky if the lab produced an implosion bomb by sometime in late 1945, and even that bomb, they thought, would be low-powered and inefficient.

To bring the implosion program up to speed, Groves, Oppenheimer, and Kistiakowsky set out on a frantic search for more personnel. To consult on the engineering aspects of implosion, Groves brought in Hartley Rowe, an experienced engineer from the United Fruit Company and a long-time friend and associate of Conant's. At the same time, winding down the Met Lab program freed up a number of people for transfer to Los Alamos, most notably the highly respected physicist Samuel Allison.

But initially, Allison's arrival only stirred up new and unneeded conflict in the already troubled implosion division. The Chicago physicist was assigned to head Oppenheimer's new "Cowpuncher Committee" (so named because the director expected it to "ride herd" on implosion), of which Kistiakowsky was also a member. But unlike Kistiakowsky, Allison was a long-standing member of the inner circle of the physics elite. This circle included Fermi, Bethe, Bacher, and the three prestigious "consultants": Rabi, von Neumann, and Bohr. It was an exclusive circle that Kistiakowsky, as a chemist, could never hope to join, no matter how great his talent in his own field. At one point, during an argument in an Administrative Council meeting, Kistiakowsky complained, "You're all ganging up on me because I'm a chemist." Oppenheimer smiled indulgently and said, "No, George, you're an outstanding third-rate physicist."

The tension among the "Cowpunchers" only made it more difficult to solve the implosion bomb's central problem, a problem that had been giving the scientists nightmares since 1943. If the plutonium bomb were to work, the plutonium would have to be made to implode, or collapse in on itself. It would have to do so in a perfectly symmetrical configuration, for anything less than perfection would cause predetonation and result in a flop. John von Neumann, an outgoing Hungarian who had grown up with Eugene Wigner and who was one of only a handful of physicists whom colleagues unhesitatingly called "genius," had earlier become interested in explosive "lenses"—arrangements of explosives shaped in such a way that the shock waves produced by a detonation would be distributed absolutely evenly over the spherical surface of the plutonium core and hit the surface at exactly the same microsecond, causing the plutonium to implode in perfect symmetry.

Von Neumann's enthusiasm spurred other scientists—including Kistiakowsky himself and Englishmen Rudolf Peirls and James Tuck—to contribute, and soon designs for explosive lenses proliferated like rabbits. By now it was February 1945, the month Groves had originally promised an implosion bomb would be ready. The general was growing impatient with the design debates, which seemed endless to him. Under increasing pressure from Groves, Oppenheimer met with Allison, Peirls, and Cal Tech's Charles Lauritsen on February 17 to choose one design over all the others. But although the scientists debated for over four hours, they were unable to come to a decision. Dissatisfied with what seemed to be dangerous vacillation on the part of the scientists, Groves turned on the pressure, putting in a pointed personal appearance at Los Alamos two weeks later. Finally, as the general sat figuratively tapping his fingers in front of them, Oppenheimer and his men were forced to make up their minds. They adopted Tuck's scheme for the explosive lenses and finally froze the design of the implosion bomb.

With the efforts of Kistiakowsky and Robert Bacher's Gadget Division now focused on one design, Tuck's lenses were tested to the tune of rollicking explosions that shook the sides of Little Pajarito Canyon. Standing behind concrete bunkers and protected by bulletproof glass, technicians took thousands of photos of the explosions, using an amazing new "sweeping image" camera invented by the Instrumentation Group's Julian Mack. This camera could shoot at the unheard-of shutter speed of one one-one-hundred-millionth of a second. By mid-April, Mack's photos were showing a shock wave that was finally as symmetrical as the theoreticians had demanded. At the same time, Groves and Sir James Chadwick were prodding the Chrysler Corporation in Detroit to produce molds that would give the lenses precisely the required shape.

Speed was the word of the day—speed, speed, and more speed—as it had been ever since Groves took command. In Washington and in the Philippines, preparations were being made for a massive troop invasion of the Japanese mainland, an invasion that Groves fervently hoped to avoid by using the new weapon. The uranium gunbomb was almost certain to work, but it was a long-standing military principle that no new weapon should be used in isolation. Since a second uranium bomb was not expected to be ready before the fall of 1945, the necessary back-up would have to be an implosion bomb.

But that bomb, containing as it did a virtual catalogue of radically new and uncertain technologies, remained an unknown. Would it work? Groves and the scientists wondered. Only a test would tell.

Chapter Thirty-Four

Just before dawn on May 7, 1945, the sky above the New Mexico desert was suddenly illuminated by a brilliant flash of light, a glowing orange ball that could even be seen in Alamagordo, some sixty miles away. The angry fireball was the result of two hundred thousand pounds of dynamite; it was the largest such conflagration ever to be caught in the act and measured by scientific instruments. Yet this explosion, carefully planned and executed by a Los Alamos team under Harvard's Kenneth Bainbridge, was only a dress rehearsal for a much larger test that was already in the planning stages. That second test, which Oppenheimer had dubbed Trinity, would make this earlier one look like a Fourth of July firecracker. For if Bethe and his theoreticians were right, the implosion bomb would go off with an explosive force equivalent to that of five thousand tons of TNT—fifty times more powerful than the May shot and by far the most powerful manmade bang in history.

The test had been on the drawing boards since the spring of 1944, when it became obvious that a bomb based on implosion would be so radically innovative that it would simply have to be tested. Soon afterward, a squad of Los Alamos scientists and soldiers set out in search of a site big enough and isolated enough to contain the mighty bomb. At first the team concentrated their search on the area around Los Alamos, but Groves quickly ruled that out as too dangerous and too near the main body of scientists, who, he said, "in accordance with good academic custom would be trying to interfere with ideas of their own."

Oppenheimer and Bainbridge then undertook odysseys throughout the West to find an alternative. Maps were so scarce that Groves had to scrounge everything from grazing survey maps to old prospectors' charts. Finally, after trekking through most of New Mexico by jeep, Bainbridge found a site that seemed perfect, an area in the desert some two hundred miles south of Los Alamos. The tract, with its bake-oven heat and its waterless expanse of bleached white desert, had been given an eerily prescient name by the early Spanish explorers: Jornada del Muerto, they had called it—the Journey of Death.

On paper, the site seemed to fit all Groves's criteria. It was isolated (the closest sizable city was El Paso, almost a hundred miles away), yet close enough to Los Alamos to make the transportation of men and equipment a relatively easy task. But once the Manhattan District began to move in on the Jornada del Muerto, all sorts of unexpected problems cropped up. For some reason, no money for construction came from the MED, so that Colonel Rube Cole of the Army Corps of Engineers office in Albuquerque had to "rob" the money from local flood-control funds and hope that a congressional act would clear him at some future date. Then it was discovered that the entire water supply consisted of two small windmills that pumped a munificent trickle of about one quart per minute. Worse, the McDonald family, who owned the only ranch on the site and supposedly had been evacuated, suddenly reappeared to brand their cattle and mend fences; and the McDonalds, observed one officer dryly, were "known for a few notches on their guns."

But the Army managed to reevacuate the McDonalds without bloodshed, and men and materials soon began to pour into the Trinity site. In essence, the job was to build an entirely new laboratory, with testing facilities and accommodations for two hundred men, in the sandy waste. To do so, Cole tore down portable barracks and buildings in Albuquerque, trucked them 115 miles, and reassembled them at Trinity. Twenty miles of new blacktop road were built, and two hundred miles of telephone line installed. Huge generators were brought in to supply electricity, and new electric pumps increased the water output to a more reasonable twenty gallons per minute. (Still, the water was so brackish and laden with gypsum that the soldiers' skins became coated with semipermanent mineral crusts. They could only wash them off by spending hours of weekend free time under hot showers at the Albuquerque Hilton.) All in all, at least twenty buildings were erected, yet the total construction cost under Groves's frugal eye was a bargain-basement $110,000.

As the pace of construction grew more frantic, scientists at Los Alamos were buffeted by fortunes good and bad until it seemed to everyone that the project had turned into an emotional roller-coaster ride. In April, things looked very good indeed. Mack's photos showed that the explosive lenses were generating symmetrical shock waves, and the ubiquitous Luis Alvarez, who sweated over his work in an office shared with Neddermeyer and Kistiakowsky, had perfected a design for the bomb's electrical detonating circuits.

But in May the program took a sudden and severe turn for the worse. Tests on the first detonators showed an alarming failure rate, failures that no one could explain. Contractors supplying the firing circuits and the molds for the explosive lenses were running far behind schedule, meaning that the testing of these crucial components would be at best perfunctory. In June there was some improvement; the detonator problems were corrected and the lens molds finally began to arrive. Even more cheering, the experimentalists at long last established a final figure for critical mass in plutonium. By June 4, Oppenheimer could finally call Jean O'Leary in Washington to tell her that the bomb core—"the little thing that goes in the middle of the Fat Man," as he called it—had been made and that it "looked quite good."

Still, the May delays had caused a real setback. The Trinity test, originally scheduled for the Fourth of July, had to be postponed to the sixteenth. It had been calculated that the war in the Pacific was costing a thousand American lives a day; whether or not the Los Alamos scientists were aware of this figure, delays in the Trinity test were felt to be not only disappointing but potentially mortal. This in turn helped inspire the Los Alamos scientists on to increasingly frantic activity yet also plunged many of them into deep, private gloom.

No one was more affected by these swings in scientific fortune than Oppenheimer himself. Never a robust figure in the first place, the anxiety and the crushing pressure now whittled him down still further. On long walks with Robert Bacher he poured out his fears and uncertainties, saying that he no longer felt capable of steering the Los Alamos effort. He had lost thirty pounds, which left him an emaciated 115, and his suits hung on his gaunt frame like old clothes on a scarecrow. A chain-smoker and a former consumptive (he had suffered a long bout of tuberculosis as a youth), he now coughed incessantly. To make matters worse, he somehow contracted chicken pox.

Groves watched Oppenheimer's deterioration with increasing concern. He knew that the director was not the sturdiest of individuals, either physically or emotionally, but he could not afford the loss of time and morale if Oppenheimer were to break down completely. At least partially to shore up the physicist's sagging psyche, Groves asked I.I. Rabi, Oppenheimer's long-time friend, to move to Los Alamos for the duration. Rabi gladly agreed.

At the same time, Groves brought Oppenheimer's younger brother Frank—himself a capable physicist—from Berkeley to provide more emotional support. From a security point of view this move raised eyebrows, for both Frank Oppenheimer and his wife Jackie were known to have been members of the Communist Party. Still, Groves thought, Frank's potential usefulness to his brother in this time of crisis greatly outweighed any security risks his presence might have created. (In fact, it created none. Frank Oppenheimer made valuable contributions not only to his brother's state of mind but also to preparations for the test itself.)

Meanwhile, construction and preparation at Trinity moved relentlessly forward, accelerated by Groves's constant pressure for more speed. The desert sprouted a set of odd new blooms as wires were strung over towering yucca plants and dials and gauges of every description peeked out from under creosote bushes. At Ground Zero, a hundred-foot steel tower was erected with a small metal shed on top, where the bomb itself would rest until detonation. Bainbridge and his men bustled about the desert in jeeps, supervising the installation and testing of thousands of instruments as sweat poured down their faces from the merciless summer sun. At the same time, Deke Parsons and Luis Alvarez buzzed the area in a B-29 and circled the tower at Ground Zero, practicing the dangerous airborne drop of instruments at the exact moment of the blast.

During the first week in July, as the date for the test drew ever closer, a new set of crises arose. The latest explosive lens molds shipped from Detroit were found to be cracked and pitted—all but useless for the fine tolerances demanded by the implosion bomb. Simultaneously, a mysterious rash of blisters broke out on the surface of the plutonium hemispheres that made up the bomb's core. The combination of these unforeseen problems now threatened to make hash of the July 16 test.

Desperately Kistiakowsky and his group attacked the cracked lens molds with tweezers and dental scrapers, working frantically to grind out the pits and bubbles. Their eleventh-hour workload was effectively doubled when Oppenheimer insisted on fabricating a second, dummy bomb to be detonated at Los Alamos in anticipation of the final Trinity test. Meanwhile, Bacher's Gadget Division failed in their efforts to eradicate the blisters on the plutonium hemispheres by filing them down. Finally they flung themselves into a last-ditch attempt to fill in the blisters with powdered gold.

The new crises threw the lab into turmoil, reflected in growing pessimism about the implosion bomb's chances for success. For the last two years the scientists' estimates on the bomb's explosive force had ranged between five and twenty thousand tons of TNT. Now, however, the top Los Alamos scientists formed a betting pool on the eventual yield of the Trinity bomb, and only Edward Teller (forty-five thousand tons) and Hans Bethe (eight thousand tons) remained that optimistic. Kistiakowsky shook his head and hopefully guessed fourteen hundred tons. Oppenheimer's bet was a mere three hundred tons; Louis Slotin's was only two tons. And Harvard's Norman Ramsey made a bet that many Los Alamites considered the most sensible of all: he guessed zero.

Oppenheimer's miserly estimate reflected his growing pessimism. Frantically, he called Groves on July 2 to plead for a postponement of the test in the face of the new crises. But Groves would not be moved. President Truman would soon be embarking for a Big Three conference with Churchill and Stalin at Potsdam, and Stimson was insisting that the bomb be tested before the conference was over so that the President would have unique and powerful leverage to bring to bear in his negotiations with the truculent Stalin, whose troops were at that very moment ominously ensconced in Eastern Europe. The Potsdam conference was scheduled to begin on July 15, and Truman had to have his news before it broke up a few weeks later. There would be no postponement of the test date, Groves told Oppenheimer firmly.

In Washington, Groves was busy making his own final preparations for the test. To devise a code for reporting the news back to his office, he turned to the current baseball standings. *Cincinnati Reds* would mean "utter failure"; *Brooklyn Dodgers*, "as expected"; and *New York Yankees* would signify "success beyond imagination." He conferred with *New York Times* reporter William Laurence—a short, battered-looking man whose broken nose and prizefighter's demeanor belied his standing as a Pulitzer Prize–winning journalist—and together they developed a list of possible press releases that would explain the explosion away as an accident in an Army munitions dump. He sent his old colleague General Thomas Farrell to Trinity as a sort of alter ego to oversee the operation. (Farrell, a witty Irishman, had been chosen as Groves's deputy when Stimson had grown concerned about the general's irreplaceability.) Stafford Warren was ordered to send out a team of fifty psychiatrists to minister to any scientists whose nerves seemed about to crack. At the same time Groves constrained the eager Bush, Conant, and Tolman, who wanted to go out to Los Alamos early to observe the Trinity preparations. Instead, Groves took only Bush in hand; on July 11 they set out for a tour of the project's West Coast facilities. Conant and Tolman would join them later.

"The worst thing anybody can do," Groves told them, "is to go out there and look down the throats of the people who are trying to get their jobs done at the last minute."

Chapter Thirty-Five

On July 12, 1945, physicist Phillip Morrison entered a sealed and guarded vault in the Omega building at Los Alamos, near where Louis Slotin had so nervelessly "twisted the dragon's tail." As a guard and a radiation specialist watched, Morrison removed the "dragon" itself: the several polished pieces of the plutonium core. He put the separate pieces—vaguely warm from their own internal radiation—into sealed suitcases. He then set the suitcases next to him on the back seat of an Army sedan. Along with two escort cars filled with MED security men and members of the bomb's assembly team, he set out for Trinity, five hours away. The bomb was at last on its way to what everyone hoped would be a fiery debut.

The next morning was Friday the Thirteenth, a date specifically chosen by the unsuperstitious Kistiakowsky for the bomb's assembly. At nine o'clock in a sterilized room in the McDonald ranch house, eight physicists dressed in white surgical coats gathered around a table. The pieces of the bomb's core had been laid out on plain brown wrapping paper. Geiger counters clicked ominously in the background, while just outside several jeeps sat with their motors idling, waiting to speed the physicists away in case of a dangerous accident. In the breathless atmosphere, Oppenheimer fidgeted nervously about, walking in and out of the room, until his jitters began to distract the men inside. Finally, Robert Bacher and Marshall Holloway insisted gently but firmly that he leave.

One by one, over six excruciating hours, the physicists fit the pieces of the core together. Cyril Smith—tall, cool, and seemingly detached— found a series of tiny pits in the plutonium hemispheres and nonchalantly plugged these potentially disastrous imperfections with Kleenex. Finally Louis Slotin maneuvered the two hemispheres until they were almost touching. Calmly he inserted the bomb's initiator in between the two hemispheres, then closed them quickly together. The Geiger counters fairly screamed in the background. The core, or "plug" as the scientists called it, was complete, ready for insertion into the body of the bomb itself.

Under the tower at Ground Zero, Kistiakowsky and his men greeted the assembly team as they arrived from the ranch house. In a tent at the base of the tower, the shell of the bomb assembly lay waiting. The eighty-pound plug was placed on a hoist, then lowered slowly into the bomb. Sand devils whipped the tent, and sweat poured down the men's faces. Suddenly the plug stuck. Amid cursing and recriminations, a hurried conference ensued among Bacher, Holloway, Morrison, and Kistiakowsky. The four men decided that the core must have expanded slightly with the heat; inside the assembly it would cool down, contract, and eventually slip into place. About five minutes later the scientists tried again. They were right: the slightly cooled plug now clicked smoothly into the assembly.

Everyone sighed in relief, and the assembled bomb began its hundred-foot trip up the hoist to the top of the tower. About halfway up, one of the "skates" that moved the hoist suddenly broke and came clattering down. There was a collective gasp as the billion-dollar bomb swung loose and rocked back and forth on its cable. Although a stack of mattresses had been piled at the bottom of the hoist to catch the bomb if it fell, no one wanted to test those mattresses. Soldiers clambered up the tower and quickly fixed the errant skate. Without further trouble the bomb rose to the top of the tower and into its metal shed, where Army engineers Leo Jercinovic and Arthur Machen strapped it into the steel cradle that was its natal bed. Later Donald Hornig, a twenty-five-year-old physicist from the University of Michigan, climbed the tower and sat in the shed for hours, reading the *Desert Island Decameron* and calmly baby-sitting the infant through a tremendous thunderstorm.

Ironically, the MED team, which had labored mightily for three years to try to control one of the basic forces of nature, now found itself dependent on the one natural force that no one could control: the weather. It was generally agreed that the bomb could not be ignited in the rain, because rainfall might wash radioactive dust particles back down to the ground; worse, the high winds associated with a rainstorm could sweep a radioactive cloud across the desert to El Paso or even as far as Amarillo. To avoid this, the wind direction on the day of the test would have to be south so that any radioactive cloud would be carried over a relatively narrow band of desert to the north of El Paso. For this risky trick Groves found a picturesque name: "threading the needle."

To monitor the all-important weather, the test planners set up an elaborate, state-of-the-art meteorological station in one of the cattle sheds on the McDonald ranch, a station manned by some of the same Army weathermen who had watched the skies over Normandy on D-Day. But inexplicably, no one—not even Groves—seems to have thought much about the qualifications of the man in charge. Groves had passed the job of selecting someone to supervise the crucial weather operations to a Professor Krick at Cal Tech, and Krick, who was not informed about the nature of the assignment, selected his student Jack Hubbard. But Hubbard, it was later determined, was only auditing classes; he had not met the academic requirements to formally enter the university. "Of all the meteorologists I could think of," said General B.G. Holzman, an Army weatherman on the Trinity staff, "Hubbard was probably one of the least qualified for such an important operation."

On the morning of the fifteenth, Hubbard cheerfully predicted that the sixteenth would be "quite suitable" for the bomb test. He called for cloudiness during the day, with scattered afternoon showers ending after the sun went down. But the sunset brought absolutely no respite from the "scattered afternoon showers"; in fact, it began to rain even harder. Confronted about his own obvious error in perhaps one of the most important weather predictions in history, Hubbard, in Holzman's words, "became quite frantic. He was so nervous and distraught that he was actually worrying all the key people involved in the shot."

"When it started to rain," said physicist Joseph Hirschfelder, a Bainbridge assistant who was one of those key people, "Hubbard locked himself in his room and prayed."

Chapter Thirty-Six

In the meantime, Groves, Vannevar Bush, and James Conant had taken off from Pasadena and were heading for Los Alamos and the Trinity showdown. (On landing in Pasadena, Groves's plane had narrowly missed a set of high-tension wires and had limped in to land amid a welter of waiting fire trucks and ambulances.) But from the moment of his arrival in Albuquerque, the general found nothing but confusion. At the airport and at the Albuquerque Hilton he saw scientists everywhere, chatting casually in large and conspicuous groups. Horrified, he ordered them to disperse in pairs. Thus Nobel Prize winner Ernest Lawrence and Pulitzer Prize winner William Laurence ignominiously cooled their heels all afternoon at a local hamburger stand.

The general found the situation at the Trinity site little better when his black Buick pulled in just after sundown. Rain was still falling in a disturbingly steady drizzle, and the scientists' nerves, frayed by weeks of frantic and nearly sleepless activity, were scraped raw. "Oppenheimer," Groves later recalled, "was the center of a large group of excited scientists, many of whom were urging that the test be called off. I was never more reminded of a high-school football team than I was at that period, with everybody trying to talk at one time and nobody really knowing what they were doing. I broke Oppenheimer loose from this group and took him into his office, where matters could be discussed calmly. . . ."

When they reached the privacy of Oppenheimer's office, Groves called in Hubbard, Holzman, and the Army meteorologists. But Hubbard was so agitated by his faulty prediction that Groves found him useless.* After sounding Holzman for his advice, he summarily dismissed Hubbard

*Years later, Hubbard was suspended from a teaching post at San Francisco State University when he was alleged to have written threatening letters, under an assumed name, to other faculty members.

and all the weathermen. "From that time on," Groves said, "I did my own weather predicting."

Alone together as they had been so often during the previous two years, Groves and Oppenheimer discussed postponing the test. Oppenheimer relayed Bainbridge's concern about the morale of the Trinity team: any postponement, he said, would have such a deflating effect that it would take them a week, if not longer, to recover. Groves pointed out that all the test's thousands of electrical connections would get soaked through if allowed to sit out in the rain, increasing the chances of a misfire. But by far the most important factor, Groves said, was the Big Three conference in Potsdam. "The situation there was such," he said, "that we simply could not delay if it was at all possible to go on." Given even the slightest break in the weather, Groves and Oppenheimer decided that the test would go forward.

The decision made, Groves urged Oppenheimer to get some sleep. It was then nine o'clock in the evening; the two men would be awakened at midnight to review the situation. But while Oppenheimer coughed and twisted in his bed, unable to relax, Groves fell quickly and soundly asleep, oblivious to the sound of his tent flaps slapping in the violent wind.

At midnight the two leaders were roused and taken to the Base Camp mess hall, where the order of the evening was steaming coffee and lurid conversation. Fermi was entertaining a table of scientists—and incidentally frightening the wits out of a group of nearby soldiers—by postulating the most macabre of the many Los Alamos betting pools. Would the ignition of the bomb, he mused aloud, set the earth's whole atmosphere on fire, or would it merely ignite the air over New Mexico? Groves was disturbed at first by this eleventh-hour black humor, but he soon put it down as an honest, if slightly perverse, attempt on Fermi's part to lighten the collective mood.

But Oppenheimer was not to be calmed. Ghostly and agitated, he stalked the mess hall smoking cigarette after cigarette while a cacophony of conflicting advice swirled around him. Groves, watching keenly from the other side of the room, soon became concerned about the director's mental state and finally pried him loose from the din. Together the two men drove through the darkness and the drizzle to the control center, which, at ten thousand yards from the bomb tower itself, was the closest permissible observation point. Just after they arrived, the skies cracked and opened into what one officer called "the damnedest cloudburst and display of lightning I had ever seen." But despite the driving rain, the atmosphere in the concrete and steel bunker was more terse and businesslike than that at Base Camp. "Although there was an air of excitement at the dugout,"

Groves said, "there was a minimum of conflicting advice and opinions" as Bainbridge and his team went briskly about final preparations for the test.

For the next few hours Groves made the overwrought Oppenheimer his private charge. "He was in the position of the quarterback calling signals," the general said, "and I wanted him to be as calm as possible. So I stayed right with him and we talked to each other. We'd go outside; we'd look up at the clouds and try to find new stars. Each time I would say that I saw one more." Still, the rain continued to pour down. The test, which had already been postponed until 4:00 A.M., was again postponed to 5:00 and then to 5:30—the last possible minute before the sun would rise and people in surrounding towns would begin to wake up, thus ruining the chances for keeping the test and the explosion secret.

At 4:00 the rain at last began to let up. Forty-five minutes later came the crucial weather report: "Winds aloft very light . . . surface calm . . . conditions holding for the next two hours." Bainbridge consulted by phone with Oppenheimer and Groves. Should the test go on? One dissenting voice would mean postponement. But all agreed. The shot would take place at 5:30, as scheduled.

The decision made and out of their hands, Groves and Oppenheimer separated. The general returned to his allotted observation spot at Base Camp, where he joined Bush and Conant. Twenty miles away, on the crest of Compania Hill, a group of some thirty scientists—including Ernest Lawrence, Joseph Kennedy, and Charles Thomas—and reporter William Laurence shook off their brief slumber and left their tents in anticipation of the shot. Some of their preparations were slightly bizarre: their special glasses—made in Los Alamos machine shops in the form of aluminum "masks" with smoked-glass eyepieces—made them look like robots from hell. Heightening the absurdity was Edward Teller's suntan lotion to protect the group from ultraviolet radiation, now applied in pitch darkness.

At 5:00, loudspeakers throughout the Trinity site suddenly began to blare a rousing rendition of "The Star-Spangled Banner"—the signal that the final countdown had begun. At the control center, physicist Joseph McKibben, exhausted and trembling, threw the switch that activated the automatic firing mechanism. Sam Allison grasped a microphone and droned out the countdown in a steady, toneless voice that belied his own excitement. "The scene was dramatic beyond words," said General Farrell, whom Groves had stationed at the center. "It can safely be said that almost everyone present was praying." Growing tenser as the seconds ticked off, Oppenheimer held on to a post to steady himself.

With two minutes to go, Groves, Conant, and Bush lay down in one of the Base Camp observation trenches, their faces turned away from the direction of the shot. Conant remarked dryly that he had never known seconds could last so long. For his part, Groves had come to the most intensely dramatic moment in his life. Would the bomb work? Would the three years' hard labor, the two billion dollars, and the vast and sprawling facilities of the MED now pay off in the greatest manmade explosion the world had ever seen? Or would the bomb be a hopeless dud, leaving the project a laughingstock and Groves himself to face what he was already calling "the greatest congressional investigation of all time"?

"As we lay on the ground," Groves later recalled, "the quiet grew more intense. I thought only of what I would do if the countdown got to zero and nothing happened."

With ten seconds to go, a gong sounded over the public address system. Allison continued to intone the countdown, his voice backed by the incongruously dreamy waltz from Tchaikovsky's "Serenade for Strings." As he neared zero, it suddenly occurred to him that the explosion—if in fact there was an explosion—might set up an electrical discharge that would come streaming through his microphone. Finally, at the last possible instant, he flung the microphone from him and screamed, "*Zero!*"

Chapter Thirty-Seven

The first thing to hit everyone was the light, "a searing light," Farrell later wrote, "with an intensity many times that of the midday sun." Groves found it so intense that it came "right through my hands, right through my closed eyelids." Bethe was reminded of "a giant magnesium flare." Farrell marveled at the colors: "golden, purple, violet, gray, and blue. It lighted every peak, crevice, and ridge of the nearby mountain range," he wrote, "with a clarity and beauty that cannot be described. . . ."

Groves immediately turned over and stood up, covering his face with the special welder's mask. He saw the fireball rise—"It was shaped just like a derby hat," he remembered—then turn into the roiling mushroom cloud that has since come to symbolize the violent new age. The fireball in all its infernal majesty seemed as if it would rise and spread forever. "My God!" General Farrell thought in a sudden panic as the cloud reached forty thousand feet and flattened threateningly across the sky. "The longhairs have let it get away from them!"

Farrell was not the only one whose first thoughts were of apocalypse, of forces far greater than man. Oppenheimer recalled a verse from the Hindu Bhagavad Gita, which ended with the line, "I am become death, the destroyer of worlds." Among the scientists on Compania Hill, Ernest Lawrence said, "The grand, almost cataclysmic proportion of the explosion produced a hushed murmuring bordering on reverence." But perhaps the most effusively awed was *The New York Times*'s William Laurence. "It was as if the earth had opened and the skies had split," he wrote. "One felt as though he had been privileged to witness the Birth of the World—to be present at the moment of Creation when the Lord said: 'Let there be light.'"

The witnesses had a full minute and a half for silent contemplation, for despite the tremendous visual force of a light far brighter than any of them had ever seen, the desert remained eerily quiet. Then, after a pause so long that some may have wondered if it was in fact some massive optical

illusion that they were seeing, came the sound of the blast's shock wave—
"a long rumble," as one physicist put it, "like heavy traffic far away." Soon
the Jornada del Muerto was rocked by the bomb's artificial thunder. "It was
astonishing," recalled Frank Oppenheimer. "It just echoed back and
forth, back and forth. It never seemed to stop."

When the shock wave finally hit, Kistiakowsky was knocked off his
feet and bowled over into the mud. In the unearthly, hurricane "wind,"
Enrico Fermi somehow managed to stand up and let fall from his hands a
bunch of torn scraps of paper, an impromptu experiment to estimate the
bomb's force. As the wave blasted the paper from its downward path and
sent it traveling horizontally through the air, Fermi noted the distance the
paper had traveled and made a hurried calculation: about twenty thousand
tons, he thought—far greater than most of the scientists had predicted.

The blast was indeed stupendous. It tore the tower from its foundation, twisted and ripped it apart, and parboiled the heavy steel until it
turned to vapor and disappeared. In the tower's place was nothing but a
four-hundred-foot crater, in which the sand was fused by the bomb's
tremendous heat into a sort of green, volcanic glass. At a thousand yards
the first set of instruments and their shelters had been completely
destroyed, to the anguish of the scientists who had planned and planted
them so carefully. Several miles away, in nearby Old Bingham, the shock
wave tore the sheets off sleeping citizens. A rancher near Alamagordo
"thought a plane had crashed in my yard." The light was seen in Amarillo,
and the shock wave was felt in El Paso, some hundred miles to the
southeast. On the Arizona–New Mexico state line, 150 miles away, one
witness "saw the sun come up and go down again."*

But none of this was known until later in the day. In the immediate
aftermath of the shock wave, scientists and soldiers alike, their long and
bitter conflict forgotten in the triumph of the moment, broke into wild
celebration. From Base Camp to Compania Hill, a symphony of cheers
filled the air and spilled through the intercom system. At the control
center someone started a snake dance, and soon everyone in the room
joined in, twisting their way through the instruments, joined hand to waist.
Even the taciturn Sir James Chadwick was stripped of his lifelong British

*The cover-up press release drawn by William Laurence—"An ammunition magazine
containing high explosives and pyrotechnics exploded early today in a remote area of the
Alamagordo air base reservation"—effectively quieted most of the resulting rumors. But it
did not fool the DuPont people at Hanford, who quickly sent their congratulations. "This is
the first time," they said with tongue in cheek, "we've heard of the Army storing high
explosives and pyrotechnics in the same magazine."

reserve. "It worked, my God!" he cried, leaping into the air. "The damn thing worked!"

One of the few to retain his composure was Groves himself. The general simply reached over to Conant and Bush and quietly shook hands. Unexcited even in this most electric of moments, the general was amused by the ecstatic reactions of the scientists, who, he said, "reminded me of an underdog team that has just won the big game in the final minute." But he was quick to realize that "to these men it meant even more than it did to me. To me it spelled the end of the war. To them it spelled the ushering in of a new age, something they had heard about from the time they first became physics students."

Groves's own reactions, consistent with his deep-rooted practicality, were more sober. First and foremost, the success of the test brought a feeling of immense relief. "I felt like Blondin crossing Niagara Falls on a tightrope," he later said. "Only for me the tightrope had been three years long." The strength of the blast led him to superimpose the results of this handiwork on an earlier achievement: "I no longer consider the Pentagon," he wrote to Stimson, "a safe shelter from such a bomb."

His own reactions aside, Groves moved quickly to get the news to Washington. A half hour after the blast he was on the phone to Jean O'Leary, giving her the "New York Yankee" signal that the test had been wildly successful. In another code, O'Leary relayed the news to Stimson at Potsdam: "Operated on this morning. Diagnosis not complete but results seem satisfactory and already exceed expectations. Local press releases necessary as interest extends for a great distance. Dr. Groves pleased. . . ."

That night, in her Arlington, Virginia, apartment, Jean O'Leary threw a quiet cocktail party for the office staff. With the exception of Groves, Farrell, and Robert Furman, nearly everyone came. For most of the guests, it was simply another of O'Leary's efforts to maintain the close-knit togetherness that had developed among most of Groves's staff. Because of the general's intraoffice security regulations, only a half-dozen of the staffers knew what they were celebrating.

But to Groves all such celebration was premature. He knew full well that even though the test represented a signal and astonishing success from the technical standpoint, the real and ultimate goal had yet to be achieved. His realization was evident when, immediately after the blast, General Farrell came to him and announced, "The war is over."

"Yes," Groves replied, "as soon as we drop two of these on Japan."

Chapter Thirty-Eight

Captain Robert Lewis cranked the B-29's engines up to 2,300 RPM, then released the brakes. The brand-new bomber, the biggest and best the Air Force had to offer, taxied smoothly down the runway. When it reached ninety-five miles per hour, Lewis lifted it gently into the air, then into a long, steady climb. Below him the salt flats of the western Utah desert gleamed whitely in the morning sun.

Lewis quickly took the plane to thirty thousand feet, then angled off to the southwest, heading for a bombing range near California's Salton Sea. Lewis's instructions were to drop a dummy bomb, which he and his crewmates had nicknamed "The Blockbuster," from thirty thousand feet into a seven-hundred-foot circle on the northern edge of the briny lake. Once the bomb was released, Lewis was to plunge immediately into an almost impossibly steep, 155-degree diving turn. "Keep your nose down," his commander had warned him, "and get the hell out of the area as fast as you can."

Lewis was a cocky Brooklynite, an excitable street fighter who was considered a problem on the ground; he had once absconded with one of the wing's B-29s just to attend a friend's wedding on the East Coast. But he was a brilliant pilot in the air. Aggressively sure of himself, he had been miffed when his commander, Colonel Paul Tibbetts, had categorically refused to explain the reason for the strange maneuver. But, Lewis thought, he was lucky that Tibbetts hadn't court-martialed him for his earlier escapade with the "borrowed" B-29. Shrugging off his irritation, he homed in on the barely visible circle that was his target. Soon bombardier Thomas Ferebee came on the intercom to say that he had the target in sight. A few moments later came Ferebee's terse announcement: "Bombs away." Then: "Correction—*bomb* away."

The Blockbuster fell from the plane, spiraling unerringly toward a dead-center hit on the target below. At the same time, Lewis threw the

B-29 into a violent, diving bank that sent the plane bucking through the air like Pegasus gone mad. But he performed the maneuver exactly as Tibbetts had described.

On the ground, Tibbetts watched attentively while a scientist calculated the distance the plane had traveled between the moment of release and the dummy bomb's "explosion." Tibbetts had excellent reason to be attentive: J. Robert Oppenheimer, the director of the lab where the real bomb was being put together, had told him that the massive shock wave from the nuclear blast might destroy the aircraft that dropped the bomb. "I can give you no guarantee," Oppenheimer had said tersely, "that you will survive." Now Tibbetts turned to the scientist beside him, who had just finished calculating the distance traveled by Lewis's plane: seven miles. That was enough, one of the Los Alamos scientists had told him, for the plane to safely escape the bomb's shock wave.

But Tibbetts's momentary sense of relief was soon chilled by the scientist who stood beside him. "Seven miles, twenty miles, fifty miles." The man shrugged. "There's no way of telling what a safe distance is until we've dropped a real atomic bomb."

Lewis's practice run had been envisioned as early as the spring of 1944, when Groves paid a call at the Pentagon office of Army Air Force chief General H. H. "Hap" Arnold. It was time, Groves told the general, that a crew for dropping the bomb ("the most perfectly trained crew that could be put together," as Groves put it) was organized and educated—even though at that point there was no assurance that the bomb would actually work. Still, Groves told Arnold, "the bomb could be ready by March 1945. We want that crew ready, sitting and waiting when we finally get it."

Arnold responded vigorously. A bomber squadron, the 393rd, was just coming out of training in Nebraska; it had the highest collective marks yet seen during the war. That group, Arnold said, would become the bomb's delivery men. In addition, he would provide the squadron with twenty-eight spanking-new B-29s—the only American plane, so Deke Parsons and his Los Alamos ordnance section had determined, capable of being modified to carry the bomb. Groves had not expected such generosity, but Arnold, who was actually skeptical about the bomb's possibilities, was merely keeping himself covered. "If anything goes wrong with this project now," he told Groves, "it won't be the Air Force's fault."

His die firmly cast in support of the MED, Arnold went looking for the best pilot he could find to command the elite group. His eye came to rest on Colonel Paul Tibbetts, a highly regarded flier who had taken the first B-17 across the English channel and had led the first American air raid on North Africa. Although introverted almost to the point of aloof-ness—his exclusive devotion to flying was known to be placing a considerable strain on his marriage—Tibbetts had been in charge of the testing program for the B-29 Superfortress and knew the plane as well as any man alive. Here, Arnold thought, was the perfect choice.

Groves was not so sure. He personally preferred Colonel Roscoe C. Wilson, an Army Air Corps officer with whom he had worked in the past. But Wilson had no combat flying experience, and Groves did not yet have the leverage to force his personal choice on the Air Force. Tibbetts took command, but not without considerable strain in his relationship with Groves.

As a training site, the general chose an airfield near Wendover, Utah—an isolated, barren patch of desert that Tibbetts characterized as "the end of the world: perfect." His men could not have agreed less. One hundred and twenty-five miles from Salt Lake City, Wendover was suffocated by heat and dust and ridden with rats, snakes, and bad water. But for the boisterous crew, there were certain compensations. The Nevada state line was only a few miles away, and that meant slot machines, card tables, and affordable women. (Venereal disease swept through the crew during their second month of training.) The frustrated fliers, their energies bottled by Tibbetts's demanding schedules, found that the commander took their spare-time fist fights, gambling losses, and skir-mishes with civilian law all in stride. And, they found, the mere mention of the training operation's code name—"Silverplate"—could bring fresh fish from Miami or San Francisco and melt the resistance of even the sternest MP.

All through the winter and spring of 1944–45, the 255 officers and 1,542 enlisted men who made up the newly christened 509th Composite Group (including some three hundred MED "creeps" who infiltrated the group under Lansdale's orders) flew their mock missions and practiced their curious maneuvers. With the lone exception of Tibbetts, no one knew precisely what it was all about. ("Don't ask what the job is," Tibbetts had told the men at their first group meeting. "Do what you are told, when you're told, and you'll get along fine.") But no one could stop the men from indulging in some intramural speculation. One pilot thought they would be sent to Germany to knock down Nazi V-2 rockets. Others had brought nylons and cigarettes to give to the French girls whom their secret European mission was sure to liberate. Soon enough, though, it became common knowledge that the group was going to hit Japan with "a very big bomb." Expectations, and with them tensions, began to rise.

In the meantime Groves pressed General Marshall to plan the military aspects of the drop itself. Groves had assumed that these plans would be made under Marshall's supervision by the Operations Planning Division of the War Department's general staff. But Marshall had other ideas. "Is there any reason," the Chief of Staff asked Groves, "why you can't see to that yourself?" Shocked and surprised—"General Marshall," said one Groves secretary, "was the only person on earth who could intimidate my boss"—Groves could only answer, "No, sir." In one swift move, and by order of the top man in the American military, Groves became what he had wanted to be since the end of World War I: a fighting general.

But Tibbetts almost stole his thunder. A staging base had been established on the South Pacific island of Tinian, some thirteen hundred miles from the Japanese mainland. There the bomb would actually be armed, and from there the final flight to Japan would begin. In April 1945, as complaints of major drunkenness and minor assaults poured in from the Salt Lake City police, Tibbetts became concerned about his men's growing restlessness. More important, he was afraid that the Los Alamos physicists, who never seemed quite satisfied with the bomb's current design, would "still be tinkering when the war was over." With this in mind, Tibbetts took a bold step: using the "Silverplate" carte blanche, he called Washington and on his own ordered an advance contingent of his men shipped out to Tinian. On May 6 the first members of the 509th boarded ship in Seattle, finally on their way to war.

Tibbetts knew that by independently ordering his men to Tinian he was risking dismissal from command and even court-martial. The heat came soon enough. Within days Tibbetts was ordered to report to Groves's office in Washington. "As I came through the door," Tibbetts recalled, "he erupted. Who did I think I was, ordering my outfit overseas? For ten solid minutes he raked me over the coals, up one side and down the other, never repeating himself. I never had such a flaying. I had never seen him so mad. Then suddenly he stopped and gave me a big smile. [Apparently], he was tickled to death that I had done it.

" 'You've got us moving,' he said. 'Now they can't stop us!' "

If the 509th was in motion, it remained to be determined just what Japanese target they were in motion toward. Ever since the spring of 1943, when the Military Policy Committee had settled momentarily on the port of Truk, Groves had considered the target decision his personal charge. In December 1944 he and Tibbetts had briefly discussed Tokyo; the Japanese capital would, in Groves's mind, administer the biggest possible psychological shock to a population that seemed increasingly inured to war. But like the Military Policy Committee earlier, Groves and Tibbetts rejected Tokyo. Frequent rainfall made it too difficult for Tibbetts's bombardier to sight in on the target, and besides, the city had already been so battered by conventional bombing that it was, in the words of one of Groves's officers, practically rubble.

Over the next few months, Groves appointed a Target Committee to attack the problem in detail. In addition to General Farrell of his own staff and a contingent of top scientists from Los Alamos—Oppenheimer, John von Neumann, William Penney, Norman Ramsey, and Deke Parsons— Groves included two scientists and an officer from General Arnold's Air Force office. This committee developed a list of seventeen potential target cities, each of which conformed to a greater or lesser degree to criteria established by Groves himself. The targets, the general said, should be undamaged by earlier conventional raids and should be of a configuration that would enable the Americans to study the effects of the blast. But most important, Groves said, the targets should be "places the bombing of which would most adversely affect the will of the Japanese people to continue the war."

By appointing members from Arnold's office to the Target Committee, Groves made a gesture in the direction of participation as equals with the Air Force. But on May 11, when the Committee convened to narrow down its recommendations, the Air Force members were nowhere to be seen. In fact, only the Los Alamos contingent—all scientists except for Parsons, who was rapidly becoming one—was present. Were the Air Force members simply negligent no-shows, or had Groves purposely neglected to inform them of the meeting? The record gives no evidence in either direction. But if the latter was true, it may have been an attempt on Groves's part to keep the preparations for this momentous decision "in house" instead of farming them out and subjecting them to the vagaries of a basically uneducated Air Force. Further, it would have meant that any target decisions made by the American high command—up to and including Truman himself—would be based on information and recommendations made exclusively by Groves's own men.

At the May meeting, the temporarily pared-down Committee spent two days closeted in a Los Alamos conference room, poring over aerial maps of Japan and the Far East. When they emerged, they had narrowed the possible targets down to four cities, rating them as to their perceived suitability. In category A were the important Pacific port of Niigata and the enormous military arsenal at Kokura. The "winners," classified AA, were Hiroshima—a city whose neighboring hills were "likely to produce a focusing effect that would considerably increase blast damage"—and the ancient Japanese capital Kyoto, which, said Oppenheimer and his collaborators, had an advantage from the psychological point of view because "it is an intellectual center for Japan, and the people there are more apt to appreciate the significance of such a weapon."

Groves was particularly pleased with the choice of Kyoto. The city was obviously humming with military activity: intelligence had identified some twenty-six million square feet of industrial plants there, one of which was turning out four hundred airplane engines a month. More important, Kyoto was over twelve hundred years old, and with its three thousand temples and Shinto shrines, it was of "great religous significance to the Japanese." As such, Groves thought, its destruction in a single, mighty blow would have a symbolic importance and a psychological impact unmatched by any other Japanese city.

But he soon found that Secretary Stimson did not agree. On June 12, while conferring with Stimson on another matter, Groves was surprised to hear the secretary ask if the targets had been selected yet. The report of the Target Committee was ready, Groves replied, but it had yet to be approved by General Marshall.

"I'd like to see it," Stimson said mildly.

"Well," hemmed the general, "it's across the river, and it would take a long time to get it."

"I have all day," Stimson said, "and I know how fast your office operates. Here's a phone. Call your office and have them bring it over."

The order put Groves in a bind. "I was stewing and fretting internally," he said later, "over the fact that I was shortcutting General Marshall. Anybody who'd been in the Army as long as I had . . . wouldn't want to be put in that position. It just wasn't wise."

But when Groves protested to Stimson that Marshall should see the report first, the aging secretary cut him short. "This is one time," he said firmly, "that I'm going to be the final deciding authority. Nobody's going to tell me what to do on this."

He then asked Groves which cities had been chosen as the principal targets. When Groves mentioned Kyoto as the top choice, Stimson cut him short again. The secretary had visited Kyoto at least three times during the 1920s, when he had been Governor-General of the Philippines, and he had, he told Groves, been "very impressed" by its ancient culture.

"I don't want Kyoto bombed," he said.

When the Target Committee report arrived, Stimson called in General Marshall from his adjacent office. "Marshall," he said, "Groves has just brought me his report on the proposed targets. I don't like it. I don't like the use of Kyoto."

Hemmed in and uncomfortable, Groves could do nothing for the moment but demur. But he had remained unconvinced by Stimson's reasoning. He continued to press almost to the last minute to have Kyoto reinstated as the principal target. Not until years after the war would he come to appreciate Stimson's point of view. In the meantime, Kyoto was spared the role of the world's first atomic target.

That role, and the misery that accompanied it, would be assigned to Hiroshima.

Part Five

THE END AND THE BEGINNING

Chapter Thirty-Nine

To the ordinary San Franciscan it might have looked like a funeral, or a wedding party. A motorcade of unmarked but identical cars undulated over the city's humps and hills, staying tightly together, heading toward the Embarcadero and the great port. But had a curious citizen chosen to follow the convoy, he or she would have been astonished by the strange skill of the drivers. For the line simply never stopped. Somehow, the drivers were able to exquisitely time every traffic light and train crossing so that their progress was not interrupted.

It was essential that this unlikely convoy not be stopped, for it was carrying World War II's most precious cargo: half the uranium core for the "Little Boy" atomic bomb. (Its more rotund companion, the plutonium implosion bomb, went by the name "Fat Man.") The core was headed for the South Pacific island of Tinian and ultimately, in a very different form, for Japan.

The core's personal escorts were Groves's designated troubleshooter Robert Furman and James Nolan, a pediatrician-turned-radiologist from the Los Alamos hospital. To disguise their Corps of Engineers affiliation, they wore the patches and insignia of artillery officers, but the disguise was thin; in their haste, Furman and Nolan had put the insignias on upside down. Waiting for them at the dock was the heavy cruiser USS *Indianapolis*, an aging survivor of the terrible battle for Okinawa. In preparation for this unique sailing, the entire Pacific Coast was on naval alert, an alert that would not be lifted until the *Indianapolis* was well clear of coastal waters. The date was July 15, one day before the Trinity test.

The *Indianapolis* made the dangerous Pacific crossing without incident but amid a constant buzz of rumors inspired by the two "artillery officers" and their mysterious cargo. (Fearing that the rolling of the ship might somehow disturb his precious package, Furman welded the lead bucket containing the uranium core to the floor of his cabin.) The only clue

229

to the importance of the cargo was in the instructions given *Indianapolis* Captain William McVay by Deke Parsons: "Every day you save on your voyage," Parsons said, "will cut the length of the war by just that much."

On arrival in Tinian, Furman and Nolan found what one of the scientists later called a "miracle." Six thousand miles from San Francisco, the United States armed forces had built the largest airport in the world. There were six runways, each the equivalent of a ten-lane highway two miles long. The hangar areas bristled with hundreds of planes. "The whole island," wrote physicist Phillip Morrison, "looked like a gigantic aircraft carrier." From that daylong hubbub, with bombers perpetually taking off and landing from combat raids over Japan, the B-29s of the 509th stood isolated and mysterious, flying phantom missions to no one knew where. In fact they were making practice bombing runs, dropping high-explosive bombs known as "Pumpkins," the same size, weight, and shape of the two atomic bombs being prepared at Los Alamos, over isolated targets on the nearby Japanese-held island Rota. But the rest of the fliers on Tinian, kept ignorant by the security surrounding the 509th, could not be convinced that Tibbetts's squadron was doing anything at all. One waggish clerk even wrote out his sarcasm in a song:

> *Into the air the secret rose*
> *Where they're going nobody knows.*
> *Tomorrow they'll return again,*
> *But we'll never know where they've been.*
> *Don't ask about results and such,*
> *Unless you want to get in Dutch.*
> *But take it from one who is sure of the score,*
> *The 509th is winning the war.*

The 509th's nervous wing-fluttering symbolized the country's growing readiness to drop an atomic bomb on Japan. To Groves it represented the last stages of a mission for which he had been preparing since 1943, a mission that increasingly seemed the furious and fiery consummation of his personal destiny. Doubts as to the moral propriety of using the bomb never entered his mind. The Japanese had started the Pacific War, after all, and now it had fallen on him and his creation to end it. "There was never any question in my mind," he would say, "but that when the bomb was ready we should use it."

Others were not so sure. At the Met Lab, where Groves had already dealt with endless rebellions, another revolution was taking shape, this one over the use of the bomb. During the spring of 1945, when news from the ALSOS mission was making it more and more evident that Germany would not produce an atomic bomb, some of the scientists had grown concerned. If the Germans were no longer a danger, they wondered, why should America so single-mindedly continue to develop a weapon that might be unnecessary? Indeed, by June some of the more prominent Met Lab scientists were speculating that the American project might be scrapped altogether.

In any case, a substantial contingent of the scientists thought the time had come to put the brakes on the MED or at least to think hard about whether the bomb should be dropped on a civilian population. Led by the gentle, pacifistic German refugee James Franck, this group labored mightily through the spring of 1945 to produce a landmark report that subjected use of the bomb to serious analysis and doubts. The military advantage and the saving of American lives achieved by a sudden use of the bomb against Japan, the Franck Report concluded, "may be out-weighed by . . . a wave of horror and repulsion sweeping over the rest of the world." To avoid this moral backlash, the Franck Report called for what was in essence an atomic sideshow—an experimental, casualty-free demonstration of the bomb, with representatives of all nations present, in the desert or on a barren island. That way, the report argued, the Japanese might be frightened into surrendering a priori, in which case "America could say to the world, 'You see what sort of weapon we had but did not use.'"

For all its rather wide-eyed idealism (the framers of the report themselves confessed that their suggestion sounded "fantastic"), the Franck Report and the idea of a test demonstration found a receptive ear in Arthur Compton. The Met Lab director was a thoroughly religious man and so was deeply troubled by the prospect of using the bomb, especially on civilian populations. He was also determined to accurately represent the opinions of his scientists to Groves and to the country's political leaders. Appointed one of four scientific advisers—the others were Oppenheimer, Lawrence, and Fermi—to a top-level committee headed by Stimson, Compton brought the concerns of himself and the Franck contingent straight to Washington and the power elite.

During the lunch break of a committee meeting on May 31, Compton saw his chance. In the Pentagon dining room he took a seat next to Stimson and asked him "whether it might not be possible to arrange a nonmilitary demonstration of the bomb," a demonstration that would conceivably leave the Japanese "so impressed they would see the uselessness of continuing the war." Stimson asked for opinions. Oppenheimer thought that a "purely technical demonstration" of "an enormous nuclear firecracker" was not likely to turn the stubborn heads of the Japanese military. Others were concerned that the test might be a dud or that, if given advance warning, the Japanese would simply shoot down the plane carrying the test bomb. Presidential adviser James Byrnes was worried that the Japanese might bring in American POWs as unwitting human sacrifices at the test site. In any case, the men at Stimson's table argued, if the test failed, the Japanese would emerge psychologically stronger and more resolved than ever to go on fighting.

Lunch was over, and so was the discussion. "Though the possibility of a demonstration that would not destroy human life was attractive," Compton later wrote in conclusion, "no one could suggest a way in which it could be made so convincing that it would be likely to stop the war." For the moment, at least, the demonstration idea was dead. Later that day, the influential committee unanimously recommended that the bomb be dropped as soon as possible, without advance warning, on a major military installation in Japan so as to achieve "the maximum psychological impact." The committee was anticipating from the bomb a mighty show of destructive force—in Stimson's words, "a tremendous shock which would carry convincing proof of our power to destroy the [Japanese] empire."

The committee recommendation, endorsed as it was by the MED's scientific leadership, might have been expected to silence the Chicago rebels. But Groves's old nemesis Leo Szilard refused to take yes for an answer and hoisted the flag of rebellion on his own. Szilard had earlier written a long memo to the President suggesting that the United States avoid using the weapon on Japan and instead stage a test demonstration. (Just how and where this demonstration would be given and who would be invited, Szilard's memo did not say.) But when the Hungarian tried to deliver the memo to Truman, the President deflected him to James Byrnes, who, forewarned and suspicious of Szilard's motives, stonewalled the demonstration idea and showed the distraught physicist the door.

Frustrated in his first attempt to deal directly with the top, Szilard soon tried again. In early June he developed a petition for Truman that asked the President to rule that the United States "shall not resort to the use of atomic bombs in this war unless the terms which will be imposed on Japan have been made public in detail and Japan knowing these terms has refused to surrender. . . ." Interestingly, this petition made no mention of a demonstration but simply outlined the conditions under which a bomb should be dropped—*conditions with which Truman, however unwittingly, later complied.*

Szilard circulated his petition in the Met Lab, garnering sixty-nine signatures. The move immediately raised Groves's hackles. The general was sure that the petition and its signatories did not represent the majority opinion among the project scientists, and he was not about to let Szilard represent it as such. In the first place, the general had developed an almost pathological hatred for the Hungarian physicist. Throughout the war he had treated Szilard as an enemy alien, and now he suspected that with the defeat of Germany the physicist had all but lost interest in pursuing the war with Japan.

Groves also knew that the Met Lab was the likeliest place in the project to foster a full-blown scientific rebellion. From the time he had introduced DuPont, the contingent of Met Lab scientists led by Szilard and Eugene Wigner had complained loudly and often that Groves was pulling the project out from under them. In many respects they were right. The general's placement of the Los Alamos bomb lab under the aegis of the University of California had been his first step toward wresting scientific power from the Met Lab's hands. In October 1944 he started actively reducing the number of Met Lab personnel, and by March 1945 he had cut its budget in half. His plan was to retain only enough money and men at Chicago to be available in case of unforeseen problems at Hanford— "much," he would say, "as you would keep a fire department."

Arthur Compton, who had so boldly and cleverly moved to make the Met Lab the country's preeminent center for nuclear research and who had encouraged his men to think of themselves as the guardians, if not the sole owners, of the nation's nuclear future, was not going to be relegated to fire department duty without a fight. As Groves cut back, the Met Lab director wrote aggrieved and urgent letters to Stimson, to Bush, and to Groves himself. He even went to Washington to personally deliver a copy of the "Prospectus on Nucleonics"—Chicago's homegrown guidebook through the wonders of the peacetime nuclear industry—to Secretary Stimson. But his campaign did little good. Finally, in frustration, he told Kenneth Nichols in March that the reduction of Chicago's role had him "perturbed to the extent of wanting out."

If this was a threat to resign, Groves paid it no notice. In May the general wrote to Compton that the efforts of the Met Lab "should not be diverted in any way toward postwar problems." The letter amounted to the Met Lab's death warrant. Defeated and all but displaced, Compton resigned within a few weeks to take a position as Chancellor of Washington University in St. Louis, although he agreed to stay at his Met Lab post until he could be replaced smoothly. The rest of the Met Lab scientists—those who had not already been transferred to Los Alamos—would now be, in the words of Luis Alvarez, "a bunch of guys without a job."

Knowing all this, Groves must have felt that the Szilard petition was more a result of the war-long battles between himself and the Met Lab than an indication of how the majority of project scientists felt about the bomb. Apparently convinced that most of the scientists' voices remained unheard, he ordered Compton to take a poll of all Met Lab personnel. When the results of the poll came in on July 12, the great majority of the Chicago scientists, some 61 percent, had voted in favor of using the bomb on Japan.*

As far as Groves was concerned, the results of the poll showed that Szilard's petition represented a minority opinion even at the rebellious Met Lab. Reactions—or lack of them—at other laboratories seemed to confirm the general's view. At Hanford and Columbia, there appears to have been no discussion at all of the use of the bomb. At Oak Ridge, where administrative ties to the Met Lab might have meant a stirring of antibomb feeling, the presentation of Szilard's petition surprisingly gathered no signatures at all but instead inspired a number of counterpetitions in *favor* of using the bomb.

At Los Alamos Szilard made an attempt to have his petition circulated by Edward Teller, but Oppenheimer deflected it, saying that his men were free to express their concerns to him personally. With the exception of Teller himself, there is no evidence that anyone did. Robert Wilson had organized a meeting in early 1945—"I called it 'The Impact of the Gadget on Civilization,'" he remembered, "or some very pretentious title such as that"—but when the meeting, which Oppenheimer attended, was over, Wilson recalled the scientists' concluding that "yes, we should keep doing this [work on the bomb] in spite of the fact that the Germans seemed to have been beaten." In general, said Los Alamos physicist David Frisch, there was among his colleagues "a natural tendency to finish the job and hope that someone at a higher level would think things through."

Although his petition had been singularly unsuccessful elsewhere in the project, Szilard stuck doggedly to his course. He wanted to send it directly to Truman, but the other Chicago signatories demurred, insisting that it go through Compton and MED channels. With extreme reluctance, Szilard turned it over to Compton the day after the Trinity test. For more than a week it sat in Compton's office until the director finally forwarded it

*Fifteen percent of the scientists voted to use the bomb "in the manner . . . most effective in bringing about prompt Japanese surrender"; 46 percent "to give a military demonstration in Japan, to be followed by a renewed opportunity to surrender"; 26 percent to "give an experimental demonstration in this country, with representatives of Japan present"; 11 percent to "withhold military use of the weapons, but make public experimental demonstration of their effectiveness"; and 2 percent to "maintain as secret as possible all new developments of our new weapons and refrain from using them in this war."

to Nichols at Oak Ridge. On July 24, the day he received it from Compton, Nichols fired the petition, along with the Compton poll and the Oak Ridge counterpetitions, off to Groves. There it sat for another week until, on August 1, the general sent it off to Truman, who was just winding down his participation in the Potsdam Conference and getting ready to sail for the United States. The President, by all accounts, never saw the petition.

Groves was often later accused of pigeonholing Szilard's petition until the dropping of the bomb was all but a fait accompli. In fact the petition had been equally delayed in Compton's office. And Groves actually had no reason to delay it. From his point of view, the petition had been effectively swamped by the Oak Ridge counterpetitions and by the Compton poll. The minority opinion of Szilard and the Chicago rebels had been stopped not as much by Groves as by the opinions of the scientists themselves. In the feverish push to make the bomb ready, the petition had become unimportant, simply another, as historian Alice Kimball Smith later concluded in regard to the Franck Report, of "an endless succession of memoranda to be read if time permitted."

Chapter Forty

If there were to be a decision on whether to use the bomb, that decision would be made—theoretically, at least—not by Leo Szilard and the disaffected Chicago scientists but by the nation's leaders. Yet during the long spring of 1945, few of the men at the top seemed willing to even talk in detail about the bomb, let alone make a decision about its use.

In a series of crucial meetings to plan strategy for the last stages of the Japanese war, President Truman failed to so much as bring the subject of the bomb up. When it *was* brought up by Undersecretary of War John McCloy in a June 18 meeting, Truman, after a brief and summary discussion, simply directed McCloy to send a memo on the subject to, of all places, the State Department. (Mention of the bomb, McCloy later recalled, created "sort of a shock. You didn't mention it out loud; it was like mentioning Skull and Bones in polite society at Yale. It just wasn't done.")

Throughout this period Secretary of War Stimson, who out of all the top officials probably did the most personal soul-searching about the bomb, remained for the most part curiously quiet about actually using it. General George Marshall, who as Army Chief of Staff should have taken a direct hand in any decision, seems to have developed in place of a bomb policy a series of orders to Groves to "see to that yourself."

Both Stimson and presidential adviser James Byrnes did discuss the bomb with Truman during the first week of June 1945. On June 1, Byrnes reported the recommendation to drop the bomb on Japan made by Stimson's Interim Committee. According to Byrnes, "Mr. Truman told me he had been giving serious thought to the subject for many days . . . and that with reluctance he had to agree that he could think of no alternative and found himself in accord. . . ." Five days later, Stimson reiterated the recommendation in a meeting with the President. The two then discussed whether to reveal the secret of the bomb to the Soviets at the upcoming

Potsdam Conference, after which Stimson expressed his fear that widespread area bombing of Japan might leave the country "so thoroughly bombed out that the new weapon would not have a fair background to show its strength." In both discussions, the "decision" to drop the bomb was already in fact a fait accompli, implicit in the recommendation of the Interim Committee.

Whether this strange reluctance to discuss the bomb represented skepticism about whether it would work — most of the shuffling and buckpassing took place before the Trinity test — or a deep-seated and collective discomfort with this potentially most destructive of all war toys, it was evident that where the bomb was concerned America's leaders were for the most part curiously reluctant to debate its use head-on.

Into this breach in atomic decision making, Groves himself was more than willing to leap. While Marshall and the Joint Chiefs of Staff methodically continued to plan for an invasion of the Japanese mainland — an invasion that was expected to cost as many as *half a million* American casualties*—Groves continued to spearhead planning for the use of the bomb. After all, it was a far less costly alternative to a protracted land invasion and its gruesome casualties, and not to use it under those circumstances, Groves felt, would amount to a tragic waste not only of American lives but also of a potentially winning weapon.

But the general had another, more personal reason for wanting to use the bomb. In March 1945, with Germany on the point of surrender, Undersecretary of War Robert Patterson had asked him if anyone in the project was "flinching" from using the bomb on Japan. Groves was horrified. "Flinching," he told Patterson, would make a "complete mess" not only of the project but of the reputations of "everyone who authorized or urged or even permitted the work in the first place." Although Groves had neither "authorized" the project nor "permitted the work in the first place," he had, once in charge, most certainly "urged" it with all the energy at his command, and he was not in the least interested in having a "complete mess" made of his reputation.

While the leaders continued to tiptoe around the subject, Groves made his moves. From the time when General Marshall had first delegated to him the task of overseeing military preparations for dropping the bomb, Groves had maneuvered to keep control of the operation in his own hands

---

*The minimum estimate for invasion casualties was General Douglas MacArthur's fifty thousand. But Army Corps of Engineers General Sam Sturgis, who inspected Japanese shoreline fortifications immediately after the war, found them so imposing that he thought an invasion might have cost as many as a million American lives.

as much as possible. He stepped lightly around the Air Force leaders who would under normal conditions call all the signals of a bomb attack and managed to wrest from General Arnold—who, like other generals, seemed skeptical about the bomb's possibilities—an agreement that orders for the bombing mission would be issued not in the field but in Washington itself. And as far as the MED director was concerned, *Washington* was a synonym for *Groves.* He then secured an agreement from General Marshall that the order would originate with Groves personally and would only be *approved* by Marshall.

With control firmly his, Groves could now actually set a date. As early as mid-May he drafted the order that set the atomic bombing of Japan in motion. The order directed General Carl Spaatz, commander of the Army Air Force in the Pacific, to deliver the first atomic bomb on either Hiroshima, Kokura, Niigata, or Nagasaki, if weather permitted, on about August 3. Under the signature of General Thomas Handy, on July 24 Groves sent the order to Potsdam, where Truman, Stimson, and the Joint Chiefs of Staff were busy carving up the map of Europe with Russian premier Josef Stalin.

There, in a fading yellow villa alongside beautiful Griebnitz Lake, some fourteen miles southeast of Berlin (the tree-rimmed lake had been the home of the Nazi motion-picture colony), America's leaders had one final chance to debate the loosing of the terrible force of the atom on an obviously ill-prepared world. Instead, in the wake of news of the successful Trinity test, most of the discussion among the Americans and British centered on whether Russia's entrance into the war against Japan was still needed now that the bomb was a reality. There is no evidence to indicate that this reality inspired any second thoughts about whether the bomb should be used at all. With the exception of the Joint Chiefs of Staff, who curiously recommended that the invasion of mainland Japan proceed as planned—without so much as mentioning the existence of the bomb— American leaders continued to regard the decision not only as a fait accompli but apparently as immutable. In that atmosphere, Groves's bombing order was received and read by Stimson, then passed on apparently without comment to Marshall, who signed it. No one has yet produced convincing evidence that President Truman ever saw the order.

Had Groves himself actually made the decision to drop the bomb by initiating and sending the bomb order? The general thought otherwise. As far as he was concerned, any "decision" had been made as long ago as 1942, implicit in President Roosevelt's early and enthusiastic moves to support and fund the MED. "From then on," Groves wrote, "the project ran downhill. . . . It was impossible for anyone to back out." The only

"decision" Truman made, to Groves's thinking, was one of "noninter-
ference—basically a decision not to upset existing plans." In other words,
once under way, the atomic bomb had acquired a momentum that simply
could not be stopped, even by the President himself.

That momentum, with a considerable extra push from Leslie Groves,
had brought the bomb into existence and now guaranteed that it would be
used to end the war.

Chapter Forty-One

It was a cool, still Sunday morning, a time when Groves might have enjoyed a few sets of weekend tennis before the typical August humidity turned the Washington air heavy and the sky white. But as he drove alone toward his office in Foggy Bottom, tennis was probably the last thing on his mind.

For this was no ordinary Sunday. The day before, a cable had arrived from General Farrell on Tinian bearing a message that Groves had been waiting to hear for almost a week. The twenty-four-hour forecast for weather over Japan was good, Farrell said, and the bombers of Colonel Tibbetts's 509th squadron were confidently expected to take off at midnight, Tinian time. This time, though, the 509th would not be flying a practice run to Rota. This time the belly of Tibbetts's lead plane, the *Enola Gay*, would be filled not with the lookalike Pumpkins but with the real thing: a uranium-fueled, gun-operated Little Boy atomic bomb.

This time they would be headed not for some bare-rock island in the Pacific but for Japan itself.

Once the signed bombing order was delivered to Tinian on July 29, Groves had left the final shots to be called by the men on the spot: Farrell, Tibbetts, and Deke Parsons. In the meantime the general had plenty of work. Already thinking beyond the dropping of the first two bombs, he was busily making plans for assembling a third, another Fat Man, and he was keeping the phone lines to Los Alamos and Hanford hot. The need for speed, paramount throughout the war, now became most intensely and terribly urgent. As Oppenheimer frantically pleaded for faster shipments of plutonium, Groves ordered Matthias to ignore all previous safety precautions and send the precious fuel to Los Alamos by the quickest possible plane.

At the same time, Oppenheimer seems to have been attacked by a bad case of last-minute jitters. Suddenly insecure in the knowledge that only two bombs were ready, the physicist phoned Groves to suggest "murdering the Little Boy and devoting all his clothes to the Fat Man"—meaning that the uranium core of the Little Boy could be gutted, then used to help produce plutonium to make more Fat Men. Instead of dropping a few solitary bombs now, said Oppenheimer, these new bombs—he envisioned as many as fifteen—could be held back, then used to support the November invasion of the Japanese mainland.

But Groves was not about to have his plans upset by what he saw as one more example of untimely vacillation on the part of scientists. Immediately he cabled Oppenheimer a crisp message: "Factors beyond our control prevent us from considering any decision other than to proceed according to existing schedules. . . ."

Now, as Groves checked into his empty office on that quiet Sunday morning, all the chattering voices were stilled. There was no one to see, no reports to write, no phone calls to make. For almost three years, that office had been the scene of nonstop activity. Now there was nothing to do but wait.

At 2:27 A.M. on Tinian, Paul Tibbetts started the engines of the *Enola Gay*. As the four motors rumbled to life, co-pilot Robert Lewis carefully noted the moment in an impromptu log he was keeping for *The New York Times*. Behind them gunner Robert Shumard fingered a tiny doll that he kept as a good luck charm, while radar operator Jacob Beser folded and unfolded a slip of rice paper on which he had written the bomb's radar frequency. While the other six crew members fiddled with their instruments, Deke Parsons and Morris Jepson crouched in the back of the bomb bay, baby-sitting the Little Boy.

For his part, Tibbetts was relieved to finally be perched in his beloved cockpit. The last hours had been hectic. When the colonel and his men had walked out onto the landing strip to begin a final check of the *Enola Gay*, they had been astonished to find a full press and motion picture crew, complete with klieg lights and rolling cameras, waiting for them. "I expected," Tibbetts later recalled, "to see M-G-M's lion walk out onto the field." But this had been a minor nuisance compared to the upsetting news reported by Luis Alvarez. The final test of the bomb's four-stage firing mechanism had been a dismal failure: the test bomb had simply dropped quietly into the sea.

Once at the controls, though, all Tibbetts's worries faded away, and he could apply himself without distraction to the job at hand. "I was working on pure adrenaline," he later recalled. At 2:45, with all four engines turning smoothly, he turned to Lewis and said quietly, "Let's go."

Two minutes later, after a harrowing approach—the *Enola Gay* was fifteen thousand pounds overweight, and Tibbetts had to take her at top speed to the very edge of the runway—the plane gave a mighty shudder, then finally lifted painfully off the airstrip just as it gave way to cliff and ocean. The atomic bomb was airborne. Within four minutes the *Enola Gay* was followed by her two support planes, the *Great Artiste* and *No. 91*, which between them carried several scientists who would measure the effect of the bomb's blast, and newsman William Laurence, who would record it for posterity. Three weather scout planes were ahead, monitoring the cloud cover and the high-altitude winds over three of the four alternative targets. A bevy of specially equipped "Superdumbo" B-29s and Navy "flying boats" were already patrolling the flight path, ready to fight off any opposition. Below, a fleet of cruisers, destroyers, and submarines were waiting to rescue any crew that were shot down—ready, as one briefing officer had put it, "to come almost onto the enemy beaches to pick you up."

What one officer called "the most perfectly planned bombing operation in history" was at last under way. Its target, some seven hours ahead, was the city of Hiroshima.

In his Washington office, Groves settled in for the long wait. Joining him were Jean O'Leary, duty officer John Derry, and several other staff members. Expecting to get word by one o'clock that the planes had taken off, the general spent the morning doing some routine paperwork. When no word came at one, then two, then three, Groves shrugged off his increasing concern and decided to get in that game of tennis after all. At three he left for the Army-Navy Club, taking an officer with him. While the general played, the officer sat at the courtside telephone, calling back into the office every few minutes. By the time the general was finished playing, over an hour later, there was still no word from Tinian.

At 3:00 A.M. in the back of the bomb bay, Parsons and Jepson crouched over the Little Boy, whose outer casing bore a message for the Japanese emperor scrawled in lipstick by General Farrell: "To Hirohito," it read, "with love and kisses." Now, with Jepson illuminating the work by flashlight, Parsons went one by one through the eleven painstaking steps necessary to prepare the bomb for arming. In doing so, the captain knew that he was disobeying one of the strictest of Groves's orders, for both the general and Oppenheimer had wanted the bomb armed before take-off, feeling that in-flight arming invited a full-scale disaster. But Parsons had seen the wreckage of crashed B-29s on Tinian and was not about to take off with a fully armed bomb. Besides, the Little Boy had been his personal project for two years, and Groves was seven thousand miles away.

Several hours later, with the new light turning the Pacific sky an iridescent pink, the *Enola Gay* reached the island of Iwo Jima, where she went into a circling orbit. At 4:55, precisely on time, the *Great Artiste* and *No. 91*, circled in behind. Forming a tight V at just over nine thousand feet, the three bombers headed north.

A few minutes later, Jacob Beser's radar screen suddenly came alive. As Beser watched, mesmerized and sweating, the early warning signal of Japanese radar swept across his screen. The signal made one pass, then a second. This time it locked firmly onto the *Enola Gay*'s position. To Beser, the implications were chilling: now, he knew, there would be no surprise attack. The Japanese knew they were coming.

At 6:00 P.M., Groves left his office for a second trip to the Army-Navy Club, this time for dinner with his wife and daughter and Stimson's assistant George Harrison. "I think I'll have some chocolate ice cream for dessert," he announced as he sat down. To Harrison he whispered in a more troubled voice, "Still no news." A few minutes later General Thomas Handy, who had first signed the bombing order, stopped by the table, but Groves could only shake his head and say, "Nothing." Grace and Gwen, who had absolutely no inkling of what was going on, barely noticed.

At 6:45, Groves was suddenly called to the telephone. Seeing him go, Harrison and Handy immediately stopped eating. "I could feel their eyes," Groves later said, "boring into my back." Now, as he picked up the phone, Derry's excited voice reported that the cable had finally come from Farrell: the planes had taken off from Tinian without incident. There was no further information.

Returning to his table, Groves discreetly passed the word to Harrison and Handy, then calmly finished his dessert. He was somewhat relieved but still concerned: by now he should have had word that the bomb had been dropped. For the first time in his three years at the head of the project, he could not push things ahead with a phone call, a threat, or a fiery speech. Like a condemned man or an anxious bridegroom, all he could do was wait.

Sometime after 6:30 A.M. Japanese time, Morris Jepson unscrewed three green safety plugs from the bomb's midsection and replaced them with three red plugs. "*This,*" the normally phlegmatic Jepson recalled, "was a moment." Indeed it was. With the insertion of the three red plugs, the Little Boy, the first atomic bomb to be dropped in anger, was finally and fully armed.

Back in his office, Groves and his staffers did their best to dispel the growing tension. In the supercharged atmosphere, someone started a poker game. Although Groves did not play, the scene inspired him to make a gambling analogy. "I'm not a betting man," he said later, "but I must say that waiting for news of the bomb was like betting on a horse when you're not at the track: all you can do is wait at a telephone without seeing anything until your horses come in."

Still, the usually unemotional Groves was not about to give in to the tension.* Seeing his outward calm, the exasperated Jean O'Leary finally exclaimed, "Don't you ever get excited about anything?" Perhaps in response, the general unbuttoned his collar and loosened his tie—the only time his men had ever seen him do so and thus a sure sign that he, too, was finally beginning to feel the intense pressure.

In Japan it was 8:12 on the morning of August 6. The *Enola Gay* and her two sisters had reached a point only nineteen miles to the east of Hiroshima. Two minutes later Tibbetts came on the intercom to tell his men to put their welder's glasses—the same aluminum masks that had been invented for the Trinity test—in place. In his notebook, Lewis wrote a laconic message: "There will be a short intermission while we bomb our target."

Below them, the city of Hiroshima was spread out, bounded by the dark blue of Hiroshima Bay and dissected by the six tributaries of the Ota River. Bombardier Thomas Ferebee, now exquisitely alert, watched intently as his target, the T-shaped Aioi Bridge, appeared at the edge of his scope. As Tibbetts threw the plane into its 155-degree turn, the bridge shimmered in the perfect center of Ferebee's cross-hairs.

"Bomb away!" he shouted.

The Little Boy dropped from the plane, wobbling slightly at first, then correcting itself as it gathered speed. Forty-three seconds later, after a free fall of over thirty thousand feet, the bomb's final switch was triggered. The Little Boy exploded with a flash of light so intense that Tibbetts swore he could even taste it. Trapped in place by the violence of the plane's sweeping dive, the crew could only watch as the shock wave, a

---

*When later accounts described Groves pacing nervously about the office, the general snorted, "I never paced in my life—not even when my children were born."

ring of air so impossibly compressed that it was actually visible, rose toward them and struck the plane with a force two and one-half times that of gravity. The plane buffeted and bounced through the sky. Four seconds later a second shock wave, this one reflected from the ground, hit the plane, knocking Beser out of his seat. Not anticipating such powerful blows, Tibbetts thought they had been hit by antiaircraft fire.

By now the *Enola Gay* was some thirteen miles from Ground Zero. With the plane entering calmer air, the crew looked down to see what gunner George Caron called "a vision of hell." The bomb had exploded with the ungodly force of 13,500 tons of TNT,* a manmade, portable inferno with an internal temperature of fifty million degrees centigrade. What had just a few minutes before been a city awakening to the routine of a new morning was now a caldron of firestorm, smoke, and ash. For the rest of his life the scene would remain vivid in Tibbetts's mind, lit by the bomb's unearthly purple glow. "The city," Tibbetts said, "was nothing but a black, boiling pallor of . . . I called it tar. But it was smoke, dust, debris, and everything.

"It was bubbling," he recalled. "Just boiling."

---

*The figure released at the time of Truman's announcement, 20,000 tons, was an estimate based on the results of the Trinity test. The figure went through several revisions before finally coming to rest of 13,500 tons.

Chapter Forty-Two

At 11:30 P.M. EST, some four and one-half hours late, the coded message from Parsons finally made its way to Groves's office. "Results clearcut," the message said, "successful in all respects. Visible effects greater than New Mexico test. Conditions in airplane normal following delivery." Although there was no indication of the damage below—those estimates would not be available for several days—Groves had heard what he wanted to hear. The Little Boy had worked. The immense three-year, multibillion-dollar gamble had paid off. Now, no matter what happened, Groves knew that all the faith, all the sweat, all his relentless pushing had been justified. His own reputation would be secure, and at the same time the waiting wolves of Congress would be calmed. Most important, he felt sure, the end of the most extensive and terrible war in history was now at hand.

As he made the announcement to his office staff—"He was all smiles," remembered one assistant—a great sigh of relief swept across the room. But there were no cheers, no celebratory histrionics. Everyone knew there was still much work to be done. He relayed the word to General Marshall; "Thank you very much for calling me," was the Chief of Staff's only reaction. Groves then retired to his inner office and began preparing his formal report for Marshall and Stimson. When he had finished the first draft, he lay down on his cot in his office for a brief nap.

At 4:30 A.M. Derry awakened him. Farrell's detailed report on the drop had just arrived from Tinian. Although there was still no precise estimate of the damage, the report described a city "covered with a dark grey dust layer . . . with flashes of fire visible in the dust. . . . It looked," according to one of the crew members, "as if the whole town were being torn apart."

This in particular was the message that Groves had been anticipating. It confirmed his supposition that the Little Boy was indeed "as husky as his big brother" and that Hiroshima had probably been destroyed. Grimly satisfied, Groves went downstairs for a shower, a shave, and a change of uniform.

By 7:00 Groves was in the Pentagon, delivering the news to General Marshall and General Arnold. After quietly registering their approval, the men turned to the next order of business: the press release with which President Truman would issue this most startling of all messages to the world.

The release had been written weeks earlier by William Laurence, and the fiery reporter had designed it to produce as much psychological impact as possible. Hiroshima, he wrote, had been "destroyed." Now, though, Assistant Secretary of War Robert Lovett warned that the Air Force had put itself in an extremely uncomfortable position when it had claimed repeatedly—and mistakenly—that its air raids had "destroyed Berlin." "After about the third time," Lovett commented, "it got to be embarrassing." At the same time, General Marshall opined that the release should not appear to gloat over the probably large number of Japanese casualties.

Groves had been in no way concerned about the Japanese. He told Marshall that he was "not thinking so much about their casualties as I was about the [American soldiers] who had made the Bataan death march." But Lovett's caution now hit home. Suddenly circumspect after the under-secretary's warning, Groves deleted the sentence in which it was claimed that Hiroshima had been "destroyed." That done, he had the release remimeographed and sent to the White House. It was just after ten. In less than an hour, the three-year secret would be secret no longer. The world would know that at hand were both the end of the great war and the beginning of the atomic age.

Grace Wilson Groves was mopping the kitchen floor when her telephone rang at 11:00 A.M. On the other end of the line an officer from the Corps of Engineers gave her a cryptic message: "There's an important announcement on the radio soon; you may be interested." Then he unceremoniously hung up.

Mildly curious, Grace turned the radio up loud, then picked up her mop and resumed her chores. A few minutes later the music was interrupted by an excited newsman. "Sixteen hours ago," he began, his voice tense with emotion, "an American airplane dropped one bomb on Hiroshima, an important Japanese army base." Grace was puzzled. She had been in Japan once as a girl; was that why the officer had called? She set down her mop to listen. "It is an atomic bomb," the announcer went on.

"It is a harnessing of the basic power of the universe." In the wake of the enormous blast, President Truman was calling on the Japanese to surrender or face "a rain of ruin from the air, the like of which has never been seen on this earth."

To Grace this was wonderful news. It probably meant not only the imminent end of the war but that her son Dick—who had just graduated from West Point and was taking Corps of Engineers training at Fort Belvoir, Virginia—would not have to join the fighting troops. This, she thought, must have been why the officer called. But then, toward the end of the announcement, she realized that the personal interest the officer had mentioned was in fact even closer to home. "The bomb project," said the radio newsman, "was directed by Major General Leslie R. Groves."

Now she understood not only the officer's call but much more. Never once in the last three years had her husband so much as hinted about the nature of his work, and she had known better than to ask. Now it was all clear: the extraordinary secrecy, the long hours and late dinners, the ceaseless travel. Grace was truly amazed; she had had no idea her husband had been working on something so important.

But her amazement lasted only a few moments. As the announcement finished, she did something that would have made her unexcitable husband proud: she picked up her mop and finished cleaning the kitchen floor.

Meanwhile, in her husband's office, the initially subdued atmosphere had over the course of the day given way to a sort of programmed pandemonium. Colonel William Consodine's public relations staff had been quadrupled in anticipation of the public announcement, but they were still barely able to handle the howling telephone and the excited mob of reporters who milled through the office, shouting, jostling, and yelling for attention.

Somehow, Consodine's secretary Patti Cox managed to escape the madhouse to meet her fiancé, a young MP who was just home from the European theater and, so he thought, soon en route to the other war.

"Quick!" Patti yelled. "We've got to get a newspaper!"

"Why?" asked her puzzled fiancé, who had not yet heard the news.

"Because it's going to tell you definitely," she exulted, "that you are *not* going to the Pacific!"

The news spread quickly through Groves's empire. At Oak Ridge, where the great majority of the seventy-five thousand workers were finding out for the first time what their real jobs had been, the initial reaction was hush and confusion. Could they now, after three years of the most rigid secrecy, suddenly talk about their work? Or would they still be silenced by the general's security agents? But the initial caution faded with Colonel Nichols's announcement, and a rush of exhilaration swept across the gigantic facility. By afternoon, people were paying as much as a dollar a copy for that day's edition of the Knoxville *Journal*, which told them more about their own work than they themselves had ever known. The enthusiasm quickly spread: in Knoxville itself, arriving train travelers from Washington were greeted by an excited porter who proudly announced, "You are now entering Knoxville, gateway to Oak Ridge."

At Hanford, Franklin Matthias had told his wife to be sure to listen to the radio. When the announcement came, she said, "tears came to my eyes and all my surface atoms turned to goose bumps." Under orders from Groves, Matthias set up an impromptu press center in the coffee shop of the transient labor quarters. By noon the area was full of reporters and local congressmen, who were finally being allowed to satisfy three years' worth of curiosity. Outside, wrote Matthias, there was "great rejoicing" among the tens of thousands of workers who had sweated out the project with their exhausted but happy commander.

Groves himself called Oppenheimer at Los Alamos. "I'm very proud of you and all your people," the general said. "Apparently it went off with a tremendous bang."

"Everyone is feeling reasonably good about it," Oppenheimer replied, "and I extend my heartiest congratulations. It's been a long road."

When the general hung up, Oppenheimer passed the news to his secretary, who had it read over the public address system. "The place went up," she recalled, "like we'd won the Army-Navy game." As the scientists came running to assemble in the Tech Area amphitheater, Oppenheimer made his triumphant appearance. To riotous applause, yelling, and foot-stamping, he took the podium, his hands clasped together over his head in the salute of a victorious boxer.

That evening, though, the first exuberance faded. A dormitory party for the scientists was quiet and subdued and broke up after only an hour. As Oppenheimer left, he came across physicist Volney Wilson in the darkness outside. Wilson was vomiting in the bushes.

"The reaction," Oppenheimer thought, "has set in."

In the world outside the project, there were also signs of an early reaction. Writer H.G. Wells, who had predicted the development of an atomic bomb in one of his novels thirty-one years before, now predicted the imminent end of mankind. "Homo sapiens," he told reporters, "is in its present form played out." Harvard anthropologist Ernest Hooton agreed. "Dropped into the hands of human beings as irresponsible as apes," he wrote, "such a weapon as the atomic bomb is to invite the destruction of civilization." American Communist Party leader William Z. Foster worried about leaving atomic power "in the hands of the reactionaries" and urged that control of the weapon be turned over to the United Nations. The Vatican newspaper *L'Osservatore Romano* lamented that "this incredible destructive instrument" would remain a temptation "if not for our horrified contemporaries, then for posterity all through history."

In general, though, the immediate public reaction was highly favorable, especially in the United States. The editorial opinions of *The New York Times* and *The Washington Post*—"What every military man has dreamed of," wrote the former, "has been found in America and is ready to be hurled against our enemies"; while the latter opined that "a struggle to the death commits all combatants to committing a maximum of destruction on the enemy"—were almost unanimously echoed in the nation's press. A Gallup poll taken a few weeks later would show that an overwhelming 85 percent of the American public favored the use of the bomb against Japan. Even among Manhattan District scientists, many of whom had some inkling of the Szilard-Franck movement in Chicago, a poll taken by sociologist Margaret Smith Stahl showed that the great majority—some 66.5 percent—also sanctioned, and even celebrated, the use of the bomb.

Chapter Forty-Three

For his part, Groves had little time to worry about the reactions of others. To rejoice over the war's end, he knew, was still premature. Long conversations with Admiral Purnell, who as Chief of Staff of the American fleet in the Philippines was a serious and knowledgeable student of Japanese psychology, had convinced him that no matter how much damage a first bomb did, it would take at least two to induce the Japanese to surrender—"The first one," Groves said, "to show them what it was like, and the second one to show we had more of them." Partly because of this conviction, Groves had purposely left the bombing order open-ended: "Additional bombs," the order said, "will be delivered . . . as soon as made ready by project staff."

No capitulatory message came from the Japanese government; Japan had essentially ignored President Truman's post-Trinity ultimatum to surrender and appeared to be more confused than impressed by the Hiroshima bombing. So Groves rode Oppenheimer with his customary relentlessness to have a Fat Man ready by August 11.

If the Hiroshima drop was relatively smooth and trouble free, the second bombing mission was a planner's nightmare. First the meteorologists on Tinian predicted bad weather for the eleventh, so, over the strenuous objections of Norman Ramsey, who was supervising the Tinian scientists, Groves summarily pushed the mission date up to the ninth. Still, it turned out that dropping a Fat Man from an airplane was a far trickier proposition than igniting it, Trinity-style, from a stationary tower. To make an already delicate situation even worse, it was found in the final moments before take-off that the lead plane, the *Bock's Car*, had a defective fuel pump.

This left Farrell in a difficult spot. At the last moment, the second bombing run was taking on the look of a suicide mission. But Groves peppered him hard, insisting on the earliest possible drop. With the hope of a quick Japanese surrender hanging in the balance, Farrell decided to take the risk at all cost.

Despite all the worrisome indications to the contrary, the *Bock's Car*, accompanied by two support planes, took off at 3:48 A.M. on August 9. She was in trouble almost from the beginning. Her faulty fuel pump was leaking gasoline, and when heavy clouds over the bomber's primary target, the Kokura arsenal, refused to dissipate after three lengthy passes, the rapidly diminishing fuel supply became a serious problem. Fifty minutes were wasted in the clouds over Kokura before the *Bock's Car* finally turned toward Nagasaki, her secondary target. On board, Commander Frederick Ashworth furiously calculated the fuel supply. There was only enough, he figured, for one run over Nagasaki and then a limping landing on Okinawa. If more than one run were needed, pilot Charles Sweeney would have to ditch the plane in the Pacific and hope against hope for a rescue by submarine.

It took the *Bock's Car* twenty minutes to reach Nagasaki. There the crew found the skies completely clouded over. Ignoring Groves's order only to drop the bomb if they could actually see the target, Sweeney and Ashworth prepared to drop it with no guidance other than the plane's radar. At the last possible moment, though, a small hole appeared in the cloud cover—tiny, but just enough to see a patch of ground below. "I'll take it!" shouted bombardier Kermit Beahan. Taking aim at a racetrack, he let the Fat Man fly.

After a fall of over thirty thousand feet, the plutonium bomb exploded. Ashworth described the hellish sight:

> The bomb burst with a blinding flash and a huge column of black smoke swirled up toward us. Out of this column of smoke there boiled a great swirling mushroom of gray smoke, luminous with red, flashing flame, that reached to 40,000 feet in less than eight minutes. Below, through the clouds, we could see the pall of black smoke ringed with fire that covered what had been the industrial area of Nagasaki.

In quick succession, the plane was hit by five distinct shock waves. As the *Bock's Car* limped back toward Okinawa, its gas gauge dropped to zero. In the last few seconds, though, Ashworth became convinced that there was enough fuel at the bottom of the tank to get them into Okinawa. Holding his breath, Sweeney agreed to go for a landing. Somehow the plane made it down to the runway. There she stalled, unable to taxi off the strip. After dropping the most powerful bomb in human history, the plane had simply run out of gas.

Groves had now dropped the necessary two bombs. But the bombing order itself remained open and in force, and the Los Alamos scientists were preparing more bombs. Some of them, Groves knew, would be ready "momentarily." In the absence of a rescinding order, these bombs would be assembled, shipped, and dropped on Japan, and Truman's "rain of ruin from the skies" would be launched as a matter of military routine.

But Groves felt that he could "smell a Japanese surrender in the air." On the morning of August 13 he went to see Marshall to try to get the Chief of Staff to allow him to delay further bombs in the hope that the Japanese were about to lay down their arms. But when he arrived, he was told by General Handy that Marshall was closeted with Stimson and that the two had left word that they were not to be disturbed by anyone under any conditions. Restless and impatient, Groves decided to act on his own. "I can't afford to sit over here," he told Handy. "I've got too many things to do. When you see General Marshall, tell him I am holding up the shipment unless I hear from him to the contrary."

Returning to his office, Groves immediately phoned Los Alamos and told them to hold the third bomb. He was just in time. Bacher had just signed the official receipt for the bomb, and its components were already loaded in a waiting car. "That bomb was all ready to go," Bacher recalled. "To stop it, Groves had acted with tremendous speed."

Groves's lightning order, in the absence of a countermanding order from Marshall, put the third bomb on hold. The man who had pushed furiously for three years to bring the bomb to the war was now pushing just as vigorously to stop it.

The war, Groves knew, was over. Two days later, at precisely high noon Japanese time, Emperor Hirohito came on the radio to confirm it. The Japanese had surrendered. The atomic bomb, the fiery creation of Groves and the Manhattan Engineer District, had brought an early end to the most tragically devastating war in the history of humanity.

The war was over. Like an expert poker player who respects the cold odds but gives precedence to his own hunches, Groves had intuited his way to a gambler's victory. His initial moves—the securing of the Oak Ridge site, the swift purchase of Sengier's uranium, and especially the bold bluff of priorities chief Donald Nelson—had put an apparently stalled bomb effort back in motion, while his vast, almost visionary expansion of the MED gave it both the money and the industrial muscle it needed to succeed. His instinctive judgment to pursue the development of gaseous diffusion despite the objections of Nobel Prize winner Harold Urey had helped make isotope separation feasible and had helped assure a supply of nuclear fuel for the Little Boy. His pushing of the implosion effort despite Oppenheimer's hesitation had validated the multimillion-dollar plutonium production and had helped provide the weapon makers with the prototype for future bombs. In general, his relentlessly aggressive approach, his almost monomaniacal attention to detail, and the thoroughgoing practicality of his engineer's outlook had helped provide the impetus, the organization, and the sharp and steady focus to a scientist's dream and turned it into the reality of a war-ending weapon.

Secretary of War Stimson, the aging battler who had been Groves's boss, summed it up in the privacy of his diary: "The case was rare indeed where a single individual had the fortune to be as effective as Groves had in the winding up of a great war."

Groves had won the greatest gamble of all time. It now remained to be seen if the victory would consume him in turn.

Part Six

REAPING THE WHIRLWIND

Chapter Forty-Four

In the immediate aftermath of the bomb's success and the Japanese surrender, Groves became a ten-minute hero. In a private ceremony at the Pentagon, as Vannevar Bush and James Conant smiled behind their identical rimless spectacles, while a beaming Jean O'Leary and Groves's proud family shuffled nervously about, Secretary of War Stimson bestowed on him a presidential Distinguished Service Medal, one of the country's highest honors. His picture was featured prominently in *The New York Times* and *Time* magazine and on the cover of *Business Week;* in it he wore the new MED insignia—an Army Services star over a mushroom cloud in the shape of a question mark—on his uniform. To *The Saturday Evening Post* he was the "Atom General"; to *Collier's* he was "The Man Who Made Manhattan." In New York City, as a crowd of over five thousand assembled around the steps of City Hall, Mayor Fiorello LaGuardia praised him for "accomplishing the impossible." At a luncheon at the Waldorf-Astoria, IBM Chairman Tom Watson said, "We have no power to award medals, but if we did we would wish to award you the medal as the number-one pioneer of the United States." Later even Hollywood came to call, as writer-producer Carter Barron developed for M-G-M a movie about the bomb entitled *The Beginning or the End*, with Brian Donlevy playing Groves and the general himself on the sidelines as a ten-thousand-dollar technical adviser.

The public, overwhelmed by news of the tremendous power of the bomb itself, was soon agape from the revelation of the enormous size and complexity of Groves's domain. The numbers were indeed awe-inspiring: three major installations encompassing a total of over half a million acres; thirty minor installations, employing a total workforce of 129,500 and dispensing an annual payroll of some $200 million. When the final tallies were in, it was calculated that the bomb had cost slightly over two billion dollars—by far the largest governmental expenditure on the production of a single object to that time. Less well known but equally impressive was the fact that over a five-month period the MED had used some nine million dollars in top-priority (AAA) certificates—more than all extra-Army research projects combined. In the end, the project had generated a staggering 5,600 separate and patentable inventions, any one of which, declared Kellex engineer Yale Baker, would ultimately save more money than the bomb cost. In sum, as they studied the lengthy list of MED-generated "world's firsts" and "world's largests," observers both inside and outside the District were left to conclude that the bomb project had been, in the words of writer Stephane Groueff, "the greatest single achievement of organized human effort in history."

But Groves had little time to bask in the glow of his postwar heroism. In Chicago, the storm that had been gathering for three years and that had been held off only by wartime demands for secrecy and teamwork now began to drizzle on the general's parade. Secrecy itself was the issue, and Samuel Allison, one of the Army's most vocal critics during the war, sounded the opening salvo. In a speech at the Shoreland Hotel on September 1, he complained that Groves's security restrictions had rendered himself and his colleagues virtual prisoners of war. In Allison's mind, Los Alamos was a "luxurious concentration camp." And now, he said, the scientists were determined to return to the pursuit of research unfettered by Army watchdogging. If security regulations were not lifted, Allison threatened, scientists would leave the nuclear field and "devote themselves to the study of the color of butterfly wings."

The speech, which was flamboyantly quoted in that evening's Chicago *Tribune*, brought a swift reaction from Groves. The next day he sent Colonel Nichols to Chicago to lunch with Allison, Harold Urey, and Enrico Fermi. The colonel was not impressed by Allison's explanation that lunch had been late the previous day and that hunger had put him in a bellicose mood. As far as both Groves and Nichols were concerned, MED security restrictions were still in place until the scientists were told otherwise. In the meantime, Nichols said firmly, there would be no more talk about butterfly wings.

Witnessing this dressing-down, Fermi "squirmed" and Urey "sort of flopped around." But Allison himself was astonished at what he saw as a heavy-handed attempt to keep the scientists muzzled. Groves had already moved to declassify a substantial body of technical information and his office soon issued a public explanation of how the bomb had been put together, in a lengthy report compiled by Henry DeWolf Smythe. But the scientists were not calmed. Groves and the Army, they were increasingly sure, were trying to regulate and control them in peacetime just as they had during the war.

The continuation of tight security was anathema not only to Allison but to the three physicists—Urey, Leo Szilard, and Edward Condon— whom Groves had found most troublesome during the war. All three had substantial and deeply personal reasons for disliking Groves as a man and opposing his policies as a leader. Motivated by drawn-out patent disputes and by his self-avowed disrespect for all authority, Szilard had clashed openly and repeatedly with Groves; Groves had responded by hounding him to the fringes of the project. Urey had felt undermined by Groves's decision to overrule him on the continuation of the gaseous diffusion process, then embittered when the general finally replaced him at Columbia. Condon had quarrelled early with Groves over security at Los Alamos and had quickly left the project. Later, in the last days of the war, he had been particularly angered when Groves denied him permission— again on security grounds—to attend an academic conference in the Soviet Union.

With these three alienated but respected physicists as their public spokesmen, other project scientists soon began to organize. Some were merely disgruntled over personal wartime inconveniences, but most were genuinely concerned about what they saw as overly restrictive and potentially damaging Army security policies. By the end of September coalitions of scientists opposing the Army sprang up at Los Alamos, Chicago, Oak Ridge, and Columbia. Six weeks later some of these groups combined to form the Federation of American Scientists (FAS). It made little difference that with the exception of Urey, Condon, Allison, and a few other senior spokesmen, very few of the MED scientific leaders joined the FAS. With the organization of this central group, the battle lines were effectively drawn. For Groves it meant the beginning of the longest, the bitterest, and in the end the most damaging of his private wars.

The skirmish represented by Allison's butterfly speech and Groves's quick response soon escalated to full-scale conflict. The battleground was the floor of Congress, and at stake, it seemed, was nothing less than the peacetime control of atomic energy. Both sides knew that the MED, with its sweeping powers and its virtually autonomous authority, was a child of wartime necessities that could be neither expected nor desired to survive once the war was over. The question was, What kind of organization would take the MED's place, and when?

Groves, as usual, was inclined to move fast. Months before the war was over, he and his staff—especially attorney John Lansdale—had developed the skeleton of a new organization that would take over after the MED was legislated out of existence.* In the weeks following the Japanese surrender, the MED was suddenly enervated by the rush of its scientists back to academia. Groves and the War Department tried to hold the line and shore up the American nuclear enterprise by pushing the new organization through Congress. This alarmed Urey, Condon, Szilard, and the FAS, to whom this May-Johnson Bill, with its heavy fines for security violations and its vaguely MED-like organization, looked suspiciously and unappetizingly Grovesian.

The scientists were quick to react. From a tiny, one-room Washington office with little more than a telephone, a typewriter, and twenty dollars' worth of stationery, they mounted a surprisingly effective campaign against the bill. Their rumpled earnestness soon won them important allies both in Congress—where an ambitious freshman senator from Connecticut named Brien McMahon made them his personal charge—and in the national press. Wiser in the ways of politics than the scientists themselves, these new partners seemed to quickly realize that the questions that most seriously concerned the scientists—restrictive security and limitations on academic freedom—were only of back-page interest as public issues. The reporters soon fastened onto a far more arresting topic: the possibility that the May-Johnson Bill was a poorly disguised effort by Groves and the War Department to keep the atomic bomb and the development of atomic energy under tight military control.

Flogged mercilessly by the press, military versus civilian control soon became the watchword of the fight against the May-Johnson Bill. The FAS scientists, who originally had not cast the struggle in such simplistic terms, soon appeared to believe that Groves was trying to hoard control of the bomb for the Army, and specifically for himself.

As far as Groves was concerned, the issue of military versus civilian control was "a phony from start to finish." Even during the war he had told Stimson that as soon as the war was over the War Department and the Army should get out of every aspect of the nuclear business except that having directly to do with the bomb. "Otherwise," he said, "the entire time of the Chief of Staff would be taken up by atomic energy." In his first postwar

---

*History has mistakenly assigned the original drafting of the May-Johnson Bill to War Department attorneys Kenneth Royall and William Marbury. In fact the bill was first drafted in Groves's office by John Lansdale—a fact that, during the ensuing debate, both men kept entirely to themselves. Lansdale did not reveal it until an interview with the author some forty years later.

appearance before Congress, he told the Military Affairs Committee that he was "appealing for an opportunity to give up our existing powers." At the same time, he told his wife that his war-long struggle as head of the MED had left him exhausted and that he "never wanted to run anything again."

The FAS scientists were disinclined to believe him. Still sure that he was trying to retain the American nuclear enterprise as a personal fiefdom, they banded together with a pair of Washington lawyers and quickly introduced a competing bill under Senator McMahon's name. That bill pointedly refused to establish specific penalties for security violations and even more pointedly eliminated the military from all participation in the management of nuclear research.

To Groves, the McMahon Bill was like a glove across the cheek; he responded with the most powerful ammunition he had. To revive congressional concern for tight security, he carefully leaked the explosive news that British physicist Alan Nunn May had spent much of the war turning over MED secrets to the Russians. In an atmosphere of growing American suspicion of Soviet tactics and Soviet motives, the news had its desired effect. As headlines across the country trumpeted the spy story and proclaimed Russian perfidy, support for the McMahon Bill evaporated overnight. In its wake came compromise: amendments that included specific penalties for security violations (ironically these penalties, which included death for certain kinds of security crimes, were far stricter than those encoded in the original May-Johnson Bill) and that created a Military Liaison Committee as an adjunct to the civilian-run Atomic Energy Commission. The amended bill, which was grudgingly deemed satisfactory by both Groves and the FAS, finally passed Congress in late June 1946—a full nine months after the debate had begun. Senator McMahon, who had bitterly opposed both Groves and the amendments but had finally been outvoted in his own committee by ten to one, joked that he "now knew what it was like to be atomized."

No sooner had the bill passed than a new controversy arose, this one over the chairmanship of the new Atomic Energy Commission. By the end of July, Truman let it be known that he favored David Lilienthal, a professional administrator whose rapid rise to national prominence had been little short of spectacular. Round-faced, big, and imposing, Lilienthal had ascended from an obscure law practice in Madison, Wisconsin, to the directorship of the Tennessee Valley Authority (TVA) at the age of thirty-three. TVA was an $800 million government electric utility that, with its twenty-seven dams and 140 distinct electric cooperatives, was one of the few enterprises in the country that rivaled the Manhattan District in megalithic vastness. In the course of his accelerated climb, Lilienthal had developed an often noted ability to handle reporters ("The press loved him," recalled subsequent AEC General Manager Kenneth Fields) and a reputation for extreme quickness of mind and exceptional analytical capacity. But even while he was making friends in government and in the press, Lilienthal's high-handed attitude—he once kept no less a figure than the Baron de Rothschild waiting for hours in his office—alienated not only his own subordinates and superiors but one General Leslie R. Groves.

Groves and Lilienthal had first clashed during the war. When in late 1942 a hurried Groves had called Lilienthal to discuss the provision of electric power for Oak Ridge, the director of the TVA had refused to see the director of the Manhattan District outside office hours. Miffed by what he saw as an arrogant slight, Groves decided not to consult with Lilienthal at all and left all further contact with the TVA to Nichols. Later, when General Somervell suggested inducting Lilienthal into the Army and placing him over Matthias at Hanford, Groves refused outright.

Against this stormy background, Groves now let it be known that he was not pleased with Lilienthal's appointment. Aware of the general's antipathy, Lilienthal himself struck a hostile attitude. The mutual bad feeling made the transition of atomic authority from the MED to the Atomic Energy Commission (AEC)—a transition already fraught with complex practical problems—all the more difficult. On the one hand, Lilienthal all but refused to consult directly with Groves during the six-month transition period. On the other, Groves balked at providing the Commission with a new and detailed inventory of project holdings, and he continued to fight to keep custody of atomic weapons and weapon facilities in the hands of the military.

In the end, of course, transition was inevitable. On the afternoon of December 31, 1946, in an official ceremony in President Truman's office, Groves symbolically handed over the keys to the atomic kingdom to Lilienthal and the AEC. The general himself took one of the four seats on the Military Liaison Committee—in effect, a long step into the background.

That step marked the end of one of the most remarkable stewardships in American history. Starting with little more than a body of scientific theory and a series of preliminary experiments, Groves had built the mightiest production establishment known to man. It had been, in the words of Undersecretary of War Robert Patterson, "an unprecedented feat of organization and management." Driving and pushing, bullying and cajoling with great daring and extraordinary effectiveness, he had directed the making of the weapon that not only ended the war but changed forever the shape of both war and peace.

In the aftermath of this unique achievement, Groves found himself constitutionally unable to go quietly into the night. From the sidelines, he continued to prick and prod at Lilienthal and the AEC. The Commission, he complained, "pointedly avoided using the men [presumably Nichols and himself] who are the most experienced in the field of atomic energy." He quickly found the Military Liaison Committee a toothless bear, essentially ignored by the Commission itself. Worst of all from his point of view, the custody of atomic weapons had been taken from the military and given to the civilian AEC, meaning that the soldiers who would be charged with delivering the weapons in case of a nuclear war would have to waste precious time garnering the permission of five scattered commissioners.

Obviously and publicly disgruntled, Groves was considered by many a pest and an obstruction. When the general's long-time ally Senator Kenneth McKellar launched a vitriolic campaign against Lilienthal— after which a congressional investigating committee completely exonerated the AEC chairman—the general was widely thought of as having had a hand in its orchestration. He was also widely suspected of trying to generate spy scares to discredit the AEC. Although these suspicions were never confirmed, they lingered in the minds of many—especially scientists and reporters—as evidence of Groves's obdurate reluctance to surrender his personal authority.

If it was true, as Groves said so often, that he had no further personal ambitions in regard to atomic energy, why did he seem so unwilling to turn over the reins? Undoubtedly, the general was of two minds. On the one hand, the tremendous pace and pressure both of his wartime and his peacetime battles had left him genuinely and thoroughly exhausted, so much so that immediately after turning over authority to the AEC he ensconced himself in a Florida hospital for a three-month rest. It was in that depleted frame of mind that he had written to a friend that his continuing responsibilities for the MED "will be the end of me" and that he had told his wife that he "never wanted to run anything again."

On the other hand, he felt a powerful emotional attachment to what he saw as his personal creation. "I feel," he told one AEC commissioner, "like a mother hen watching strangers take all her chicks." He also felt— perhaps with some reason—that no one in the world knew as much as he did about running an atomic energy program and that the AEC commissioners (with the possible exception of Robert Bacher) were little more than well-intentioned amateurs. With this in mind, it was impossible for him to remain detached, impossible for him not to feel hurt and puzzled when he found himself unceremoniously steered to the sidelines. Bitter and frustrated—"I've gone from being the admiral of the fleet," he wrote one friend, "to being the captain of one destroyer"—he retired from the Army in January 1948, leaving behind him the only career he had ever known.

In the end, this battle was extremely costly. Although he had succeeded in restoring to the military at least some role in atomic energy administration, without custody of nuclear weapons that role turned out to be limited and essentially symbolic. In the meantime, an Army career that had occupied most of his lifetime and that was studded with brilliant achievements had been sadly sacrificed. His lone-wolf style of operating and his almost monumental ego—he had at one point likened his administration of the MED to that of an "absolute monarch"—had alienated many of his associates in the Army. His intense and at times heavy-handed insistence on the rights of the military and on the exclusive priorities of national defense had distanced him from many of his most important scientific allies, including Bush, Conant, and Oppenheimer. As he faded swiftly into what he saw as an enforced retirement, Groves found himself, as he had most of his life, virtually alone.

Chapter Forty-Five

Ⅰt should have been a gratifying day. General Leslie R. Groves (retired) had come down from his new home in Darien, Connecticut, to give a seminar at the National War College in Washington. The subject of the seminar was on everyone's mind that September day in 1949: how long would it take the Russians to match the American achievement and explode an atomic bomb of their own? As the officer students listened attentively to the distinguished graduate—the one man who could have been expected to best know the state of the Russian bomb effort—Groves made a prediction that he had made many times during the four years since the end of the war: "The Russians may have scientific ability, but they don't have the practical skills, the industrial know-how, or the ability to mobilize resources that we do. It'll be ten to twenty years before they make an atomic bomb."

On the dais beside Groves, Colonel Kenneth Fields squirmed uncomfortably. An outstanding West Point graduate and former football player whom Groves had maneuvered into MED service at the end of the war ("Groves looked for two things in his officers," Fields recalled, "a top ten academic standing and a place on the football team"), the colonel was now a weapons development specialist at Los Alamos and an Army liaison officer to the Atomic Energy Commission. As such, he had received the night before the most distressing news he had heard since the end of the war, news that he had not yet had a chance to communicate to Groves. Two days before, monitors in a B-29 flying over the Pacific had picked up signs of intense radioactivity emanating from somewhere in the Soviet Union. Furious calculations had confirmed the worst: the Russians had detonated their first atomic bomb. Now, Fields knew, Groves had inadvertently put his foot in his mouth. Not wishing to embarrass his former boss, Fields could only hedge when asked to make his own prediction. "You never know," he hemmed. "It might happen tomorrow."

The incident was only one of a long series of public embarrassments that Groves suffered after the war. They had begun in the fall of 1945, when it was revealed that he had ordered American occupation troops in Tokyo to destroy the experimental cyclotrons of Japanese physicist Yoshio Nishina. Although Nishina had indeed been charged by the Japanese Army with the task of building an atomic bomb, it was obvious to American scientists that their effort had been even less successful than the German. In fact, Robert Serber, who inspected Nishina's lab just after the war, found it "pathetic." Still, the order was processed, and Nishina was forced to watch in tears as American soldiers destroyed his cyclotron with welding torches and crowbars. The act brought screams of protests from American physicists. Groves later tried to explain it away as carelessness, but Robert Furman, who says he actually sent a letter to Farrell trying to get the order stopped, called it "stupidity on the Army's part; a terrible mistake." It was a mistake that many physicists remained unwilling to forget.

At the same time, his use of a spy scandal to advance the Army's ends was backfiring on him. After the transition of authority to the AEC in 1947, a new rash of spy stories had erupted, one involving a pair of Army sergeants who were accused of taking some secret MED documents from Oak Ridge, the other concerning a Princeton student named Alexander van Luft who had somehow lifted a single document from Los Alamos and had taken it home as a "souvenir." Although both these escapades turned out to be harmless, the widespread publicity they received—out of all proportion to their true significance—prompted anti-Groves elements in the press to proclaim that the general had purposely leaked the stories in order to discredit the AEC. Although the general vigorously denied the charges, he never quite lived them down.

Three years later, the far more serious treacheries of Klaus Fuchs and David Greenglass were revealed. Greenglass, a sergeant in the SED detachment at Los Alamos who had had a minor job assembling lens molds for the Fat Man, had turned over some crude sketches of those molds to Soviet agent Harry Gold. Although the value of those sketches to the Russian atomic-bomb effort was hotly disputed, few doubted that the information gleaned from Fuchs, who had far greater access and far more comprehensive knowledge than Greenglass, had effectively advanced the Soviet cause—some scientists said by as much as eighteen months. These sensational revelations enabled Senator Brien McMahon, who was still embittered from his earlier battle with Groves, to turn the tables, charging that Fuchs's treason had been the general's exclusive "fault and failure" and that the MED security system had been in effect a "cafeteria service for enemy spies."

For his part, Groves could maintain with some reason that the British were to blame for Fuchs's infiltration, that agreements between Roosevelt and Churchill had prevented Groves from carrying out his own investigation of Fuchs and the British contingent. But his curiously offhand dismissal of the Greenglass incident—"We had over 150,000 employees in the Manhattan District," he shrugged; "We couldn't watch them all"— seemed to many inconsistent with his wartime preoccupation with security in general, and in particular with his almost rabid pursuit of Leo Szilard, who although troublesome was hardly an enemy spy. Groves later attempted to blame the Los Alamos scientists; their insistence on open and free-wheeling colloquia, he maintained, had given Greenglass far more information than he needed to do his relatively insignificant job. This struck many scientists as being both essentially inaccurate and blatantly unfair.

Equally embarrassing was a spy story in which the central figure turned out to be Groves himself. In the winter of 1949, a bony-faced New York businessman named George Racey Jordan, who as an Air Force major had been a wartime liaison officer with the Russians, loudly claimed that in 1943 he had uncovered three shipments of uranium, totaling some 2,850 pounds, that had been made directly to the Soviets— shipments that, Jordan claimed, had been authorized and signed off by Roosevelt adviser Harry Hopkins. He also accused Hopkins of turning over a group of top-secret documents on the Manhattan Project to the Russians, documents that purportedly came directly from Groves's office. In the public uproar created by Jordan's sensational charges, Groves was called to testify before Congress. He emphatically exonerated the White House aide: "At no time did I ever meet Harry Hopkins, talk to him on the phone, receive any letters from him or write any to him, or have any dealings with anyone who pretended to be talking for him. . . . Furthermore, I can't imagine any request from Mr. Hopkins along those lines ever occurring without my knowledge."

But in clearing Hopkins, Groves implicated himself. The uranium shipments to the Russians, he admitted, had indeed taken place, authorized not by Hopkins but by Groves himself. The story unfolded slowly. In January 1943, William Moore of the Lend-Lease Administration received a request from a Soviet purchasing officer for some 465 pounds of uranium in various chemical forms. Moore contacted several chemical companies, and all of them appeared eager to supply the Russian request. But because uranium had been placed (by Groves and the MED) on the War Production Board's critical materials list, the request was denied. But the Soviets were encouraged by private correspondence with the chemical companies, who obviously stood ready to do business despite the government restrictions, so they tried again. This time the request reached Groves.

The general, who might have been expected to indignantly turn the request down, did a surprising thing: he decided to indulge the Russians. In the first place, he reasoned, consistent turndowns might arouse Soviet suspicions as to why the uranium was being held so tightly to the American chest. In the second place, he thought, sending uranium to the Russians might actually present a splendid opening for American espionage: if MED agents could somehow track a shipment to its Russian destination, they might be able to find out something concrete about the state of the Soviet bomb program, which was at the time a deeply troubling mystery.

In the context of a wartime alliance that nearly everyone considered temporary, this reasoning might have seemed sound. But in 1949, with the alliance long since shattered and the Cold War heated by the recent explosion of the Russian bomb, the uranium shipment and Groves's approval seemed—to much of the public and press, at least—a dangerous and ill-conceived folly.

Without doubt, though, the most substantial and the longest-lasting of the controversies in which Groves was embroiled was the ongoing bitter debate over the effects of radioactivity on the decimated Japanese cities. Two days after the Hiroshima drop, Harvard University physicist Harold Jacobson, who had no connection with the Manhattan District, made a dramatic public announcement: radiation, he said, would render Hiroshima virtually uninhabitable for as long as seventy-five years. MED security agents immediately tried to silence Jacobson by threatening him with jail for security violations; on hearing this, Jacobson promptly fainted and had to be driven home by his doctor. But the announcement, which was carried in newspapers across the country, had made both the public and the scientific community understandably nervous.

Groves moved immediately to counter the growing public unease. Assured by Oppenheimer that Jacobson's statement was "lunacy" and by MED radiologist Stafford Warren that the injuries and deaths at Hiroshima had been almost entirely due to burns, the general organized a publicity event in which he and Oppenheimer sought to allay fears of lingering radiation by personally escorting a contingent of reporters and photographers to the Trinity site. Ensconced in a squadron of postapocalyptic white tanks, the group drove directly to Ground Zero, where, near the stunted, twisted steel stubs of what had been the bomb tower, Groves and Oppenheimer stepped out and nonchalantly posed for pictures. At the same time, Phillip Morrison and Robert Serber scoured the ruins of Hiroshima with a Geiger counter, picking up absolutely no unusual radiation levels. In fact, Morrison was heartened to see new growth already appearing on Hiroshima's bomb-blackened water lilies.

Still, the radiation controversy refused to die. Other reports from Hiroshima spoke of scores of patients whose hair had fallen out, whose white blood cell counts were radically low, or who were suffering from nausea and internal hemorrhaging—all symptoms of radiation sickness. The 1946 publication of John Hersey's book *Hiroshima*—a moving eyewitness account of a city struggling to recover from the horror of the bomb blast—further fanned public indignation. Over the ensuing forty years, estimates on radiation deaths at Hiroshima have varied extravagantly, from as high as twenty thousand by the Radiation Research Effects Foundation in Hiroshima to a low of one thousand by Joseph Hirschfelder, the Los Alamos physicist who was responsible for predicting the bomb's aftereffects.

A recent study of twenty thousand Hiroshima survivors by the National Research Council (in cooperation with the Japanese government) sheds little new light on the controversy. It concluded that although the radiation count at Hiroshima was 30 to 50 percent lower than earlier studies indicated, health hazards remained essentially the same. Indeed, the precise nature and extent of radiation effects on the human body still remains a topic of heated debate among radiologists. Although the controversy over radiation-caused deaths at Hiroshima will probably never be settled scientifically, it has continued to serve as powerful ammunition for anyone who wishes to paint Groves as a heartless villain or a mad bomber.

The controversy that perhaps most enmeshed Groves and that lingered longest in the public mind involved the perplexing figure of J. Robert Oppenheimer. In the nine years immediately after the war, Oppenheimer became perhaps the closest thing since the third-century alchemist Hermes Trismegistus to a scientific deity. He became chairman of the General Advisory Committee to the AEC, an elite scientific panel (Fermi, Rabi, and Conant were among its members) that was in effect an Olympian scientific council on atomic affairs. In 1948 he left Berkeley to become head of the Institute for Advanced Study in Princeton, perhaps the world's most prestigious think tank. There as director he became the putative boss of such legendary physicists as Albert Einstein and John von Neumann. His ubiquitous porkpie hat became a symbol of the entire physics enterprise; one science writer even devised a complex tongue-in-cheek formula for gauging the importance of any given physicist: by measuring the length and number of contacts he had with Oppenheimer.

But Oppenheimer did not enjoy this heady ascent for long. In 1954, a large part of the nation was gripped by the hysterical viciousness of McCarthyism; the physicist's marginally and harmlessly pink past then came back to haunt him. In the inquisitional atmosphere, in which any deviation from a conservative political norm was seen as an indication of dangerous red leanings (if not outright communism), the Atomic Energy Commission—whose general manager was none other than Kenneth Nichols—decided to act on the wildly extravagant charges of congressional staffer William Liscum Borden. Borden accused Oppenheimer of being "an espionage agent operating under a Soviet directive."

Whether or not they took Borden's charges seriously, the commissioners knew that Oppenheimer's political background had for a time been something less than lily-white. Perhaps fearing the wrath of McCarthy and FBI Director J. Edgar Hoover, who at that point gave the impression that they alone were running the country, the AEC suspended Oppenheimer from the General Advisory Committee and in April 1954 opened a special hearing to determine whether the physicist constituted an ongoing security risk. The AEC billed the procedure as a "hearing," but it was in effect a trial—one that quickly and spectacularly became public. As the nation, and particularly the scientific community, looked on in horrified fascination, as reporters battled each other for copies of the transcript, Groves made a dramatic appearance.

Earlier, the general had written that in reviewing Oppenheimer's record before appointing him to head Los Alamos, "it was apparent to me that he would not be cleared by any agency whose sole responsibility was military security. Nevertheless, my careful study made me feel that, in spite of that record, he was fundamentally a loyal citizen and should be employed." Now, in the heat of the hearing, he stood by that estimate, saying that if Oppenheimer had ever committed a disloyal act, he would be "amazed."

A few minutes later, Oppenheimer's attorney Lloyd Garrison asked Groves a key question: in light of his knowledge of security matters and of Oppenheimer's background, would he give the physicist a security clearance today? Groves's answer, though preceded by a rather tortured interpretation of 1954 security requirements, seemed straightforward enough: "I would not clear Dr. Oppenheimer today if I were a member of the commission." But later, when Garrison asked if Groves thought that Oppenheimer should be fired from his AEC position, the general was equally emphatic in the opposite direction: firing Oppenheimer, he said, especially given the glare of public controversy, would be "most unfortunate."

In the end the AEC did fire Oppenheimer, removing him both from his job and from his security clearances. "They even came to Princeton," he said later, his eyes flashing with anger, "and took my files." It was a shameful episode in American history, and it galvanized the scientific community in support of its exiled colleague.

To many of those scientists, Groves's testimony had been confusing. Those who were inclined to support the general could say that he had given Oppenheimer a virtually unqualified character reference and had specifically recommended that he *not* be fired. But those who saw Groves as an enemy of science could cite his statement that he would not clear Oppenheimer in light of present-day restrictions, and they could say that the general had effectively pulled the rug out from under his long-time ally. Although in the last analysis it seems that Groves's ambiguous testimony was largely self-annulling, that it neither helped Oppenheimer nor hurt him, the fact remains that to many scientists—especially those connected with the FAS—Groves's statements amounted to a deep and personal betrayal. As far as they were concerned, that betrayal constituted one more black mark on the general's ever-growing list.

In the end, all these controversies chipped away at Groves's public reputation. Increasingly he came to be seen—especially in the eyes of the FAS scientists and their allies in the press—as a red-necked military bully, a blustering martinet who, when all was said and done, was an enemy of scientists and the scientific cause. Yet even in the midst of battle, even as he was criticizing his scientific opposition as loudly, as insistently, and often as inaccurately as they were criticizing him, he was at the same time taking quiet but important steps to ensure that in the long run science in general and nuclear research in particular would reap lasting benefits from his work.

Chapter Forty-Six

Norris Bradbury looked incredulously at his new boss. Bradbury, freshly chosen to replace J. Robert Oppenheimer as director of the Los Alamos laboratory after Robert Bacher turned the job down, had heard all the scuttlebutt about Groves. "I was told," he recalled later, "that he was unpleasant, unfriendly, not very loyal to his subordinates, and at his worst when talking to scientists." Yet here he was, in the heart of the ogre's Washington lair, listening to the general say in a dispassionate and even friendly tone, "All right, Dr. Bradbury, what can I do to help you?"

Bradbury was ready to test the general's good intentions. A Stanford physicist and former Navy commander, his small, almost frail body masked boundless energy, a prodigious memory, and a mental toughness that had won him the respect of everyone he had worked with at Los Alamos. Bradbury knew that his number-one priority was to halt the flow of scientific talent that had already seriously depleted the Los Alamos staff, or at least to replace those who had left with equally capable scientists. To do that, he knew, Los Alamos would have to be changed from the rude scientific Dogpatch it had been during the war to a modern and commodious facility that could attract and hold scientists not only by virtue of the challenging work it offered but by virtue of its creature comforts.

"General," said Bradbury, "what I need most of all at this point is some good housing."

Groves instantly agreed. He was pleased that Bradbury's priorities almost exactly matched his own. There had already been some talk in Congress about closing the laboratory entirely, and Oppenheimer had wanted to pack up the whole facility and move it to the more civilized confines of South San Francisco. By the end of July 1946, models for three hundred new homes, to be built that fall amid the pines and meadows to the west of the Tech Area, were ready for inspection. When some of the wives complained about the thin walls, the lack of floor insulation, and even the placement of the kitchen sinks, Groves—perhaps remembering his wartime struggles with the scientists' wives—doggedly had all those features upgraded and changed. "It was good housing," Bradbury said. "Groves didn't ask anyone for permission; he just went ahead and did it."

During this period, when the future of the lab was still in considerable doubt, Groves continued to mother-hen the operation as best he could. When one in a seemingly endless series of water crises had Los Alamos housewives lining up with pots and pans at the nearly dry tanks, the general was on the phone every day, ordering water trucked in to relieve the immediate shortage and spurring the digging of new wells and the installation of new lines to solve the problem for the long term. When Robert Wilson wrote a letter complaining about wartime censorship, Groves immediately called the new military commander, Colonel Lyle E. Seeman, and told him that the peacetime policy would be "to correct and improve for the future, and to express regret for any mistakes that may have been made in the past. . . ." It was an uncharacteristic show of contrition on Groves's part and a recognition of his own role in the wartime squabbles between the scientists and the Army. It left many Los Alamos scientists both relieved and slightly amazed.

While he was shoring up Los Alamos, Groves at the same time was working tirelessly—again, in the virtual absence of his wartime authority—to hold the line throughout the MED. He considerably streamlined the Oak Ridge operation, junking the Rube Goldberg-ish liquid thermal diffusion plant and the already outmoded Alpha electromagnetic building. He concentrated instead on expanding the far more efficient gaseous diffusion facility, which, now that the barrier problem had been solved, was clearly the isotope-separation process of the future. The Hanford plant continued to produce plutonium in a steady hum and as such needed little attention, but Groves did have to replace DuPont, which now wanted out of what it had seen as a strictly wartime obligation, with General Electric.

At the Met Lab he enthusiastically supported the efforts of Eugene Wigner and Walter Zinn to develop the next generation of nuclear reactors: devices that would actually "breed" more nuclear fuel than they consumed. In Berkeley, where, according to Molly Lawrence, Groves "seemed genuinely concerned that the Rad Lab get back to what it had been doing before the war," he repaid Ernest Lawrence for his wartime performance by allocating $170,000 to complete his enormous 184-inch cyclotron. He also found money to support Edwin McMillan in the development of the "synchrotron," a new type of particle accelerator. At the same time, he spurred the creation of new national laboratories at

Argonne, Illinois, and in Brookhaven, New York, laboratories whose sole order of business was to develop the atom for peacetime applications.

Szilard, Urey, Condon, and the FAS scientists continued to excoriate Groves for his stand in the debate over the AEC, but scientists who had been closer to the center of the project were more apt to see the constructive side of his actions. Robert Oppenheimer, who perhaps better than anyone else was in a position to evaluate Groves's performance, was moved to write the general that "there is no need for me to add words of appreciation for what you did during the war. . . . The United States knows that it is in your debt, and will forever remain so." But, Oppenheimer said, "it is much harder to recognize the many wise, disciplined, and constructive things you have done in the most difficult months since the end of the war, under circumstances where you were seldom free to act as you would have wished, yet bore a very heavy responsibility." Citing the general's unwavering support for basic science, the physicist went on to appreciate "the wise restraint that you have brought to the maintenance of healthy relations with the working scientists of this country, under circumstances of unparalleled difficulty." In conclusion, Oppenheimer said, "Let me offer a word of encouragement for all you have done to keep intact a going, and in some ways a growing organization for the future."

It was a stirring testimonial from the man whom Groves had plucked from near-anonymity to lead one of the most urgent scientific projects of all time, from the man with whom he had performed one of history's most unlikely pas de deux. And from the point of view of nuclear science and nuclear scientists, it was both a lasting eulogy and a final good-bye.

Chapter Forty-Seven

By the time he received Oppenheimer's letter, Groves was already on the point of becoming a private citizen. He was leaving the Army with great reluctance, motivated in part by the conviction that neither the military nor the government could ever again offer him a job that would equal the Manhattan Project in challenge, in satisfaction, and in pure excitement. "It would be impossible," he wrote wistfully in 1958, "for any job to be as interesting as mine was."

Nevertheless, Groves's obvious skill and daring as an administrator made him a prime catch. No sooner was the ink on his retirement papers dry than a number of potentially intriguing employers came to call. The Intercontinental Corporation tried to hire him to upstage his earlier feat at Galveston and build a series of enormous ports on the coast of India, but the general turned the job down as unappetizingly far from home. The newly formed All-American Football Conference, aware that the general was a former player and a great fan, wanted to make him its first commissioner, but the general wanted more autonomy than the club owners were willing to grant. Supreme Court Justice Felix Frankfurter, who had been thoroughly disgruntled during the war when Groves sent John Lansdale to confiscate the notes of the Justice's many conversations with Niels Bohr, now amazed the general by offering him a standby position as a top-level consultant to the Supreme Court in cases involving engineering—one or two of which cases, the Justice assured him, would "give a comfortable income for life."

But for Groves, by far the most tempting offer came from industry. As a sort of by-product of the Manhattan Project, the general had become greatly interested in the electronic computer, which had first been developed by MED consultant John von Neumann. During the war Groves had put a number of primitive IBM computers to work at Los Alamos, and both he and the scientists had been greatly impressed by the amount of

279

calculating time the machines had saved. After the war, Groves continued to stay in contact with von Neumann, and he had become increasingly excited about the computer's potential, convinced that these electronic wizards would soon revolutionize the way the world did its business.

In 1948, Remington-Rand seemed to agree. Already committed to developing the UNIVAC, one of the first of the gargantuan modern mainframes, Chief Executive James H. Rand saw in Groves the ideal man to push that development through to fruition. Groves enthusiastically agreed, and in February 1948 he signed on as vice president in charge of research and development—specifically, so he understood, to shepherd the UNIVAC to market.

Within a month Groves packed up and moved his family to a two-story Garrison home set deep among the pines and maples of Darien, Connecticut, Rand's corporate headquarters. There he launched himself with his customary vigor into his new job. Over the next five years he saw his efforts starting to pay off: UNIVACs found places at the United States Bureau of the Census and at the Metropolitan Life Insurance Company; they were even used by a University of Cincinnati astronomer to calculate the exact position of the infinitesimally faint eighth moon of Jupiter.

But in the mid-1950s Rand decided to de-emphasize the computer, and as IBM slowly but surely filled the gap left by Rand's withdrawal, Groves found himself inexorably kicked upstairs. Trading on his name and reputation, which helped them recruit no less a figure than General Douglas MacArthur as Chairman of the Board, the company turned him into a glorified traveling salesman, sending him on national whistle-stop tours to promote the sales of typewriters and electric shavers. A director's title and business lunches on Rand's yacht were no substitute for a challenging and substantial job, and Groves ultimately grew dissatisfied. "He never said anything," recalled his friend Willard Holbrook, "but it was easy to see that he was bored."

On a brisk New Mexico day in 1946, Groves was driving down from the Los Alamos mesa with Norris Bradbury. The two men had spent the previous day in a nonstop series of planning sessions, and now both lapsed into a weary and contemplative silence. Suddenly, apropos of absolutely nothing at all, the general turned to the physicist and said, "Bradbury, why don't people like me?"

The question, which left the disconcerted Bradbury fumbling for words, was indicative of a deep change in Groves's personality and in his personal priorities. It was certainly not a question that would have occurred to him during the war, when, as he often said, "I was not running a popularity contest," or even before, when stepping on people's toes had seemed an unavoidable and in some ways inconsequential part of getting a job done. But now, with the biggest of all jobs successfully accomplished, with the pressure off (or at least relaxed) and his reputation established— at least in his own mind—Groves began to pay attention to the human values for which he had previously had neither skill nor patience.

The signs of this change, of his newfound sociability and relaxation, were perhaps most evident in Groves's home. He and Grace now found time to travel for pleasure, although even in the culinary paradises of Europe she never let him forget his undisciplined waistline. Richard, or "young Dick," as their friends called him, was making his own mark in the Army—to his father's intense although often well-concealed pride—and would eventually, after his father's death, rise to become a lieutenant general and an adviser for NATO officers to the Secretary of Defense. At Princeton Gwen met a young computer scientist named Alan Robinson, who survived the general's intense and protracted scrutiny to become his son-in-law and the father of three of his grandchildren, with whom, Gwen said, her own father was "super—he would get right down on the floor and play with them all day long."

If his family noticed a change in the general, so did nearly all the scientists who had close private contact with him—as opposed to his detractors in the FAS, who saw him only through the haze of wartime mythology. "During the war," commented Luis Alvarez, "he was a hundred percent business. But afterwards he seemed to be a good deal warmer." On visits to Berkeley, where, perhaps, he felt best understood and most respected, Groves found time for dinner parties at Trader Vic's with Ernest Lawrence and the Rad Lab scientists, and time to sneak off with Lawrence for a few sets of tennis at the Berkeley Tennis Club. "He didn't think Ernest was a very good player," Molly Lawrence recalled, "but he let him win because Ernest liked to win so much."

The wartime effort had brought him close not only to Lawrence, with whom he shared much in the way of background and basic temperament, but also to some scientists who on the surface seemed worlds apart. With Oppenheimer he maintained a friendship that, although never intimate, was always marked by mutual respect and even a certain warmth. On his postwar trips to Princeton, generally to consult with von Neumann on computer matters, he often stayed with Robert and Kitty; and when Gwen graduated from Bryn Mawr, Oppenheimer helped her get a job at the Institute for Advanced Studies. He maintained a warm correspondence with both James Conant and Richard Tolman, and on his rare visits to Pasadena, Tolman, of whom the general was particularly fond, became, as he put it, "one of the *must* people for me to see."

But undoubtedly his closest friend among the scientists was Sir James Chadwick. Forged by their close contact during the war, their friendship continued to grow because, Groves said, "each of us recognized the other as being wholly straightforward and honest." Others may have found the British physicist pinched and dour, but to Groves he was "a true gentleman—it stood out all over." The two corresponded frequently, and Groves and his wife paid the Chadwicks an occasional visit at their summer cottage at Denbigh, in the damp Neolithic forests of North Wales. "I am afraid," Groves wrote in a subsequent letter, "that as we get along in years we are going to constantly lose friends of long standing." The letter was painfully predictive, for Chadwick, whose health had been poor for years and who could sleep only with the aid of barbiturates, died in 1974.

The change in Groves's personality was equally obvious to his nonscientist friends. When he moved back to Washington after his retirement from Rand in 1961, he took steps to reestablish and rebuild lapsed acquaintances with West Point classmates Charles Holle and Willard Holbrook, and he was an amiable guest at parties thrown by old Army friends William Wanamaker and Albert C. Wedemeyer. Everyone remarked that Groves had mellowed, that he had in large part dropped the sarcasm that kept people at a distance all his life. "People started to like him," said Holbrook, "and he found out that he liked being liked."

The only real shadow on Groves's private life was cast by his own heart. After the war, Stafford Warren had warned him that "you are playing things a little close to the margin of your cardiac reserve." From a distance Dr. Charles Rea continued to monitor the weight and diet of the man who during the war had been his "most unruly patient." In addition to atherosclerosis, which put his already weak heart under even more strain, the general suffered from chronic nephritis and was continually plagued by pains in his knees and elbows.

Still, he was not the sort of man to let health problems still him. His retirement from public life, although final, was never quite complete. A lifelong Republican conservative, he now became an active campaigner, an intimate of Herbert Hoover and a behind-the-scenes promoter of the presidential candidacies of Robert Taft and Douglas MacArthur. His residence in Darien made him, ironically enough, a neighbor of Brien McMahon (a cartoon in a local newspaper once showed the two men eyeing one another suspiciously from their respective lockers in the country-club dressing room), and for a time there was serious talk among local party leaders of running Groves against McMahon for his seat in the Senate. Although he appeared to toy with the idea for a time—certainly, he must have felt, it would have been an interesting race—the general eventually backed away, deciding instead to support another Republican candidate.

He also became something of a public spokesman on nuclear affairs, the man whom reporters trotted out whenever atoms, and especially atom bombs, were in the news. The detonation of the first Russian bomb had left him surprisingly nonplussed, despite the spectacular inaccuracy of his earlier prediction. "I'm not losing any sleep over it," he said. "We're still considerably ahead." Nonetheless, he used the opportunity to publicly urge that the United States push ahead with all speed to develop the hydrogen bomb that Edward Teller had been promoting since MED days. He consistently supported the development of nuclear power and especially the nuclear-powered submarine, through which he formed a long-term friendship with fellow military maverick Hyman Rickover. In the mid-1950s, when government-sponsored Operation Plowshare seriously entertained the audacious idea of using nuclear explosives to excavate a second Panama Canal, Groves assisted with the survey. (Ultimately and fortunately, the idea was dropped because of the possibility of setting off massively destructive earthquakes in the region.)

But by the 1960s, Groves's activities were severely limited by his weakening heart. He began to have fainting spells, and he found it increasingly difficult to climb stairs. One day, while approaching the tenth green at the Chevy Chase Country Club (he had long since traded the serious exertions of tennis for the gentler exercise of golf), he began to walk around in circles—circles that grew increasingly smaller until he collapsed. Although on his revival he insisted on driving himself home, it was soon found that he had suffered a heart attack.

From that point on Groves went into a steady decline. As his arteries grew increasingly constricted by atherosclerotic plaque, the fainting spells and falls became more frequent. On Sunday, July 12, 1970, he had lunch with his son Dick and his family at the Chevy Chase Country Club. At nine o'clock the next morning, he complained of severe chest pains. His wife immediately drove him to Walter Reed Army Hospital, where for two hours doctors worked furiously to keep him alive. But it was no use. At eleven o'clock, still in the emergency room, Groves died. Three days later, after a funeral service in Fort Meyers, Virginia, he was buried with honors at Arlington National Cemetery, within walking distance of the Pentagon.

*   *   *

A few years before Groves's death, his old friend Charles Holle had taken a trip to Oak Ridge. For Holle it had been both a sentimental journey and a matter of curiosity, for despite his long-standing friendship with Groves, he had never actually visited any of the MED installations. Now, Holle thought, the enormous, thrumming facility, with its mammoth factories for separating uranium, its hundreds of miles of roads, its thousands of homes, and its dozens of churches, schools, and hospitals should have represented one of Groves's most triumphant legacies, a personal monument to the skill and resolution of the man who more than anyone else was responsible for its creation.

As he was about to leave, however, Holle stopped in one of the local stores to buy a postcard. He filled it in, addressed it to Groves at his Connecticut Avenue home, and started to drop it in the mailbox. Then, on impulse, he showed it to the girl who was clerking behind the counter. Pointing to the side of the card where he had written Groves's name, he said, "Is that name familiar to you?"

The girl looked quizzically at the name, then turned the card over, as if expecting the answer to be revealed on the other side. When it wasn't, she handed the card back to Holle and shrugged.

"Sorry, sir," she said, hardly stirred from her apathy. "I never heard of him."

Postscript

How did Groves come to lose the place in history that he had so apparently earned? World War II created a pantheon of heroes — Eisenhower, MacArthur, Patton, Bradley. Why is Groves's name so conspicuously missing from the list?

Without a doubt, the general was in large part a victim of his own ego. "After the war," recalled former Groves assistant Joseph Volpe, "I used to help him with his speeches. I'd cross out the *I* and put in *we* or *they*. Then he'd cross that out and put the *I* back in." "It was a little ridiculous," remembered Emilio Segrè. "He tried to take credit for *everything*." Even the general's personal papers reflect his propensity for bragadoccio. When complimented for his sharp recall of a diplomatic report, whose authors included not only future Secretary of State Dean Acheson but also Lilienthal and Oppenheimer, he wrote, "I think it was because I was more interested than any of the others, and maybe I had a better mind to start with." In the 1950s a television interviewer asked him to characterize the administration of the MED. "The whole thing," replied Groves without hesitation, "was centered on me."

That ego, in combination with his brusque and often sarcastic style, alienated many of the people who might otherwise have championed him. It especially alienated the former MED scientists who later became so influential in the FAS. Among those scientists, it became something of a parlor game to circulate uncomplimentary stories about Groves: his alleged mania for security, his malapropisms, his scientific naïveté, his supposed tightfistedness with a budget. Some of these stories were probably true; others, such as his "welcome speech" to the Army personnel at Los Alamos, for example — in which he was widely quoted to have said, "Gentlemen, we have gone to great trouble and expense to assemble here the greatest collection of crackpots the world has ever seen" — were almost certainly apocryphal. These stories would later congeal to form a sort of Groves antilegend, squeezed by reporters and writers into a picture of the general that was more a caricature than a portrait, distorted in proportion to its lack of dimension.

But it may be that the single factor that contributed most to the displacement of Groves was the tragic fall of J. Robert Oppenheimer. Even before he was pilloried by the AEC in 1954, reporters tended to exaggerate the physicist's role in the success of the MED. Oppenheimer's charm, his articulate and quotable fluidity, and his sparkling intellect made him excellent copy, so that it was easy to forget that he had been director of only one MED facility and to make him, as one *New York Times* story did, the "scientific director of the Manhattan Project" or, even more inaccurately, "The Man Who Built the A-Bomb."

But with his figurative death on the sacrificial altar of McCarthyism, the Oppenheimer legend began to take on almost mythical proportions. Appalled by what seemed a terrible and senseless martyrdom, scientists and reporters alike rushed to defend him, to eulogize him, and at the same time to stand in the shade of his suddenly immense shadow. For the rest of Oppenheimer's sadly shortened life—he died of throat cancer at sixty-two, thirteen years after the AEC hearings—realistic estimates of his contribution to the bomb project were drowned in sheer hyperbole. To the press and public, he became "a scientific genius, the technocrat of a new age for mankind." At a reunion of physicists, the normally restrained Norris Bradbury declared that Oppenheimer had built Los Alamos "by the sheer force of his personality and character." To more than one physicist, he was "Mr. Los Alamos." To a subsequent biographer, he was the "Shatterer of Worlds." But during the AEC hearings themselves the sobriquet emerged that stuck most firmly in the public mind: Oppenheimer was, according to *Newsweek* magazine, the "Father of the Atomic Bomb."

As time went on, the Oppenheimer story was told and told again. It was, after all, an extremely good story, almost Promethean in scope: the physicist had dared the gods with his aspiration, had angered them with his success, and had paid the final price for his hubris. As the story was repeated, it was increasingly told from the point of view of the scientists. Since many of those scientists were unsympathetic to Groves and the military, Groves himself was either pushed aside in the telling or assigned a role that smacked either of villainy or of comic relief. That role reached a ridiculous extreme—and at the same time probably its widest and most unfortunate public acceptance—with the release of a 1981 BBC "docudrama" on Oppenheimer, in which Groves was presented as a candy-chewing, foul-mouthed martinet with the accent of a rednecked Southerner. The characterization was done for the sake of dramatic conflict but with no regard at all for reality.

It is curious that the scientists who knew Groves best, those who were close to the top and center of the MED, have been nearly unanimous in their praise for the general's execution of his job. "There were many people at Los Alamos who took a rather dim view of General Groves," recalled Robert Bacher. "But the fact is that he was an extraordinarily able man, a genius at getting things done under very adverse circumstances." To George Kistiakowsky he was "difficult, but extraordinarily capable as a manager. The thing he did with the Manhattan Project was next to a miracle." I.I. Rabi felt that Groves did "a great job, and not only at Los Alamos. It was an incredible achievement; there was never anything like it in history." Even Groves's antagonist David Lilienthal was moved to remark that "a comparable feat [to the MED] would have been the development of diesel engines and oil-burning ships five years after the discovery of oil."

Like Lilienthal, some of the other figures with whom Groves had had the most troublesome relationships during the war eventually came to see the value of his contributions. When the Senate was considering a special bill to give Groves a permanent retirement rank of Lieutenant General, Edward Condon wrote that it was a "splendid and long overdue recognition for a man whose really superior accomplishments during the war should have been recognized. . . . It is most unfortunate that in the heat of the controversies·which developed after the war . . . there was a tendency to detract from General Groves's accomplishments as an engineer and administrator. . . . I am sure that every fair-minded person realizes that General Groves did an amazing job." A few months before the general's death, Eugene Wigner wrote, "Few of us realized in the days of the Manhattan Project how great your contribution was thereto, and even though I always had the most profound regard for you personally, I did not realize it at that time either."

. But perhaps the strongest summary tribute came from Luis Alvarez.

I have been most embarrassed by the treatment you have received publicly at the hands of some of the younger scientists. Those of us who disagree strongly with their views have refrained from replying in public . . . , but you can rest assured that we have defended you stoutly in scores of private debates, and have in fact convinced many of your detractors that they were wrong. It has been my observation that those most critical of you had absolutely no idea of the job you did. With one exception, I never met a man who worked at all closely with you who was not overwhelming in his praise. My own feeling is that your handling of the Manhattan District was superb and advanced the end of the war by at least a year. I shudder to think what a flop the whole project would have been without your direction.

In the end Groves's contributions stand immutable and ultimately unaffected by either praise or condemnation. The great wartime facilities he built still exist and are still on-line. Oak Ridge still separates U-235 from uranium ore, and the gaseous diffusion method, although it will eventually give way to sophisticated laser techniques, is still the industry standard. The Hanford plant has had a more checkered and controversial history; a 1986 government report indicated several escapes of dangerous radiation during the plant's lifetime. But none of these occurred during Groves's tenure. Los Alamos is not only one of the world's foremost weapons development centers (still administered by the University of California), it is also the site of advanced research on the controlled fusion reactors that may eventually make present-day nuclear power facilities safely obsolete. The Argonne and Brookhaven National Laboratories that Groves helped start after the war have contributed everything from new knowledge of the subatomic particles that are the basic stuff of the universe to special diets for avoiding jet lag.

And what about the atomic bomb, certainly, in terms of its impact on the world, the most important of Groves's many legacies? The general himself never showed the slightest regret or remorse over the building of the bomb or its use on Japan. "I wish the people who complain so loudly about the Japanese who were killed," he once wrote to Jean O'Leary, "could take a trip to the war cemetery in Honolulu and see the graves of the thousands of American boys who were killed by the Japanese." To the end of his days, he continued to see the bomb as a war-shortener and an ultimate life-saver.

It would be too easy, although perhaps in some ways true, to dismiss Groves's responsibility for the bomb's development, to say that he was simply doing a soldier's job in wartime. It would likewise be too easy, although, probably true, to say that if Groves had not done it, someone else would have—and that someone else might have been the Germans, the Russians, or even the Japanese. The responsibility was certainly not his alone; if the scientists could not have built the bomb without his managerial leadership, he himself could not possibly have done it without the scientists, the engineers, the industrialists, and the laborers who moved the Manhattan District at its roots. But he was probably the one figure whose subtraction from the picture might have erased it altogether, and as such he must bear the weight of his own handiwork.

But precisely what is it that Groves's achievement wrought? Undeniably the bomb is, in terms of its impact on the lives of men, perhaps the single most important object ever invented. Yet in terms of its original purpose, as a weapon of war, it has been a phantom, a loud but ghostly voice bellowing from the closets in which it has been firmly locked for forty years. Ever since Nagasaki, despite the almost constant state of warfare in which the world has found itself, not one nuclear bomb has been dropped in anger. In fact, the bomb's greatest impact has been not actual but psychological: the great and certainly justified fear of future bombs rather than the horror of bombs actually employed. In the context of World War II this is precisely what Groves and its makers had in mind: not so much the actual horror of death and destruction, which the far bloodier conventional bombing of Tokyo had already shown to have little effect; but the psychological shock of death caused by a single and radically efficient new weapon.

Probably with this in mind, Groves came to see the atomic bomb as an antiwar weapon, as a sort of terrible and ultimate prophylactic against wars of all kinds. He was in large part wrong; the present existence of some forty small- to medium-size wars is awful testimony to the bomb's failure as a peace-keeping device. But he was, or has been up to now, right in terms of nuclear war. The bomb has in essence canceled itself out, and the very dread of its potentially apocalyptic effects, so forcefully portrayed in thousands of books, articles, and films, has made it increasingly unlikely that it will ever be used. This is not to say that the world should simply dismiss the bomb or underestimate its awful possibilities. Dread has engendered vigilance and sobriety, and they must be maintained if the world is to keep its apparently inevitable wars on something less than a planet-destroying scale.

But in the context of the present day, at least, perhaps the greatest atomic tragedy is the almost inestimable amount of money spent to maintain a weapons system that is, as former Secretary of Defense Robert McNamara has said, "militarily useless."

It is a relevant and perhaps hopeful irony that Groves's former offices are now occupied by the director of the Arms Control and Disarmament Agency. In fact, the deemphasis on nuclear bombs and on the baroque delivery systems that surround them, the freeing of that money for the feeding of the hungry, the healing of the sick, and the construction of a more genuinely humane human community would, in a convoluted way, make the bomb what Groves seems to have wished it were: a weapon of peace.

NOTES

Chapter One

Background: Lingeman, *Don't You Know There's a War On?*

"Edith Plant" is fictional, a composite of the 600,000 citizens who made up the Ground Observer Corps.

Page 4, paragraph 3: Ansel Talbert, New York *Herald-Tribune*, 10/9/39; William Laurence, *The Saturday Evening Post*, 9/7/40, and *The New York Times*, 5/5/40

Chapter Two

Background: Groves, *Now It Can Be Told*

Page 7, paragraph 2: Styer–SPEX, 5/4/42; Groves Personal Papers, passim

Chapter Three

Background: Jungck, *Brighter Than a Thousand Suns*
   Hewlett and Anderson, *The New World*

Page 9, paragraphs 1–3: Axelsson, George, "Is the Atomic Terror Exaggerated?" *The Saturday Evening Post*, 1/5/46

Page 11, paragraphs 3–4: Hooper–*The New Yorker*, 8/27/54

Page 12, paragraph 1: Sachs–Groves, 9/12/63

Page 12, paragraph 3: Eugene Wigner interview, 5/80

Pages 12–13: Sachs–Groves, 9/12/63

Page 13, paragraphs 5–6: Jungck, *Brighter*, pp. 110–11

Chapter Four

Background: Hewlett and Anderson, *The New World*
   Gowing, *Britain and Atomic Energy*

Page 15, paragraph 2: Luis Alvarez interview, 5/23/85

Page 15, paragraph 3: Sachs–Groves, 9/12/63

Page 18, paragraph 1: Richard Groves interview, 8/31/85

Chapter Five

Background: Fine and Remington, *The Corps of Engineers*
    Groves, *Now It Can Be Told*
Page 19, Fine and Remington, *Corps*, pp. 651–52
Page 21, paragraphs 2–4: Groves Personal Papers, passim
Page 22, paragraph 4: Bush–Bundy, 9/17/42; Groves Personal Papers, passim

Chapter Six

Page 25: Groves Personal Papers, passim
Pages 25–26: "Chronology of District X," MED Files, Library of Congress, pp.
    21, 43, passim

Chapter Seven

Background: Hewlett and Anderson, *The New World*
Page 28, paragraph 2: "District X," p. 83
    paragraph 3: Groves Personal Papers, Haley interviews, B6; "District X,"
    p. 126
    paragraphs 4–5: Groves Personal Papers, undated notes

Chapter Eight

Background: Lingeman, *Don't You Know There's a War On?*
    Nelson, *Arsenal of Democracy*
Page 33, paragraph 1: Clay–Styer 6/10/42; "District X," p. 83
    paragraphs 3–6: Groves Personal Papers, undated notes on General Lucius
    Clay
Page 34, paragraph 1: Nelson–Groves, 9/19/42
    paragraphs 2–3: Groves, *Now It Can*, p. 22
    paragraph 4: Groves Personal Papers, notes on *The New World*, p. 27

Chapter Nine

Background: Jungck, *Brighter Than a Thousand Suns*
    Hewlett and Anderson, *The New World*
    Groueff, *Manhattan Project*
Page 37, paragraph 1: *Business Week*, 8/18/45
    paragraph 2: Bunyard, *The Nuclear Britain*
    paragraph 4: John Gunther, "The Mystery Man of the A-Bomb," *Readers
    Digest*, 12/53, p. 19; Richard Groves interview, 8/30/85
Page 38, paragraph 2: Robert Furman interview, 7/24/85
Pages 38–39: Sengier–Groves, n.d.
Pages 39–40: Toronto Sunday *News*, 9/2/51

Page 40, paragraph 2: "District X," p. 66
   paragraph 4: Ibid., p. 147

Chapter Ten

Background: Groves Personal Papers, biographical notes

Page 46, paragraph 1: Richard Groves interview; A.S. Daggett–Military Secretary, 11/24/06

Page 48, paragraph 2: Gwen Groves Robinson interview

Page 49, paragraph 2: Groueff, *Manhattan Project*, p. 107

Chapter Eleven

Background: Groves Personal Papers, biographical notes

Page 52, paragraph 2: Willard Holbrook interview, 8/3/85; Holbrook interview; United States Military Academy, *The Howitzer*, 1918

Page 53, paragraph 2: Richard Groves interview; Holbrook interview
   paragraph 3: William Wannamaker interview, 8/20/85; Holbrook interview
   paragraph 4: Richard Groves interview

Page 56, paragraph 2: Richard Groves interview
   paragraph 3: Groves Personal Papers, speech to Officer Candidate School Graduation Class, Fort Belvoir, Virginia, 11/3/67
   paragraph 4: Charles Holle interview, 7/24/85

Chapter Twelve

Background: Groves Personal Papers, biographical notes

Pages 59–60: Richard Groves interview; Geraldine Elliott interview, 7/13/85; Donald Antes interview, 8/6/85; Groves–Shelley, 1/25/69; Fred Sherill–Groves, 10/28/47

Page 60, paragraphs 2–4: Hearing of Congressional Committee on Military Spending, 4/30/41

Pages 60–61: Gurney, *Pentagon*

Page 61, paragraph 2: Richard Groves interview
   paragraph 3: Holle interview; Antes interview

Page 61, paragraph 4: Wannamaker interview; Furman interview; Holle interview; Connie Watson interview, 7/28/85

Page 62, paragraph 2: William Potter interview, 8/15/85; Alan Robinson interview; Goodchild, *Oppenheimer*
   paragraph 3: Andrew Walker interview, 6/26/85; Ralph Carlisle Smith interview, 5/20/85; Joseph Volpe interview, 8/2/85
   paragraph 4: Robert Bacher interview, 5/16/85

Page 62, paragraph 3: Groves, Personal Papers, Ermenc interviews, pp. 23–24; Holbrook interview

Page 63, paragraph 2: Groves Efficiency Reports, in possession of Richard Groves
paragraph 4: Patricia Cox Owen interview, 8/2/85; I.I. Rabi interview, 8/4/85
Page 64, paragraph 2: Alvarez interview

Chapter Thirteen

Background: Groves Personal Papers, Haley interviews
Hewlett and Anderson, *The New World*
Groueff, *Manhattan Project*
Page 68, paragraph 3: Groves Personal Papers, notes dictated 11/6/64
Page 70: Loc. cit.
Page 71, paragraph 6: Groves Personal Papers, Ermenc interviews
Page 72, paragraphs 3–5: Groves Personal Papers, Haley interviews

Chapter Fourteen

Background: Groves Personal Papers, Haley interviews, Ermenc interviews.
Compton, *Atomic Quest*
Hewlett and Anderson, *The New World*
Groueff, *Manhattan Project*
Page 73, paragraph 2: Groves Personal Papers, Haley interviews
Page 74, paragraph 2: Compton–Conant, 5/18/42; Szilard, *His Version*, p. 147
Page 75, paragraph 1: AEC press release, 9/10/62
Page 76, paragraph 3: Groves Personal Papers, Haley interviews
paragraph 4: Groves Personal Papers, George Tressel interview, 7/12/67
Pages 77–78: Groves Personal Papers, Haley interviews
Page 78, paragraph 4: Wyden, *Day One*, p. 60
paragraph 5: Ibid., passim
Page 79, paragraph 1: Wigner interview
paragraph 2: Groves Personal Papers, Szilard memo, "What is Wrong With Us?"
paragraph 3: Groves Personal Papers, Haley interviews
paragraph 4: Szilard–Compton, 12/4/42
Page 80, paragraph 2: Compton–Groves, 10/26/42; Groves–Stimson, 10/28/42
paragraph 3: John Lansdale interview, 3/19/85
paragraph 4: Groves Personal Papers, Haley interviews
paragraphs 5–6: Compton, draft of *Atomic Quest* in Groves Personal Papers

Chapter Fifteen

Background: Groves Personal Papers, Haley interviews
Hewlett and Anderson, *The New World*
Groueff, *Manhattan Project*

Page 84, paragraph 4: Groves Personal Papers, Haley interviews

Page 85, paragraph 1: Ibid.

paragraph 2: Groueff, *Manhattan*, pp. 38–39

paragraph 3: "District X," p. 63

Page 86, paragraphs 1–3: Groves Personal Papers, Haley interviews

Page 88: Groves Personal Papers, undated notes

paragraph 3: Compton–Conant, 10/8/42

Chapter Sixteen

Background: Groves Personal Papers, Haley interviews

Groueff, *Manhattan Project*

Pages 89–90: Franklin Matthias interview, 8/20/85

Page 90, paragraph 3: Groves Personal Papers, Haley interviews

paragraph 4: Compton, *Atomic Quest*

Page 91, paragraph 1: Wigner interview

paragraph 2: Groves Personal Papers, passim

paragraph 3: *Investor's Reader*, 4/44

paragraph 4: Groves Personal Papers, Haley interviews

Page 92, paragraph 7: Groves Personal Papers, undated notes on DuPont

note: *Investor's Reader* 4/44

Page 93, paragraph 7: Matthias interview

Chapter Seventeen

Background: Groves Personal Papers, Haley interviews

Smith and Weiner, *Robert Oppenheimer*

Goodchild, *J. Robert Oppenheimer*

Page 95, paragraphs 1–2: John H. Dudley, in Badash et al., *Reminiscences*, pp. 3–4

paragraph 4: Groves Personal Papers, undated notes

Page 96, paragraph 2: Manley–Oppenheimer, 7/28/42

paragraph 4: Correspondence between Chicago and Berkeley during the first two weeks in October shows that before his arrival in California, both Groves *and* Oppenheimer had been thinking in terms of a bomb lab at the Oak Ridge site. On October 6, Manley wrote Oppenheimer, saying, "Groves was here yesterday, and there is a resulting increase in definiteness about the plans for site X [Oak Ridge]. He favors having everything concerned with production *and military applications* there." Oppenheimer had already telegrammed Compton on October 3 to say that he thought "proximity of fast and slow laboratories [i.e., bomb assembly and plutonium laboratories] desirable. Obviously, before the first Groves–Oppenheimer meeting on October 8, one of the two men—or both—had changed his mind. Since Groves had been somewhat disquieted by his experience at Chicago, it seems likely that the idea of isolating the bomb lab had occurred to him independently of any suggestion from Oppenheimer.

Page 98, paragraph 2: Groves Personal Papers, Haley interviews
paragraph 4: "District X"; Priscilla Green Duffield interview, 6/14/85

Page 99, paragraph 3: Dudley, op. cit.; Chambers, *Technically Sweet Los Alamos*, p. 44

Page 100, paragraph 2: AEC, *In the Matter*, p. 28
paragraph 3: Chambers, *Technically*, p. 56
paragraph 4: Smith and Weiner, *Oppenheimer*, p. 77; Manley, in Badash et al., *Reminiscences*, p. 24
paragraph 5: Jungck, *Brighter*, p. 20

Page 101, paragraph 2: Groves Personal Papers, undated notes on Oppenheimer
paragraph 4: I.I. Rabi interview, 8/13/85
paragraph 5: Compton, *Atomic Quest*, p. 151

Page 102, paragraph 2: AEC, *In the Matter*, p. 28

Chapter Eighteen

Pages 103–104: Bacher interview; Rabi interview

Page 104, paragraph 3: Groves Personal papers, undated notes
paragraph 5: Oppenheimer–Conant, 2/1/43

Page 105, paragraph 1: Groves, Conant–Oppenheimer, 2/25/43
paragraph 5: Bethe–Oppenheimer, 3/3/42; Kunteka, *City of Fire*, p. 40

Page 106, paragraph 1: Oppenheimer–Conant, 10/21/42; Conant–Groves, 12/24/42
paragraph 2: Conant–Groves, 1/7/42
note: Conant–Oppenheimer, 3/22/43; Conant–Oppenheimer, 3/13/43
paragraph 3: Oppenheimer–Rabi, 2/26/43; Rabi–Oppenheimer, 3/8/43; Bacher interview

Page 107, paragraph 2: This count was made by comparing lists developed by Oppenheimer, Bacher, Bethe, et al.—as found in Tolman–Groves, 7/26/43—with actual personnel records on file in the Los Alamos National Laboratory (LANL) Archives.

Chapter Nineteen

Background: Groueff, *Manhattan Project*

Pages 111–112: Groves Personal Papers, undated notes on Colonel James Marshall; Groves–Styer, 8/16/61; Richard Groves interview; Alan Johnson interview, 8/21/85; Bradbury interview

Chapter Twenty

Background: Groueff, *Manhattan Project*
Hewlett and Anderson, *The New World*
Jones, *Manhattan*

Page 113, paragraph 2: Matthias interview
    paragraph 3: Matthias Diaries, 6/19/43
Page 114, paragraph 2: Ted Van Arsdale, in "Hanford . . . The Big Secret,"
    Columbia Basin News, 1958
    paragraph 3: Groves–Patterson, 11/1/43
Page 115, paragraph 3: Groves Personal Papers, undated notes
Page 116, paragraph 3: Compton-Wigner, 7/23/43; Wigner–Compton, 8/5/43
    paragraph 4: Groves Personal Papers, undated notes
Page 117, paragraph 1: Compton, *Atomic Quest*, p. 169

Chapter Twenty-One

Background: Hewlett and Anderson, *The New World*
    Groueff, *Manhattan Project*
Page 118, paragraph 3: Richard Groves interview; Kenneth Fields interview,
    8/16/85; Goodchild, *Oppenheimer*, p. 56
Page 119, paragraph 4: Nichols, speech to National War College, n.d., in Groves
    Personal Papers; Groves Personal Papers, undated notes
Page 122, paragraphs 1–2: Groves Personal Papers, undated notes
Page 124, paragraph 1: Groves Personal Papers, Haley interviews
Page 125, paragraph 2: Ibid.

Chapter Twenty-Two

Background: Goodchild, *J. Robert Oppenheimer*
    Stern, *The Oppenheimer Case*
Page 127, paragraph 4: Goodchild, *Oppenheimer*, p. 72
Page 128, paragraph 2: Rabi memo, 4/28/43; Bethe–Oppenheimer, 12/22/42;
    Manley–Oppenheimer, 10/12/42
    paragraph 3: MED Organization Chart, 5/29/45; Groves, *Now It Can*,
    p. 154; Groves–Crane, 2/6/54; Groves Personal Papers, undated notes;
    Conant–Bush, 10/20/43; Tolman–Groves, 7/7/43
    paragraph 4: Oppenheimer–Groves, 5/27/43; Bradbury interview
    paragraph 2: Groves–Parsons, 2/26/48; Hirschfelder, in Badash et al.,
    Reminiscences, p. 83; Groves Personal Papers, undated notes; Bradbury
    interview
Page 129, paragraph 2: Bradbury interview
    paragraph 4: Tolman–Oppenheimer, 3/27/43
Page 130, paragraph 1: Minutes of Governing Board, 10/28/43; Neddermeyer–
    Parsons, 10/30/43
    paragraph 2: Bacher interview
Page 130, paragraph 3: Groves, *Now It Can*, p. 63
Page 131, paragraph 1: Goodchild, *Oppenheimer*, p. 93
    paragraph 3: Goodchild, *Oppenheimer*, p. 96

paragraph 4: Lansdale interview
paragraph 8: Emilio Segrè interview, 5/28/85; Minutes of the Governing Board, 7/15/43
Page 132, paragraph 1: Oppenheimer memo, 1943; Minutes of the Governing Board, 5/6/43
paragraph 2: Groves Personal Papers, "Comments on Oppenheimer in Los Alamos," n.d.
paragraph 4: Minutes of the Governing Board, 9/23/43, 10/28/43; Groves–Oppenheimer, 11/1/43; DeSilva–Lansdale, 11/8/43

Chapter Twenty-Three

Background: Jungck, *Brighter Than a Thousand Stars*
Pages 135–136: Alvarez interview
Page 136, paragraph 4: Seaborg Diaries, 12/6/43
Page 137, paragraph 1: Bethe, Teller–Oppenheimer, 8/21/43
paragraph 2: Lansdale–Groves, 2/1/60; Groves Personal Papers, notes dictated 11/24/65
paragraph 3: Furman interview; Matthias interview
paragraph 4: Groves Personal Papers, Re: General Marshall, notes dictated 10/16/63
Page 138, paragraph 1: Oppenheimer–Fermi, 5/25/43
paragraph 4: Jungck, *Brighter*, p. 56
paragraph 5: Jones–Groves correspondence, late 1943

Chapter Twenty-Four

Page 141, paragraph 1: Correspondence with Anne Wilson Marks, Winter 1986
paragraph 2: Smith interview
paragraph 3: Robert DeVore, "The Man Who Made Manhattan," *Collier's*, 10/13/45
Page 142, paragraph 3: Patricia Cox Owen interview, 8/21/85; Johnson interview; Watson interview
Page 143, paragraph 1: Elliott interview; Groves Personal Papers, Haley interviews, E3; Johnson interview
paragraph 2: Watson interview
paragraph 4: Smith interview; Groves Diaries, passim
Page 144, paragraph 2: DeVore, "Man Who Made"
paragraph 4: Groves Diaries, passim
paragraph 5: Elliott interview
Page 145, paragraph 2: Groves Diaries, passim; Groves Personal Papers, interview with Jerry Wallace, 3/19/48; DeVore, "Man Who Made"
paragraph 3: Groueff, *Manhattan*
paragraph 4: Rabi interview; Johnson interview; Watson interview; DeVore, "Man Who Made"; Bacher interview

Page 146, paragraph 1: Groves Personal Papers, Haley interviews, E3
    paragraph 2: Bacher interview; Duffield interview
    paragraph 3: Bernice Brode, "Tales of Los Alamos"; Duffield interview
    paragraph 4: Bradbury interview; Harold Agnew interview, LANL
Page 147, paragraph 1: Alvarez interview; Owen interview; Walker interview
    paragraph 2: Groves Personal Papers, passim
    paragraph 3: Richard Groves interview; Rea–Groves

Chapter Twenty-Five

Background: Groueff, *Manhattan Project*
    Hewlett and Anderson, *The New World*
    Jones, *Manhattan*
    Robinson, *The Oak Ridge Story*
Page 150: Groueff, *Manhattan*, p. 272
Page 151, paragraphs 3–4: Volpe interview
Page 153, paragraph 4: Jones, *Manhattan*, p. 148
Page 155, paragraph 2: Lawrence interview

Chapter Twenty-Six

Background: Groueff, *Manhattan Project*
Page 157, paragraph 1: Van Arsdale (1958)
    paragraph 3: Van Arsdale (1958)
Page 159, paragraph 2: Groves, *Now It Can*, p. 82
    paragraph 3: Matthias interview
Page 160, paragraph 4: Matthias interview
Page 162, paragraph 2: Groves Personal Papers, undated notes

Chapter Twenty-Seven

Background: Fine and Remington, *The Corps of Engineers*
    Hewlett and Anderson, *The New World*
Page 163, paragraph 5: Alvarez interview; Duffield interview
Page 164, paragraph 2: Alvarez interview; Brode, "Los Alamos"
    paragraph 3: Duffield interview; Johnson interview
Page 165, paragraph 1: Manley–Oppenheimer, 2/12/43
    paragraph 2: Groves Diaries, 1/44; Antes interview
    paragraph 3: Brode, "Los Alamos"
Page 166, paragraphs 1–2: Smith interview
    paragraph 3: Duffield interview
Page 167, paragraph 1: Unsigned War Department report, 11/12/46
    paragraph 2: Groves Personal Papers, Haley interviews, p. 43; Minutes of
the Governing Board, 5/25/44; Smith interview

paragraph 3: Rabi interview
paragraph 4: Walker interview; Duffield interview; Marks correspondence
Page 168, paragraph 1: Oppenheimer–Conant, 7/23/43
paragraph 2: Robert Duffield interview; Smith interview; Minutes of the Governing Board, 9/30/43; Seaborg interview
Pages 168–169: Kunetka, *City of Fire*, passim

Chapter Twenty-Eight

Background: Kunetka, *City of Fire*
Goodchild, *J. Robert Oppenheimer*
Page 171, paragraph 1: Segrè interview
Page 172, paragraph 1: Minutes of the Governing Board, 10/43; Los Alamos Personnel Report, 2/44
paragraph 3: Kistiakowsky–Conant, 11/1/43

Chapter Twenty-Nine

Background: Groves, *Now It Can Be Told*
Pash, *The ALSOS Mission*
Goudsmit, *ALSOS*
Pages 175–176: Lansdale interview; Groves Personal Papers, notes dictated 10/10/63
Page 176, paragraph 4: Joseph Marshall, "How We Kept the Atomic Bomb Secret," *The Saturday Evening Post*
paragraph 5: Groves–Kahn, 8/16/61; Lawrence interview
Page 177, paragraph 2: Walker interview; Groves Personal Papers, notes dictated 8/1/65
paragraph 3: Groves Personal Papers, undated notes
paragraph 4: Winacker–Groves, 6/3/75; Groves Personal Papers, notes dictated 9/24/63
paragraph 5: Groves Personal Papers, passim
Page 178, paragraph 2: Engel–Patterson, 1943; Matthias Diaries, 7/15/44
Page 179, paragraph 1: Lamont, *Day of Trinity*, pp. 66, 79
paragraph 2: Furman interview
Page 180: Goudsmit, *ALSOS*, p. 71

Chapter Thirty

Background: Hewlett and Anderson, *The New World*
Groueff, *Manhattan Project*
Jones, *Manhattan*
Page 181, paragraphs 1–2: Minutes of Meeting of the Military Policy Committee, 5/5/43

Page 182: Groves Personal Papers, Hoover Institute, pp. 20–21; *The Washington Star*, 10/7/65

Chapter Thirty-One

Background: Hewlett and Anderson, *The New World*
    Groueff, *Manhattan Project*
    Jones, *Manhattan*
Page 187, paragraphs 1–6: Matthias interview
Page 188, paragraph 2: Bacher interview by Mario Balibera, LALN
    paragraph 3: Matthias interview
Page 189, paragraph 3: Groueff, *Manhattan*
Page 191, paragraph 3: Groves Personal Papers, undated notes on Secretary Stimson

Chapter Thirty-Two

Groves Personal Papers, notes dictated 2/25/46; Groves Diaries, 4/25/45

Chapter Thirty-Three

Background: Goodchild, *Oppenheimer*
    Kunetka, *City of Fire*

Chapter Thirty-Four

Background: Lamont, *Day of Trinity*
    Kunetka, *City of Fire*
    Groves, *Now It Can Be Told*
Page 201, paragraph 2: Groves Personal Papers, notes dictated 5/13/63
Page 202, paragraph 2: Davalos–Tyler, 8/17/61
    paragraph 3: LANL, "Los Alamos: Beginning of an Era" p. 39
    paragraph 4: Alvarez interview
Page 203, paragraph 1: Groves Diaries, 6/4/45
Page 205, paragraph 4: Oscar Schisgall, "Background of the Bomb," *Liberty*, 10/13/45; Groves Personal Papers, undated notes on General Farrell; Elliott interview
Page 206, paragraph 2: Groves Personal Papers, undated notes

Chapter Thirty-Five

Background: Lamont, *Day of Trinity*
    Kunetka, *City of Fire*
Page 208, paragraph 4: Groves Personal Papers, Freed interview, 2/25/46

Page 209, paragraph 1: Davalos–Tyler, 8/17/61; Holzman–Groves, 4/17/63
 paragraph 2: Holzman–Groves
 paragraph 3: Hirschfelder, in Badash et al., *Reminiscences*, p. 76

Chapter Thirty-Six

Background: Lamont, *Day of Trinity*
 Kunetka, *City of Fire*
Page 211, paragraph 2: Groves Personal Papers, undated notes
 paragraph 3: Ibid.
Page 212, paragraph 6: Davalos–Tyler, 8/17/61; Groves Personal Papers, undated notes
Page 213, paragraph 2: Groves Personal Papers, Freed interview
 paragraph 5: LANL, "Los Alamos," p. 51
Page 214, paragraph 2: Groves Personal Papers, Freed interview

Chapter Thirty-Seven

Background: Lamont, *Day of Trinity*
 Kunetka, *City of Fire*
Except as indicated, all quotes in Chapter 37 are from Lamont
Page 215: Groves Personal Papers, Freed interview; LANL, "Los Alamos"
Page 216, paragraph 1: LANL, "Los Alamos," pp. 53–54; Frank Oppenheimer interview, LANL, 2/81
Page 217, paragraph 2: Groves Personal Papers, Freed interview
 paragraph 3: Groves–Stimson, 7/25/45
 paragraph 4: Giovanniti and Freed, *Decision*, p. 198
 paragraph 5: Elliott interview
 paragraphs 6–7: Groves, *Now It Can*, p. 298

Chapter Thirty-Eight

Background: Thomas and Witts, *Enola Gay*
 Groves, *Now It Can Be Told*
Except as indicated, all quotes in Chapter 38 are from Thomas and Witts
Page 220, paragraph 4: Groves Personal Papers, Freed interview
Page 220, paragraph 3: Groves Personal Papers, notes dictated 9/25/63
Page 221, paragraph 2: Groves Personal Papers, G. Carroll interview, p. 32
Page 222, paragraph 1: Ibid.; Elliott interview
Page 223, paragraph 2: Groves, *Now It Can*, p. 267
Pages 224–25: Groves Personal Papers, Freed interview

Chapter Thirty-Nine

Background: Thomas and Witts, *Enola Gay*
 Smith, *A Peril and A Hope*

Giovanniti and Freed, *The Decision to Drop the Bomb*
Compton, *Atomic Quest*
Groves, *Now It Can Be Told*
Szilard, *His Version of the Facts*

Pages 229–230: Furman interview

Page 230, paragraph 2: Morrison, in MED Decimal Files
paragraph 4: Groves Personal Papers, undated notes

Page 231, paragraph 2: Franck Report, reprinted in Jungck, *Brighter*, pp. 348–60

Page 232, paragraph 2: Compton, *Atomic Quest*, p. 238
paragraph 3: Giovanniti and Freed, *Decision*, p. 108
paragraph 4: Szilard, *His Version*, p. 212

Page 233, paragraph 2: Groves Personal Papers, undated notes
paragraph 3: Groves Diaries, 3/3/45, 3/27/45; Compton–Groves, 10/6/44, 12/7/44
paragraph 4: Groves–Compton, 5/28/45; Alvarez Interview

Page 234, paragraph 3: Robert Wilson interview, LANL, 5/20/80; Frisch, "Scientists and the Decision to Bomb Japan," unpublished ms. in Groves Personal Papers

Page 235, paragraph 2: Smith, *Peril*, pp. 78–79

Chapter Forty

Background: Giovanniti and Freed, *The Decision to Drop the Bomb*
Groves, *Now It Can Be Told*
Hewlett and Anderson, *The New World*

Page 238, paragraph 4: Groves Personal Papers, Bryson interview
note: Groves Personal Papers, undated notes on Robert Patterson

Chapter Forty-One

Background: Thomas and Witts, *Enola Gay*
Wyden, *Day One*

Except as indicated, all quotes in Chapter 41 are from Thomas and Witts

Page 242, paragraph 1: Groves Diaries, 7/45/passim
paragraph 2: Ibid; Groves–Oppenheimer, 7/9/45
paragraph 6: *The Washington Post*, 7/31/85

Page 244: Groves Personal Papers, undated notes

Page 245, paragraph 1: Schisgall, "Background"
paragraph 2: Jean O'Leary interview, 11/20/82
paragraph 6: Remmick, David, "Hiroshima, With No Regrets," *The Washington Post*, 7/31/85

Chapter Forty-Two

Background: Wyden, *Day One*
Groves, *Now It Can Be Told*

Page 247, paragraph 1: Groves, *Now It Can*, p. 322
   paragraph 2: Groves Personal Papers, McCrary interview, WNBC-NY, 8/16/48; Elliott interview
   paragraph 3: Groves, *Now It Can*, p. 323; Wyden, *Day One*, p. 286
Page 248: Groves, *Now It Can*, pp. 324, 328
   paragraph 5: DeVore, "Man Who Made"
Page 249, paragraphs 5–9: Owen interview
Page 250, paragraph 1: Robinson, *The Oak Ridge Story*, pp. 106–7
   paragraph 2: Van Arsdale (1958); Matthias Diaries, 8/6/45
   paragraphs 3–4: Groves Personal Papers, transcript of telephone call Groves–Oppenheimer, 8/6/45
   paragraph 5: Wyden, *Day One*, p. 290
   paragraph 8: "The Atomic Age," *Time*, 11/19/45
Page 251, paragraph 2: Smith, *Peril*, p. 78

Chapter Forty-Three

Background: Groves, *Now It Can Be Told*
Page 253, paragraph 1: Groves Personal Papers, undated notes
Pages 253–255: Cave–Brown and MacDonald, *Secret History*, pp. 532–34
Page 255, paragraph 3: Groves Personal Papers, Freed interview
   paragraph 4: Bacher interview
Page 256, paragraph 2: Stimson Diaries, 9/12/45

Chapter Forty-Four

Background: Hewlett and Anderson, *The New World*
   Smith, *A Peril and a Hope*
   Groves, *Now It Can Be Told*
   Herken, *The Winning Weapon*
   Groves Personal Papers, passim
Page 259, paragraph 1: *The Saturday Evening Post*, 9/1/48; DeVore, "Man Who Made"; Groves Personal Papers, clippings; "Enter: The Atomic Age," *Business Week*, 8/11/45
Page 260, paragraph 1: Groueff, *Manhattan*, p. xi
   paragraph 2: Gibbons, Roy, "Scientist Drops A-Bomb: Blasts Army Shackles," *The Chicago Tribune*, 9/2/45
   paragraphs 3–4: Smith, *Peril*, p. 89
Page 262, note: Lansdale interview
   paragraph 4: Groves Personal Papers, E.P. Eagles interview, 5/8/62
Page 263, paragraph 1: Hearings before House Committee on Military Affairs, 10/9/45; Richard Groves interview; Groves Personal Papers, notes dictated 4/1/68
   paragraph 3: McMahon radio interview, "Town Meeting," 3/28/46

Page 264, paragraph 1: *Atlantic Monthly*, 2/46; *Popular Mechanics*, 5/46; Fields
   interview
   paragraph 3: cf. Tris Coffin, "Washington's Atomic War," *The Nation*,
   2/16/46; Fields interview
   paragraph 5: *The New York Times*, 1/1/47
Page 266, paragraph 1: Groves–Brereton, 2/25/48
   paragraph 2: Groves-Brereton, 2/25/48; Groves Personal Papers, preliminary draft of statement to House Committee on Military Affairs

Chapter Forty-Five

Background: Hewlett and Anderson, *The New World*
   Herken, *The Winning Weapon*
   Groves Personal Papers, passim
   Wyden, *Day One*
   Stern, *The Oppenheimer Case*
   AEC, *In the Matter of J. Robert Oppenheimer*
Page 267: Fields interview
Page 268, paragraph 1: Fields interview; Furman interview
   paragraph 3: *Newsweek*, 12/19/49
Pages 269–270: "Excerpts from USSR Supply Division Files Concerning Atomic
   Energy Materials . . ." Records of the Office of the Chief of Engineers,
   MED

Chapter Forty-Six

Background: Hewlett and Anderson, *The New World*
Page 275: Bradbury interview; Rosenfeld, Albert, "Mr. Los Alamos," *Empire*,
   11/30/52; Groves Personal Papers, notes dictated 4/1/68
Page 276, paragraph 1: Bradbury interview
   paragraph 2: Transcript of telephone conversation Groves–Seeman,
   12/26/45, LANL Archives; Seeman Diary, 12/24/45
   paragraph 4: Lawrence interview
Page 277, paragraph 2: Oppenheimer–Groves, n.d.

Chapter Forty-Seven

Page 279, paragraph 1: Groves–Kilgallen, 8/28/58
   paragraph 2: *The Washington Post*, 2/9/47; Groves Personal Papers, notes
   dictated 5/14/63
Page 280: Richard Groves interview; Holbrook interview
   paragraph 5: Bradbury interview; *Empire*, 11/30/52; Groves Personal
   Papers, notes dictated 4/1/68

Page 281, paragraph 2: Gwen Groves Robinson interview
    paragraph 3: Alvarez interview; Lawrence interview
    paragraph 4: Groves–Tolman, 10/15/47; Gwen Groves Robinson interview
Page 282, paragraph 2: Groves Personal Papers, undated notes on Chadwick;
    Robinson interview; Groves–Chadwick, n.d.
    paragraph 3: Holle interview; Holbrook interview
    paragraph 4: Warren–Groves, 3/22/48; Rea–Groves, 12/9/47
Page 283, paragraph 2: Richard Groves interview
    paragraph 3: Holle interview
Page 284: Holle interview

Postscript

Page 285, paragraph 2: Volpe interview: Segrè interview; Groves Personal Papers;
    Haley interviews
Page 286, paragraph 2: Davis, Harry M., "The Man Who Built the A-Bomb," *The New York Times Magazine*, 4/18/48
    paragraph 3: *Newsweek*, 4/26/54
Page 287, paragraph 2: Bacher, LANL interview; Kistiakowsky, LANL interview;
    Rabi interview; Groves Personal Papers, undated note
    paragraph 3: Condon–Hickenlooper, 5/13/48; Wigner–Groves, 3/19/70
    paragraph 4: Alvarez–Groves, 2/3/48

BIBLIOGRAPHY

Records and Unpublished Sources

Papers of General Leslie R. Groves. Washington, D.C.: Modern Military History Branch, U.S. National Archives.

Diaries of Leslie R. Groves. Washington, D.C.: Modern Military History Branch, U.S. National Archives.

Manhattan Engineering District History. Washington, D.C.: Modern Military History Branch, U.S. National Archives.

Harrison-Bundy Files. Washington, D.C.: Modern Military History Branch, U.S. National Archives.

Office of Scientific Research and Development Files. Washington, D.C.: Scientific Branch, U.S. National Archives.

Correspondence of J. Robert Oppenheimer. Washington, D.C.: Library of Congress.

Archives of Los Alamos National Laboratory, Los Alamos, New Mexico.

Papers of General Leslie R. Groves. Stanford, Calif.: Hoover Institute Library.

Diaries of Henry Stimsom. New Haven, Conn.: Yale University Library.

Diaries of Glen Seaborg. University of California, Berkeley, Radiation Laboratory.

Chambers, Marjorie Bell. *Technically Sweet Los Alamos: The Development of a Federally Sponsored Community.* Ph.D. dissertation, University of New Mexico, 1974.

Books

Alperovitz, Gar. *Atomic Diplomacy: Hiroshima and Potsdam.* New York: Simon and Schuster, 1965.

Badash, Lawrence, Joseph Hirschfelder, and Herbert P. Broida, eds. *Reminiscences of Los Alamos, 1943–45.* Dordrecht, Holland: D. Reidel, 1980.

Bunyard, Peter. *The Nuclear Britain.* London: New English Library, 1981.

Bush, Vannevar. *Pieces of the Action.* New York: Morrow, 1970.

Cave-Brown, Anthony, and Charles B. MacDonald, eds. *The Secret History of the Atomic Bomb.* New York: Delta, 1977.

Compton, Arthur H. *Atomic Quest.* New York: Oxford, 1956.

Conant, James B. *My Several Lives.* New York: Harper, 1970.

Dallin, David. *Soviet Espionage.* New Haven: Yale University Press, 1956.

Davis, Nuell Pharr. *Lawrence and Oppenheimer.* New York: Simon and Schuster, 1968.

Fermi, Laura. *Atoms in the Family.* Chicago: University of Chicago Press, 1954.

Fine, Lenore, and Jesse Remington. *The Corps of Engineers, Construction in the United States.* Washington, D.C.: U.S. Government Printing Office.

Giovanniti, Len, and Fred Freed. *The Decision to Drop the Bomb.* New York: Coward-McCann, 1965.

Goodchild, Peter. *J. Robert Oppenheimer: Shatterer of Worlds.* Boston: Houghton-Mifflin, 1981.

Goudsmit, Samuel. *ALSOS.* New York: Schuman, 1947.

Gowing, Margaret. *Britain and Atomic Energy 1939–45.* New York: St. Martin's, 1964.

Groueff, Stephane. *Manhattan Project.* Boston: Little, Brown, 1967.

Groves, Leslie R. *Now It Can Be Told.* New York: Harper, 1962.

Gurney, Gene. *The Pentagon.*

Hawkins, David. *Project Y: The Los Alamos Story.* Los Angeles: Tomash, 1983.

Herken, Gregg. *The Winning Weapon.* New York: Knopf, 1980.

Hewlett, Richard G., and Oscar E. Anderson, Jr. *The New World 1939/1946.* University Park, Pa.: Pennsylvania State University Press, 1962.

Holloway, David. *The Soviet Union and the Arms Race.* New Haven: Yale University Press, 1983.

Irving, David. *The German Atomic Bomb.* New York: Simon and Schuster, 1967.

Jette, Eleanor. *Inside Box 1663.* Los Alamos, N.M.: Los Alamos Historical Society, 1977.

Jones, Vincent. *Manhattan: The Army and the Atomic Bomb.* Washington, D.C.: Center of Military History, U.S. Army, 1985.

Jungck, Robert. *Brighter Than a Thousand Suns.* New York: Harcourt, 1958.

Kunetka, James. *City of Fire.* Englewood Cliffs, N.J.: Prentice-Hall, 1979.

———. *Oppenheimer, the Years of Risk.* Englewood Cliffs, N.J.: Prentice-Hall, 1982.

Lamont, Lansing. *Day of Trinity.* New York: Atheneum, 1965.

Lingeman, Richard. *Don't You Know There's A War On?* New York: G.P. Putnam's Sons, 1970.

Michelmore, Peter. *The Swift Years.* New York: Dodd, Mead, 1969.

Nelson, Donald. *Arsenal of Democracy.* New York: Harcourt, Brace and Co., 1946.

Pash, Boris. *The ALSOS Mission.* New York: Charter, 1980.

Robinson, George O. *The Oak Ridge Story.* Kingsport, Tenn.: Southern Publishers, 1950.

Smith, Alice Kimball. *A Peril and a Hope.* Chicago: University of Chicago Press, 1965.

————, and Charles Weiner, eds. *Robert Oppenheimer, Letters and Recollections.* Cambridge, Mass.: Harvard University Press, 1980.
versity Press, 1980.

Smythe, Henry DeWolfe. *Atomic Energy.* Washington, D.C.: U.S. Government Printing Office, 1945.

Stern, Phillip. *The Oppenheimer Case: Security on Trial.* New York: Harper, 1969.

Szilard, Leo. *His Version of the Facts.* Cambridge: MIT Press, 1978.

Thomas, Gordon, and Max Morgan Witts. *Enola Gay.* New York: Stein and Day, 1977.

Truman, Harry S. *Year of Decisions.* Garden City, N.Y.: Doubleday, 1955.

Truslow, Edith C. *Manhattan District History—Nonscientific Aspects of Los Alamos Project Y, 1942–46.* Los Alamos: Manhattan Engineering District History, ND.

United States Atomic Energy Commission. *In the Matter of J. Robert Oppenheimer.* Washington, D.C.: U.S. Government Printing Office, 1954.

Wyden, Peter. *Day One.* New York: Simon and Schuster, 1984.

Newspapers

Cleveland *Press*

Columbia Basin *News*

Knoxville *Journal*

New York *Herald-Tribune*

The New York Times

Oak Ridge *Journal*

Sage *Sentinel*

Richland (Washington) *News*

Santa Fe *New Mexican*

Toronto *Sunday News*

The Washington Post

The Washington Star

Magazines

Atlantic Monthly 2/46
Bulletin of the Atomic Scientists 1/50
Business Week 8/18/45
Collier's 10/13/45
Cosmopolitan 2/47
Empire 1/30/52
Fortune 3/4/41
Investor's Reader 4/44
Liberty 10/13/45
Life 9/24/45, 10/29/45, 2/13/50
Look 7/49, 3/14/50, 8/3/63
The Nation 2/16/46
The New Yorker 8/17/46, 11/16/46
Newsweek 6/11/45, 9/12/45, 2/24/47, 12/19/49, 4/26/54
Popular Mechanics 5/46
Readers' Digest 12/53
The Saturday Evening Post 9/7/40, 1/5/46, 9/1/48
Time 11/25/44, 11/19/45, 12/7/49, 3/6/50

Interviews

Luis Alvarez*
Donald Antes
Robert Bacher
Hans Bethe* (by Mario Balibrera, Los Alamos National Laboratory)
Norris Bradbury
Priscilla Green Duffield
Robert Duffield
Richard Feynman* (by Lillian Hoddeson and Gordon Baym, LANL)
Kenneth Fields
Robert Furman
Richard H. Groves
Willard Holbrook
Charles Holle
Alan Johnson
George Kistiakowsky (by Mario Balibrera, LANL)
John Lansdale

Molly Lawrence
Anne Wilson Marks (correspondence)
Geraldine Elliott Martin
Franklin Matthias
Phillip Morrison (by Mario Balibrera, LANL)
Jean O'Leary
Frank Oppenheimer (by Mario Balibrera, LANL)
Patricia Cox Owen
Isodore Isaac Rabi*
Alan Robinson
Gwen Groves Robinson
Glen Seaborg*
Emilio Segrè*
Robert Serber (by Lillian Hoddeson, LANL)
Ralph Carlisle Smith
Edward Teller (by Mario Balibrera, LANL)
Stanislaw Ulam (LANL)
Joseph Volpe
Andrew Walker
William Wannamaker
Connie O'Leary Watson
Victor Weisskopf (by Mario Balibrera, LANL)
Eugene Wigner*
Robert Wilson (by Mario Balibrera, LANL)

*Nobel laureates

GLOSSARY

atomic number: a number denoting the total number of protons in the nucleus of an atom of a given element

atomic weight: a number denoting the total number of protons and neutrons in the nucleus of an atom of a given element

centrifuge: a rotary machine for the separation by controlled centrifugal force of substances having different densities

critical mass: the amount of fissionable material necessary to promote a nuclear explosion

cyclotron: an apparatus that whirls a stream of electrons or ions at immense speeds in a strong magnetic field; also called an atom smasher

deuteron: the nucleus of an atom of heavy hydrogen

gaseous diffusion: a process for separating isotopes of uranium gas by passing the gas through a microporous metallic barrier

Geiger counter: a device for measuring ambient radiation

heavy water: water containing significantly more than the natural proportion of heavy hydrogen (deuterium) atoms

implosion bomb: a weapon in which a quantity of fissionable material has its volume suddenly reduced by compression (through use of explosives) so that it becomes supercritical and produces an explosion

ion: an electrified component of an atom or molecule

isotope: a form of an element having the same number of protons in the nucleus but with a different number of neutrons

liquid thermal diffusion: a process for separating isotopes of uranium by circulating liquefied uranium gas through two concentric pipes maintained at different temperatures

Manhattan Engineer District (MED): the official Army designation for the whole of the atomic bomb project

neutron, fast: a neutron with energy greater than approximately 100,000 electron volts

313

nuclear reactor: a device in which radioactive substances are arranged so as to promote nuclear fission

nuclear fission: the disintegration of the nucleus of a radioactive element

nuclear fusion: the joining, under great heat and pressure, of hydrogen nuclei to form helium, in the process of which a certain proportion of the mass involved is converted to energy

nucleus: the central core of an atom

neutron: an atomic particle with a neutral electrical charge

plutonium: a manmade element with an atomic number of 94, produced from uranium by the absorption of a neutron

predetonation: premature initiation of an explosion

transuranic elements: elements the atomic numbers of which are higher than uranium

uranium: the naturally occurring element with the highest atomic weight and number. Of its three isotopes (U-234, U-235, and U-238), only U-235 is readily fissionable

Index

Abbott, Henry, 53
Abelson, Phillip, 10, 68–69, 152
Adler, Edward, 123, 124
Agnew, Harold, 146
All-American Football Conference, 279
Allis-Chalmers, 121–22
Allison, Charles, 102n
Allison, Samuel, 128, 198, 213–14
  postwar security attacked by, 260–61
ALSOS mission, 179–81, 183
Aluminum, increase in production of, 31n
Alvarez, Luis, 84, 104, 105, 163–64, 202, 204, 242, 281
  in assessment of German atomic progress, 135–37
  on Groves's work, 287–88
American Legion, 4
Anderson, Carl, 101, 107
Anderson, Herbert, 74, 76
Andrews, Henry, 11–12
Argonne National Laboratory, 277, 288
Arms Control and Disarmament Agency, 289
Army. *See* United States Army.
Army-Navy Munitions Board, 32
Arnold, H.H. "Hap," 220–21, 239, 248
Arnold, Samuel, 128
Ashbridge, Whitney, 133, 166
Ashworth, Frederick, 254
Atomic bomb
  amount of uranium or plutonium needed for, 76–77
  as antiwar weapon, 289
  critical mass for. *See* Critical mass.
  Groves's final opinion on, 288
  Groves's responsibility for, 288–89
  Joliot-Curie's proposal for building of, 38–39
  "Little Boy" and "Fat Man" terms for, 229
  opposition to use of, 230–35
  political dimension of, 80–81, 83
  possibility of dud, 181, 232
  as potentially setting atmosphere on fire, 212
  power of, 80–81

  predictions of, 4–5
  problems of fabrication of, 95–96
  firing mechanism, 129–30, 171–73, 198–200
  proposed test demonstration of, 231
  sent by sea to Tinian, 229–30
  test of, 211–17
    betting pool on yield, 205
    Groves's and Oppenheimer's later visit to site of, 270
    preparations for, 201–9
Atomic Energy Commission
  formation of, 263–64
  Oppenheimer as chairman of advisory committee to, 271–72
Atomic fission
  discovery of, 10
  whether possible in a bomb, 15
Atomic fuel, proposed, 11–12

B-29 (airplane), 182, 204, 267
  in atomic bombing of Japan, 241–46
  practice dropping of bomb by, 219–20, 230
Bacher, Robert, 62, 103–5, 106, 130, 132, 146, 168, 188, 199, 203, 207, 208, 255, 275
  as AEC commissioner, 265
  on Groves's work, 287
Bainbridge, Kenneth, 201, 204, 212, 213
Baker, Yale, 260
Bank of Belgium, 37
Barron, Carter, 259
Bart, Blasius, 190
Bart, Sieg, 190
Baseball code for outcome of Trinity test, 205
Battle of the Bulge, 181–82
BBC (British Broadcasting Corporation), 286–87
Beahan, Kermit, 254
Beams, Jesse, 20, 69–70
Becquerel, Henri, 37
Beginning or the End, The (movie), 259
Bell Laboratories, 123

92
GROVES
L
  Lawren, William
      The general and the bomb.